LOCATING AUGUST STRINDBERG'S PROSE:
MODERNISM, TRANSNATIONALISM, AND SETTING

ANNA WESTERSTÅHL STENPORT

Locating August Strindberg's Prose

Modernism, Transnationalism, and Setting

UNIVERSITY OF TORONTO PRESS
Toronto Buffalo London

ISBN 978-1-4426-4199-0 (cloth)

Printed on acid-free, 100% post-consumer recycled paper with vegetable-based inks.

Library and Archives Canada Cataloguing in Publication

Stenport, Anna Westerståhl
Locating August Strindberg's prose : modernism, transnationalism, and setting / Anna Westerståhl Stenport.

Includes bibliographical references and index.
ISBN 978-1-4426-4199-0

1. Strindberg, August, 1849–1912 – Criticism and interpretation.
2. Transnationalism in literature.   3. Modernism (Literature) – History and criticism.   I. Title.

PT9816.S74 2010   839.72'6   C2010-902909-7

University of Toronto Press acknowledges the financial assistance to its publishing program of the Canada Council for the Arts and the Ontario Arts Council.

  Canada Council   Conseil des Arts
         for the Arts   du Canada

University of Toronto Press acknowledges the financial support of the Government of Canada through the Canada Book Fund for its publishing activities.

Contents

Acknowledgments

This book has greatly benefited from the generous attention it has received from many readers and discussion partners over the years. Profound thanks go to my mentor and advisor Linda Haverty Rugg, as well as to other University of California-Berkeley professors who have given of their time – Mark Sandberg, Michael Lucey, Barbara Spackman, and, in memoriam, Allan Pred. I thank Strindberg scholars Ulf Olsson, Ann-Charlotte Gavel Adams, Margaretha Fahlgren, Stefanie von Schnurbein, Anna Cavallin, and the press's anonymous readers for comments and suggestions at various stages of the project. At the University of Illinois, I have encountered a wonderfully rich and collaborative intellectual environment, and a number of people have been especially significant for making this book come together. In particular, thanks go to the Friday writing group – Ericka Beckman, Ellen Moodie, and Yasemin Yildiz – as well as to Andrea Goulet, Anke Pinkert, Brett Ashely Kaplan, Maggie Flinn, Mara R. Wade, Jonathan Ebel, Shelley Wright, and Lawrence Smith. Several graduate students have helped me along – thank you Kathleen Smith, Jon Sherman, Carola Dwyer, Benjamin Davis, and Paul Hartley. The staffs at the Royal Library in Stockholm, the University of Illinois Library, the Stockholm City Museum, and the Gothenburg University Library have provided critical assistance in all stages of the project. Editor Richard Ratzclaff at the University of Toronto Press has steered this project through with wonderful grace.

Research and scholarship cannot be imagined, let alone completed, without funding. I am very grateful for the travel and teaching release support awarded by the University of Illinois Research Board, the American-Scandinavian Foundation, the Helge Ax:son Johnson

Foundation, the Flora Hewlett Travel Fund and the European Union Center at the University of Illinois, the Gålö Sixten Gemzéus Foundation, the University of California at Berkeley, and SWEA International San Francisco Chapter. For support in the final stages of publication, I thank Stiftelsen Konung Gustaf VI Adolfs fond för svensk kultur.

Permission to reprint parts of chapter 1 from the article 'National Betrayal: Language, Location, and Lesbianism in August Strindberg's Novel *Le Plaidoyer d'un fou*,' published in *Comparative Literature* 62:2 (2010), 144–60, is granted from Duke University Press; permission to reprint parts of chapter 5 from the article 'Interiority Conceits: Domestic Architecture, Grafophone Recordings, and Colonial Imaginations in August Strindberg's *The Roofing Ceremony* (1907),' published in *Modernism/Modernity* 17:4 (2010), is granted from the Johns Hopkins University Press.

As always, much gratitude is due to the Stenport and Westerståhl families for unwavering support; to Ingegerd, especially, and to Märta and Jacob for joy and diversion. And I save the largest thank you to last: this book is for Olof and it comes with much love.

LOCATING AUGUST STRINDBERG'S PROSE:
MODERNISM, TRANSNATIONALISM, AND SETTING

Introduction

If you were to name the locations of European literary modernism, would London, Paris, Vienna, New York, or Berlin rank at the top of your list? Or Dublin and Prague, perhaps? But what about Stockholm? Or the rural countryside of France? How about the railway lines connecting Copenhagen to an anonymous boarding house in Bavaria, or an ethnographic exhibition of thousands of artefacts brought from Congo to Sweden by missionaries and military; or an Alpine landscape in Austria? Similarly, which national traditions and languages would you use initially to exemplify the movement? Anglophone or francophone, perhaps? But what about a Swedish writer who lives in exile all over Europe for a good portion of his adult life, and whose most experimental works are written in French about Stockholm and Paris, or in Swedish about peasants in France and artists in Berlin, or which may be set in an anonymous Stockholm apartment but tell a story of domination in Africa from a national perspective that does not include acknowledgment of its colonization practices? And what does literary modernism look like from the geographical periphery of Europe, when part of writing within a modernist paradigm means challenging conceptions of nation and national languages as constructs upon which a centre-margin paradigm relies?

Looking for answers to some of these questions spurred me to write this book about August Strindberg's prose narratives. In works written by Strindberg (1849–1912) in exile from Sweden – or in those of his texts that explicitly seek to destabilize concepts of nation and national language, or margin and centre – I have also sought for ways to understand how European modernism construes setting as a literary device that can supplement our understanding of the movement: its self-reflexive emphasis on experimentation, on disjointed temporality, on alienation and fragmentation, on speed and transience, on recollection and artistic creativity, and on the coincidental and contigent.

In a well-known prefatory remark to *A Dream Play* (1902), Strindberg outlines his experimental conception of the spatio-temporal. In this play, like in a dream, 'tid och rum existera icke ... Personerna klyvas, fördubblas, dubbleras, dunsta av, förtätas, flyta ut, samlas' (*Ett drömspel* 7) (time and space do not exist ... Characters split, double, multiply, evaporate, condense, disperse, and converge [trans. Robinson, 176]). Many of Strindberg's prose works suggest similarly complex approaches to space and time. This is particulary true for narratives that thematize transnational travel and linguistic displacement, and which self-reflexively address the function of literary setting. The settings of Strindberg's prose modernism explored in the five chapters of this book range from Stockholm to Paris, Berlin, and London; from the Swedish, French, Prussian, and Austrian countrysides to the Swedish involvement in the Belgian Congo; from apartments to restaurants, railway carriages to boarding houses, libraries to hospitals, and streets to farmland, incorporating practices of writers, artists, actresses, scientists, farmers, explorers, photographers, and many others.

What these locations and practices show is that Strindberg's prose is explicitly and self-reflexively transnational at a time when national allegiance remained strong in the European tradition, including the Swedish. Using his own works as a guide, I suggest that Strindberg's prose offers ways to redefine and rewrite a marginal literary identity at the end of the nineteenth century. These narratives not only reformulate what it means for a literature to be construed as 'Swedish' or 'French,' but also make apparent the multilingual complexity inherent in European prose modernism as it evolves from the late nineteenth century onward.

Gunnar Brandell, one of Strindberg's many biographers, makes the author's geographical vagabondage evident in a map in the second of his four-volume biography. He counts twenty-eight domiciles mostly in continental Europe during the period 1883–94 (*Strindberg – ett författarliv*, vol. 2) and counts another ten or so primarily in Paris, Austria, and Sweden during the period 1894–8 (*Strindberg – ett författarliv*, vol. 3). Brandell's visualization of Strindberg's extensive vagabondage is inspiring. It makes visible how Strindberg's writing challenges any stable correlation between nation and author; it also raises questions about aesthetic tensions inherent in his constructions of literary setting. Along these lines, this book proposes to read Strindberg's transnational writing in ways that emphasize its connection to European prose modernism. For Strindberg, as for many other contemporary émigré modernists (Rainer Maria Rilke, Franz Kafka, or Joseph Conrad, for example), language as a construct does not appear associated with a perceptual 'home.' Strindberg's writing in French, or in Swedish about France, Germany, Austria, and Switzerland, rarely addresses conceptual issues of writing in a 'foreign' language or about 'foreign' locations. In fact, although Stellan Ahlström has argued in an oft-repeated formula that Strindberg left Sweden in self-imposed exile in 1883 armed with the explicit desire to 'conquer' Paris and achieve literary fame in the French capital, Strindberg states in a letter to Danish newspaper editor Edvard Brandes that he actually has no intention of becoming a 'French writer,' instead making use of French 'for want of a universal language' (*Brev* 5:122; my trans.). Language and location are both intriguingly transparent as concepts in Strindberg's writing, which counteracts the language-as-a-national-marker model so influential for later literary reception.

Emphasizing Strindberg's prose as constitutive of transnational European modernism allows us to rethink some of the ways in which the author Strindberg has been construed as a delocalized psyche. He has been, we could say, construed as pure subjectivity extraneous from geography. This narrowly conceived legacy of Strindberg's delocalized authorial persona has influenced the general reception of his writing as primarily, if not exclusively, about subject-formation and (fraught) identity construction. Strindberg's authorial persona has always been marked by attributes signalling a rational subject's dissolution, such as those including medical insanity or extreme misogyny, as several scholars show (Olsson, *Jag blir galen*; Fahlgren). In the paradoxical extension of arguments in which nation and authorial persona coalesce, Strindberg's prose has been read as primarily about identity and subject formation. In this paradigm, based on assumptions of positivist construction, literary representation becomes a way to heal a problematic authorial persona and a fragmentary national literary history. Not only can Strindberg be construed as the father of modern Swedish literature in this paradigm, but his prose also becomes a way to engage with the 'crisis of representation' that is modernism's hallmark according to Pericles Lewis in the *The Cambridge Introduction to Modernism* (1).

Turning the relationship between modernist subjectivity and setting around proposes shifting the weight we have put on something we perceive to be a given (the tormented, split subject; the challenges to temporality) to perceiving it, in fact, as inseparable from something quite concrete. This identity/subjectivity interpretive tradition, which is how we have been taught to think about modernism's spaces, in part obscures what is actually original in Strindberg's prose, namely, its sophisticated and complex constructions of setting across national traditions, languages, and trajectories of travel. Focusing on the setting of his literary works conceived in exile and upon returning to Sweden, allows for the expansion of a tradition of scholarship that has coerced Strindberg's prose into both national paradigms and constructions of a cohesive authorial persona. It also allows us to understand from a different perspective Strindberg's astonishingly comprehensive output.

Though best known in an international context for the theatrical innovations of *Miss Julie* (1888), *A Dream Play* (1902), or *The Ghost Sonata* (1908), Strindberg was a prolific prose writer for over forty years in numerous genres and in two languages – Swedish and French. Strindberg's prose writing includes popular realist and naturalist novels, like *The Red Room* (1879) and the *The People of Hemsö* (1887), as well as experimental and expressionist ones like *Inferno* (1897) and *Black Banners* (1907), numerous autobiographies, short story collections, historical fiction, and essays on aesthetics, natural sciences, linguistics, and social and political issues. Expansive and prolific, Strindberg's collected works in the recent Swedish *Samlade verk* (*Collected Works*) comprise over seventy volumes, while individual pieces number in the hundreds. He also wrote over ten thousand letters. In fact, Strindberg's oeuvre engages with all major literary and aesthetic movements of the late nineteenth and early twentieth centuries and encompasses all major genres of the period – drama, novel, short story, poetry, ethnographic and historical prose, journalism, essayistic writing, criticism, and autobiography, as well as painting and photography.

Locating August Strindberg's Prose proposes that without an investigation of setting, neither the forms nor cultural contexts of European modernism can be understood, and, by extension, that two lesser-known items of the modernist tradition – the prose of August Strindberg and the concept of literary setting – are central to how we perceive the movement's formation and continuing legacy. My approach to Strindberg's prose is in line with other significant developments in modernist studies, namely, from the psychological to the spatial; from a modus operandi that traces representational 'crises,' often assumed to be based in character or author psychology, to their implementation in formal choices and to ones that propose spatial relations as distinctly formative for and representative of modernism.

As a transnational writer, Strindberg incorporates many locations into his writing and obscures and eschews others. The field of Strindberg scholarship is similarly diverse – scholars in Sweden and Scandinavia, Germany and France, and North America and the United Kingdom have often focused on very different aspects of his writing, and have tended to make those conform to their respective national traditions of literary interpretation. *Locating August Strindberg's Prose* expands on the limited number of monographs on Strindberg's prose available in English, including Eric Johannesson, *The Novels of August Strindberg*; Michael Robinson, *Strindberg and Autobiography*; Harry G. Carlson, *Out of Inferno*; and Gunnar Brandell, *Strindberg in Inferno*. In this book, I draw on my own transnational positions as a U.S.-trained scholar of comparative literature and native of Sweden, with a significant interest in French and German literature. I build on and incorporate English-language scholarship, as well as a wide range of sources in Scandinavian languages, French, and German, which may be little known internationally. The methodology I use involves close readings of spatial descriptions and a narrative's structural dependence on certain settings, while these literary readings are related to larger questions about production and reception. This book is thereby part of an explicit effort to demarginalize Strindberg's prose and challenge boundaries between different national scholarly traditions, while offering new ways for a field like comparative literature to investigate the assumptions of nation and monolingualism on which its methodological and theoretical approaches have been based.

Setting

Part of the central argument in this book is that Strindberg's prose illustrates and contextualizes fundamental conceptualizations of European literary modernism. By analysing something very concrete in Strindberg's prose, and in the prose's production and reception circumstances, I seek to illustrate how two disparate and unwieldy traditions – those of Strindberg and of modernist scholarship – can be related. The project started as a pragmatic query. I noticed there are very few critical interpretations of Strindberg's prose settings, despite the primary importance of location in his works. It made me think that if we are searching for 'this "something"' (dette 'noget') which makes Strindberg's prose modernist, in Per Stounbjerg's formulation (315, my trans.), and we have not been able to identify it, perhaps we have been looking in the wrong places. Per Stounbjerg's scholarship is suggestive in this regard, as he has consistently interpreted Strindberg's writing as a modernist. The recent essay title 'Ett subjekt intrasslat i världen: Strindbergs självbiografiska prosa' (A Subject Entangled in the World: Strindberg's Autobiographical Prose, my trans.) suggests Stounbjerg's interest in exploring spatialized conceptions of subjectivity, though his investigations remain removed from concrete engagement with geographical locations. I hope that the present book will help spur further interest in literary setting as a conceptual tool for analysing both locations represented and places imagined in the prose of August Strindberg and in European modernism. I believe this can help us expand Strindberg studies outward from its historically dominant interpretive paradigm based in subjectivity and identity studies. A concept like setting offers us a concrete way to explore other facets of Strindberg's writing and shows how these connect with prevalent strategies of European literary modernism. Such an interpretive strategy ultimately seeks to de-marginalize Strindberg in European literary and cultural history.

The concept of 'setting' is one of the terms I draw on to address this question. Place and space have been much discussed in critical theory and cultural studies, but in this book I am referring to an older term for several reasons. The term incorporates both space and time, as evident in an expression like 'the setting of Strindberg's breakthrough novel *The Red Room* is late nineteenth-century Stockholm.' Setting is also medium-specific to literature, and specifically, to narrative prose. Literary studies have borrowed terms and approaches from other disciplines and media to address the function and importance of setting, including in particular those of geography and architecture, which indicates that questions of literary location span multiple interdisciplinary interests.[1] It also suggests literary theory's problems of defining, maintaining, and critiquing its own terminology. Part of the reason literary studies needs a return to a concept like setting, I argue, is to counteract metaphorical slippage, in which catch-all spatial terminology obscures the medium-specific functions of literature or, as David Harvey writes, which 'invite[s] theorists

---

1 Some of the most important concepts have been derived from Henri Lefebvre's production of space, Michel DeCerteau's practices of the everyday, Anthony Vidler's warped space and the architectural uncanny, Gilles Deleuze's and Felix Guattari's rhizomes, Edward Soja's thirdspace, and Franco Moretti's maps.

of all stripes to simply delight in the conveniently disruptive metaphors of spatialities, cartographic metaphors, and the like' ('Cosmopolitanism' 287, drawing on Neil Smith and Cindi Katz). In this book, I use setting to address specifics of literary production, reception, and representation. The approach includes attention to how Strindberg writes about locations, where he writes, about which places, in what languages, and for which audiences.

To advocate for setting as a distinct and critical category of modernism's spatial parameters necessitates drawing out some of the reasons why the concept has been overlooked. The term itself illustrates some of its negative baggage. 'Setting,' like that of a setting of a jewel, appears to imply both secondary status and stasis, by which its function becomes one of letting the jewels of narration (plot, character, theme, linguistic formulation, narrative strategy, or whatever feature you choose to focus on) shine unobstructed. When associated with the term 'set,' images of painted theatre backdrops or cinema's sound stage particle boards suggest fakery and suspendability. From these perspectives, setting appears incongruous with dominant ideologies of modernism, including its interest in philosophy and subjectivity construction. In modernism's ideology of constructions of the self – the fragmented and alienated human psyche; the priority placed on the individual's subjective experiences – situated and localized aspects of narration may appear inconsequential and dispensable.

Setting as a literary term posits, however, that a story needs a location to take place; that location, of course, may index a recognized place name, or not. Narrative takes (a) place and produces literary space. Setting is in fact so integral to narration that any story, whether modernist or not, cannot be either conceived or analysed without it, just as the literary spaces produced span the material and imaginary. Drawing on setting as a medium-specific literary term allows us to construct a credible bridge between modernist texts and cultural constructions, such as those that have become foundational for European modernism: tensions between conceptions of centre and margin, national belonging and cosmopolitanism, public and private, emigration and travel, high culture and low, city and country, formal fragmentation and subjective displacement, and gendered and sexual hierarchies.

Setting seems to be one of modernism's present absences, overlooked at least partly because it does not appear to fit easily into still-hegemonic theoretical emphases on temporality in cultural and literary studies (Gaonkar 4–5). The term 'modernism' itself connotes time, as Peter

Brooker and Andrew Thacker argue: 'to be "modern" seems to imply an intrinsic relation to time and history, and thus to past, present and future cultural practices' (1; cf. Armstrong 10–11). The modern subject's literary constitution in space – one of modernism's most interesting aspects – is neglected in such constructions of modernist ideology. Such tight linkages between literature and history, rather than literature and geography, are evident in most national literary traditions, including the Swedish. This particular tradition tends to organize divergent and heterogeneous literary expression according to decades (those of the 1880s, 1890s, and so on), while assuming stable national and linguistic boundaries of 'Swedish' literature. In this paradigm, Strindberg's varied production, conceived during forty years in multiple nations, two languages, and in multiple genres – often in direct opposition to Swedish and French national ideologies – never really fits. In its emphasis on temporal organization, Sweden's national literary history, which includes significant emphasis on Strindberg as the designated 'father of modern Swedish literature,' correlates with the emphasis on temporality in both narrative and modernist studies.' The implicit emphasis on temporality as primary and principal in literary studies has, it seems, obscured concrete ways of addressing constructions of setting that show complexities of expression that are part of emergent transnational literary modernism at the end of the nineteenth century. Such literary modernisms, exemplified in this book by some of Strindberg's most interesting and experimental prose works, also put the spotlight on actual locations that have largely been understood as marginal to the tradition in terms of both setting and topic – including those that Strindberg put at the centre of his writings.

The disregard for setting connects with fundamentals of narrative theory, as it emphasizes temporality over spatiality. For Paul Ricoeur, a representative example, 'one presupposition commands all the others, namely, that what is ultimately at stake in ... every narrative work, is the temporal character of human experience ... narrative, in turn, is meaningful to the extent that it portrays the features of temporal existence' (3; see also Carroll 34; Bal 133–41). Though Mikhail Bakhtin's essay 'Forms of Time and of the Chronotope in the Novel' represents one of the first sustained attempts – and richly complex it is! – to investigate in conjunction spatial and temporal parameters of narrative, the concept of the chronotope prioritizes time over space. As Bakhtin writes, 'the primary category in the chronotope is time' (85) and a majority of his analyses in fact devote their 'entire attention to time' (86). Strindberg's prose settings, in fact, gesture to the limitations of a predominant critical tradition that narrowly prioritizes temporality over spatiality. *Locating August Strindberg's Prose* suggests some concrete ways to investigate settings that bridge form and cultural context, where the contributions of modernist literary technique and theme conjoin. The prose settings I will be investigating not only challenge any stable notion of 'nation,' especially during a time of increasing nationalism and constructions of national literary histories, and of language, as belonging to nation, and of fetishized metropolitan identities (particularly those of Paris, Berlin, and Stockholm), but also challenge us to rethink notions of temporality, especially as those pertain to modernist conceptualizations of selfhood and consciousness.

Transnational

A second critical concept I draw on in this book is the term 'transnational.' According to the *Oxford English Dictionary*, the term first came into use in 1921, thus reflecting its emergence from the time period under investigation here. In contrast to the term 'international,' which denotes relations between stable nations, 'transnational' signifies a more complex relationship. The term entails the idea of 'extending or having interests extending beyond national bounds or frontiers' and so presupposes the engagement of multiple nations and expresses according to its prepositional and adjectival usage connotations of 'across, beyond, over, transcending, surpassing' (*OED*). These are precisely the complextities that Strindberg's prose engages. James McFarlane began formulating a transnational understanding of European modernism in his essay 'Berlin and the Rise of Modernism 1886–1896,' included in the influential primer *Modernism: A Guide to European Literature 1890–1930*. But like later developments of these arguments, McFarlane does not address *how* texts produced in, about, for, and in reaction to multiple locations and the transnational relationships between them come to formalize modernism. Strindberg's prose provides a case study in this regard for how modernism formalizes transnational settings.

Strindberg's transnational prose narratives suggest a productive way to define European literary modernism as a movement that not only challenges simplistic oppositions between concepts like margin and centre, or import and export models of literary influence, but also as one which is founded upon movement across national borders and within and between national and primary languages. Strindberg's prose dismantles the truism that literary modernism is an international phenomenon and replaces it with a dynamic critical framework that seeks to span transnational, cultural, and literary movement(s).[2] Brooker and Thacker ask a very helpful question in their introduction to *Geographies of Modernism*: '*where* was modernism?' (rather than the more customary *when* or *what* was modernism?). They rely, however, on an established transatlantic cartographic line that links metropolitan Paris and London with New York, to emphasize the continued importance of quintessential urban locations that have usually been associated with modernism – 'streets, offices, cafes and artists' quarters' (3; see also Huyssen, 'Geographies of Modernism in a Globalizing World' 6). Rosner takes the rethinking of city space in modernism in another direction, arguing that domestic spaces, interior design, and residential architecture provided a 'conceptual vocabulary' for the modernist novel that also challenges gendered preconceptions of public and private in literary modernism (2, see also Walkowitz 11). Strindberg's prose writing offers ways to rethink the construction of European literary modernism as associated with major metropolitan centres, public locations, particular gendered constructions of space, and import-export models.

Periodization of European literary modernism has been contested: Lewis proposes the period 1850–1950; Bradbury and McFarlane narrow the range to 1890–1930; and individual national traditions, like the Swedish, tend to establish a later range, 1914–60, or so. In this book, I follow Toril Moi's lead in *Ibsen and the Birth of Modernism* to argue that Scandinavian modernism evolves earlier than often assumed. Any comprehensive understanding of Scandinavian modernism begins with the term 'the modern breakthrough,' coined by Danish Georg Brandes to describe what he, as a multilingual Europe-based literary critic, understood as important and original about Scandinavian literature in the 1880s – the ways it polemically engaged and reformulated Scandinavia's transition to modernity. Brandes's call for innovations in Scandinavian literature in his lecture series at Copenhagen University in 1871 stipulated that litera-

---

2 Cf. monographs by Thacker, *Moving Through Modernity*; Walkowitz, *Cosmopolitan Style*; Rosner, *Modernism and the Architecture of Private Life*; Briens, *Paris Laboratoire de la littérature Scandinave moderne 1880–1905*; the edited volumes by Brooker and Thacker, *Geographies of Modernism*; Wollaeger, *The Oxford Handbook of Global Modernisms*; and Bahun-Radunović and Pourgouris, *The Avant-Garde and the Margins*; and articles by Eysteinsson ('Borders of Modernism in the Nordic World'); Friedman ('Cultural Parataxis and Transnational Landscapes of Reading'); Huyssen ('Geographies of Modernism in a Globalizing World'); and Gikandi ('Preface: Modernism in the World').

ture could become *modern* and relevant by engaging social issues in new and original forms (383–4). Brandes explicitly challenged a pervasive national romanticism and a centuries-old import model of literary influence in Scandinavia. Strindberg did the same, especially in works composed outside of Sweden. Inspired by Brandes, I would argue, Bradbury and McFarlane began reconceptualizing European modernism from a comparative perspective, arguing that particularly Scandinavian modernism, in 'its most significant manifestations' was 'a good generation *earlier* than the Anglo-American' (37; see also Mitchell), and that the Scandinavian Modern Breakthrough Movement had thoroughly influenced conceptions of European modernism in Berlin, London, and Paris by 1890. Strindberg's role is paramount here, but has tended to be overlooked in international scholarship. Moi charts a similar trajectory, namely, that the Scandinavian Modern Breakthrough Movement, and particularly the early plays of Ibsen, provides the earliest and most comprehensive aesthetic critique of continental idealism and bourgeois realism, but that Ibsen's formidable importance for modernist aesthetics has been overlooked in favour of the writings of Charles Baudelaire or Gustave Flaubert, for example.[3]

Strindberg's transnational prose illustrates what European literary modernism is. It is partly what Susan Stanford Friedman calls modernism's critical 'linguistic polyvocality' and 'cultural parataxis,' which allow 'the juxtaposition of disparate [locational and linguistic] elements in non-hierarchical ways' (36). Strindberg's writing about the French or Austrian countrysides, or about Stockholm in French or Paris in Swedish is part of a body of late nineteenth-century transnational literature that gives empirical background to Friedman's claim that studies of European modernism need to deemphasize the '"culture capitals" of Europe' instead to investigate 'how local formations of modernism are continually affected by cultural traffic of all kinds' and 'the cultural hybridity that results from widespread intercultural communication' (36). This disparity, or heterogeneity, provides an important complement to Pascale Casanova's paradigm of *littérisation* (127–38). In the influential *World Republic of Literature*, Casanova claims that Strindberg's

---

3 Like Ibsen's plays, Strindberg's transnational prose modernism does not fit easily into categories of Scandinavian modernism. In its classical formulations, Swedish and Scandinavian modernism tends to emphasize a formalist approach that privileges poetic experimentation, syntactic dissolution, and fragmentary imagery, as preeminent in the canonical legacy of the 1940s generation of Swedish poets (see Brantly; Luthersson). More comparative approaches have recently begun to be explored; see Jansson, Lothe, and Riikonen.

strategies for gaining recognition in Paris serve as a 'paradigm of *littérisation*' (137), i.e., the ways in which 'a text from a *literarily deprived* country comes to be regarded as literary by the legitimate authorities' (136, my emphasis) – in this case, come to be seen as attaining the cultural, monetary, and aesthetic prestige brought by Parisian recognition. Casanova posits Paris as the 'the capital of the literary world'; the 'place where books – submitted to critical judgment and transmuted – can be denationalized and their authors made universal' (127). I propose instead that Strindberg's prose modernism, particularly in Swedish-language works about Paris, deconstruct both assumptions of Paris's iconic status in European letters and the idea that literature originating in so-called literarily deprived locations is derivative of European models. Critical attention to the setting of Strindberg's individual prose works, and the ways in which these literary locations make us rethink narrative trajectory and content, help us gain a better understanding of transnational European modernism.

Locating August Strindberg's Prose thereby engages with questions of the so-called globalization of literary studies, and more specifically with the changing field of comparative literature. In the current globalization discourse, as represented by works like *Comparative Literature in an Age of Globalization* (Saussy) or a concept like 'planetarity' (Spivak, *Death of a Discipline*), there is a clear assumption that literature has something very pertinent to do with space; that there is something geographically significant about literary production, reception, consumption, and canonization. Traditional literary history and novelistic and narrative theory has tended not to engage with these questions very openly, however. In this book I draw on terms like 'setting' and the 'transnational' because one is medium-specific and the other relates explicitly to the geographical imagination of the time period I am investigating. Both terms are critical to an understanding of literary modernism, while Strindberg's prose production thereby offers a complementary understanding of the field of comparative literature.

When studied from an international perspective, it seems that Strindberg's prose reputation has suffered from an unfortunate double-blow, which effectively has edged it out of the modernist and comparative literary context. First, few of Strindberg's novels are currently in print in any other language than Swedish, while the prose has been overlooked in favour of his drama, and, more recently, his painting and photography (see Granath; and Rugg, *Picturing Ourselves*). Second, scholars have historically had great difficulty dealing with the fact that

Strindberg's prose seems to defy any easy or stable categorization, whether national, linguistic, thematic, or stylistic. There is a problematically large body of Strindberg works to contend with and any attempt at synthesizing, generalizing, or categorizing quickly runs up against pertinent counter-examples. Scholarship has historically tried to deal with this heterogeneity in two ways, by organizing the work according to either biographical or national models. Biographical models of interpretation seem by now to have been largely relinquished, as indicated by the significant contributions of prominent Swedish Strindberg scholar Ulf Olsson (*Levande död* and *Jag blir galen*; see also Fahlgren; Hockenjos; Lönngren; Schnurbein; Stounbjerg).

National frameworks remain strong, however. The authoritative *Collected Works* is also called The National Edition, *Nationalupplagan*, and this name has become the popular moniker for the project. Another case in point involves standard Scandinavian reception of two of Strindberg's better-known French-language novels. Swedish scholars tend to label these as 'Swedish' works of literature, while scholars of French read them for their correlation with 'French' literature. In fact, both these works are explicitly transnational. *Inferno* (1897), written in French in Sweden, is set mostly in Paris and in Austria, though it was first published in a Swedish translation and only subsequently in its original version. *A Madman's Defence* was written in French in Denmark in 1887–8, and is set mostly in Stockholm, though its originating point of narration is a Bavarian pension. That work was first published in a German translation in Berlin in 1893 and subsequently in a French version in Paris in 1895. Strindberg never authorized it for publication in Sweden. Taking Strindberg's prose as a critical case study with relevance for many other marginalized texts, *Locating August Strindberg's Prose* questions constructions of national literary history and offers a model for investigating the transnational also within other literary movements, authorships, and languages; incorporating Strindberg's prose works into a context of European literary modernism, where it belongs, is part of what this book hopes to achieve.

August Strindberg's Literary Locations

Some texts discussed in this book are better known and available in English translation – in these cases, I spend less time on contextualization and move quickly into analyses of literary setting. In other cases, reframing the field of European modernist literary studies by including some of Strindberg's lesser-known works is part of the central argument, which necessitates more contextualization.

The book's first chapter investigates multiple European settings of Strindberg's French-language narrative *A Madman's Defence* (*Le Plaidoyer d'un fou*). In this work, I contextualize the stakes involved in writing a first-person novel about transnational travel and displacement that details intimate aspects of tormented love, divorce, lesbian desire, infidelity, and fear of impending insanity. This chapter focuses in particular on settings of the public and private, including apartments, railway travel, anonymous pensions, and theatre and refers to French novelistic and dramatic conventions for representing divorce and lesbian desire in certain settings. I point to the self-reflexive nature in which this work destabilizes national allegiances as part of its contribution to European modernism. The second chapter investigates how *Among French Peasants* (*Bland franska bönder*) (1889) develops the rural and agrarian as a setting for a modernist ethnographic representation that mixes methodology, literary style, anachronisms, and impressionistic techniques of the visual arts and photography. I point in particular to the technologically mediated mechanisms of recollection and remembrance that are part of this work's modernist aesthetics, and how these thematize spatial transience. The book's third chapter turns to *Inferno*, another first-person narrative originally written in French for an international audience. I show in this chapter that this novel's use of indexical street names and public locations in Paris depends on fragmentation and displacement techniques that provide conceptual models for André Breton and surrealism's renunciation of spatial description, as well as for Rilke's corporealization of Paris in *The Notebooks of Malte Laurids Brigge*. These three works are fascinating representatives of the limitations of national literary ideology and ideologies of monolingualism, as their formal experimentation in setting constructs radically new conceptions of France, Sweden, and continental Europe. Strindberg's French narratives have not previously been incorporated into the canon of early European modernism, whereas their experimentation, not least in construction of literary setting and migrant practices, I argue, requires inclusion.

In the final two chapters of the book, I turn to overlooked texts whose use of setting illustrates in new ways how Strindberg's writing relates to German and British prose modernism. Chapter 4 discusses how settings in the novel *The Cloister* (*Klostret*), written in Swedish in 1898 and set partly in Berlin of the early 1890s (it was first published in its entirety in 1966), emphasizes transience and speed as a rhetoric of displacement fully operable in the *Großstadt*, which connects the work to Georg Simmel's theories of urban alienation. Read in conjunction with Berlin's anaemic prose modernism of the 1890s, *The Cloister* appears strikingly different, as it introduces homosexual culture, divorce practices, and New Woman figures as given aspects of emergent transnational modernism in ways that construe setting as paramount to literary experimentation. In chapter 5, I turn to Strindberg's last works of modernist prominence, the short novel *The Roofing Ceremony* (*Taklagsöl*) (1906) and the series of expressionist chamber plays (1907–9), which were written in Swedish in Stockholm upon the author's return from many years of vagabondage around Europe. These works investigate interiors of Stockholm's modern apartment buildings and use setting to conceive new models for introspection and psychological interiority. Claustrophobic apartments become harbingers of psychological torment and anxiety, while ghastly multi-units either grow of their own accord or go up in flames. In *The Roofing Ceremony*, narrative construction of consciousness, of recording and recollection, and of a suppressed colonial imagination (the extended Swedish presence in the Belgian Congo) demonstrate close affinity with Joseph Conrad's *Heart of Darkness* (1902) and seem to presage to Samuel Beckett's *Krapp's Last Tape* (1958). *The Roofing Ceremony's* emulation of a first-person stream-of-consciousness technique posits both a domestic apartment setting and the recording practices of a grafophone as prerequisites, as the novel destabilizes many of the tight connections between Paris, Stockholm, and, to some extent, Berlin, previously established by Strindberg's prose.

What the chosen texts have in common is their dependence on spatial figurations to convey the experience of modernity; these texts, moreover, are integral to a European modernist aesthetic that challenges ideologies of nation, practices of national literary history, and a neglect of setting for prose construction. By reading Strindberg's transnational prose narratives, we can understand the foundation upon which literary modernism relies.

1 National Betrayal: Public, Private, and Railway Travel in *A Madman's Defence*

Location is critical to Strindberg's drama and prose from the late 1880s. Settings are marked by experimentation and transformation, while these reconceive ideological foundations for national and gendered public-private paradigms. This is evident in the plays *The Father* (1887), *Miss Julie* (1888) with its famous manifesto preface, and *Creditors* (1888; first published 1890), which provide the foundation for Strindberg's international reputation. *The Father* is set in the drawing room of a country manor that figuratively turns into an insane asylum, *Miss Julie* in a kitchen of a count's estate where characters talk repeatedly of escaping by train to continental Europe, and *Creditors* in a boarding room in an anonymous boarding house, which could be a resort anywhere in Europe. The plays from the late 1880s are written expressly for international audiences; Strindberg himself translated *The Father* into French in 1887 to promote it for production in Paris. Designed for a small migrating cast without the resources of an established (national) theatre, these plays are short, use real everyday objects as props, limit make-up, oratory, and exaggerated gestures, and can be inexpensively produced in unconventional locations, including the student association in Copenhagen where *Miss Julie* was first performed in 1889 (it premiered in Berlin in 1892 and in Paris in 1893). This play – with its explicit references to sex and menstruation, as well as implicit degradation of the nobility – was not produced in Sweden until 1905. These plays are transnational and European in their conception and reception.

Strindberg's narrative prose from the mid-1880s challenges national and gendered paradigms even more explicitly than the plays. In the prose, production and reception are displaced from nation and mother tongue – Strindberg is writing in French and Swedish while living in self-imposed exile in different locations in Europe. Narrative settings are similarly employed as vehicles that cross Swedish and French conventions of literary spatial representation. Written in French in 1887–8, the long first-person narrative *A Madman's Defence* (*Le Plaidoyer d'un fou*) engages explosive topics. These transcend national borders in their threat to constructions of bourgeois subjectivity and public-private paradigms, as they include divorce, lesbian desire, and constructions of male insanity. *A Madman's Defence*, I argue in this chapter, is actually critical for our understanding of budding European transnational modernism in its radical hybridization of settings, literary genres, themes, language(s) of composition, plot and character construction, and reception and publication. As the first-person narrator of *A Madman's Defence* appears increasingly irrational, boundaries of nation, of public and private, and of gendered conventions disintegrate in ways that illustrate how literary setting, rather than primarily character psychology, becomes a vehicle of modernist experimentation for Strindberg. Aligning itself with French nineteenth-century novelistic and dramatic conventions for the representation of marriage, domesticity, adultery, and lesbian desire, *A Madman's Defence* straddles a public European domain of literary convention as well. If Strindberg's plays from this time have been read as emblematic of modern drama, *A Madman's Defence* should be understood as one of Europe's definitive modern – indeed modernist – novels.

Composed in the first person as an extended chronological flashback, the narrator Axel gives two primary reasons for his project. The first is concern over his wife Maria's presumed adultery with men and women. The second involves a desire to write the story of his courtship and marriage in an attempt to defend himself against Maria's presumed allegations of his insanity – hence the title 'A Madman's Defence.' The text's first and longest part (about half of the total number of pages) is set in Stockholm and its surroundings and tells the story of Axel's gradual infatuation with Maria, an aspiring actress married to the baron and military officer Gustaf. Maria's scandalous elopement with Axel and subsequent divorce from Gustaf is the critical plot event, occurring at the end of part 1. The second and third parts are set in Stockholm as well, in rented rooms and in the new apartment Axel and Maria inhabit after their marriage. The later parts chronicle an accelerating dissolution of the relationship. Part 4 is told as one successive move after another, as the couple and their children travel from Stockholm to Paris and on to temporary residences in rural Switzerland, France, and

Germany. The quick relocations, Axel writes, serve to hide Maria's erotic relationships with men and women.

By the end of the nineteenth century, third-person omniscient narration set in a city, for example, had become coded as a rational and 'male' genre. First-person narration in autobiographical form, on the other hand, was a subjective 'female' genre, implicitly composed in solitude in a location removed from the urban public, such as a bourgeois domestic apartment or a rural estate. The tension between third- and first-person novelistic narration in French is critical to *A Madman's Defence* intervention in Swedish and French national literary traditions. The narrative formulates a complexity of modern transnational existence by writing it as remarkably private and intimate when composed in the first-person and in an alien language, French. By privatizing transnational and linguistic migration, *A Madman's Defence* challenges the legacy of Strindberg as Sweden's most famous and first modern writer. As an artefact of a modernist literary tradition that offers the possibility of writing oneself out of a national context, this French-language text challenges both Swedish and French national literary traditions – it is a work demonstrably alien to both national canons. Though some scholars have noted that Strindberg may have written *A Madman's Defence* to compete with contemporary and fashionable French authors such as the Goncourt brothers or Henri de Maupassant (Rossholm, 'Kommentarer' 524), others remark that especially for the later parts of the novel 'there are no French or other precursors' (Brandell, *Strindberg – Ett författarliv* 2:195, my trans.).

A Madman's Defence formalizes its frustration with rigid nineteenth-century gender and architectural conventions by use of two social transgressions – a divorce and lesbian desire – through settings that construe these transgressions less as private, intimate, or personal than as deliberate actions that rupture national and narrative conventions. These settings include street scenes and excursions to the countryside, but crystallize in locations that span public and private as reflective of the transnational: domestic apartments, a railway station, theatrical performance, and anonymous pensions.

The idiosyncratic geography of the text's production and reception circumstances reflect the transnational tensions intrinsic to it. Strindberg, having left Sweden for France in order partly to write an ethnography about French peasants (the subject of this book's next chapter), travels through Europe and then settles in poverty with his family in Denmark in the fall of 1887. Here he begins an extended first-person narrative in an adopted language, French, about earlier experiences in Stockholm: *A Madman's Defence*. The narrator of *A Madman's Defence* professes his experiences to be true, while the author in correspondence with friends in Sweden describes related events as too intimate ever to be published. As a seemingly private artefact, the text is nevertheless named after a public defence speech in a French court (*plaidoyer*). *A Madman's Defence* was first published in a German translation in 1893, *Die Beichte eines Thoren*. Obscenity charges were laid against it a year later in Wilhelmine Berlin. Its notoriety got it quick press and favourable reviews in Parisian journals before its publication in a heavily edited French version by Georges Loiseau in 1895. Only posthumously published in Swedish in 1914, that version was translated from the edited French publication because Strindberg's original manuscript had been lost. Deposited with Edvard Munch in Paris, it had been grouped with the painter's remaining property at the anatomy department of Oslo University. Here it was eventually discovered in 1973 and published in a new Swedish translation in 1976, on which both the Swedish and the French versions in the *Samlade verk*-edition are based (Rossholm, 'Kommentarer'). I include references from Anthony Swerling's translation from the French, *A Madman's Manifesto* [*sic*], with modifications as necessary.[1]

The trajectory of the manuscript and subsequent editions indicate on a material level that *A Madman's Defence* is an artefact of transnational modernity on multiple levels. Such a reading offers a departure from several main lines along which *A Madman's Defence* has been previously interpreted. In the first line of critical interpretation, which I call a narrative identity line, the text has been analysed or questioned as a form of autobiographical document (events appear to resemble some of those of Strindberg's first marriage) or, in a related strand, as fiction about the construction of narratorial identity (cf. Johannesson; Robinson; Stounbjerg; Beschnitt; and Teilmann, 'Hekseproces og ægteskabsroman'). In the second line, the work has primarily been studied for its aesthetic, social, and cultural constructions of modernity, gender, and sexuality (cf. Fahlgren; Olsson, *Levande död*; Schnurbein; Borgström; Stounbjerg; Lönngren; and Stenport, 'Inledning').

---

1 Swerling's translation is antiquated, but more reliable than other English versions, which are largely dependent on the German translation from 1893 (*Die Beichte eines Thoren*). Swerling oddly translates Le Plaidoyer d'un fou as a Madman's Manifesto, whereas I retain the literal translation A Madman's Defence in this chapter. A modern English translation of Le Plaidoyer d'un fou is long overdue.

1 Settings of Now and Then

The originating setting of *A Madman's Defence* is one of the many anonymous boarding houses that transient artist and writer émigrés would frequent at the end of the nineteenth century, and which effectively served as centres for a certain kind of impoverished, cosmopolitan, and at least temporarily denationalized *bohème*. In the introduction's first sentence, Axel, a professional writer, is interrupted at his desk in his nondescript hotel room by an attack of fever so fierce that the pen falls from his hand, preventing him momentarily from writing the narrative we are about to read. This interruption proves instrumental. Regaining consciousness means recuperating rational thinking, Axel claims, which leads him to frame his project within a naturalist methodology of objectivity, authenticity, and scientific observation. This is also a distinctly French and European approach.

Axel introduces himself, the first-person narrator, as an honest and trustworthy impartial observer, whose textual project is to publicly prove his own sanity (and discredit his wife's allegations of his madness) by conducting 'une enquête, profonde, discrète, scientifique … utilisant toutes les ressources de la nouvelle science psychologique' (*Le Plaidoyer d'un fou* 279) (a profound, discreet and scientific inquiry into my life. I will seek out everything at last, using all the resources of the new science of psychology [trans. Swerling, *A Madman's Manifesto* 11]). This scientific enterprise is also designed to prove that he is a respectable family man and father, a writer to be taken seriously, and an innocent victim of an increasingly demonized wife's scheming. Naturalism's interest in stable gender conventions and polarizing constructions of sexuality (as demonstrated in many of Zola's novels – including *Nana's* version of an actress's uninhibited libido) correlate with ideas of masculine systematicity, medical science, and legal discourse that thematically motivate the narrator's project also in *A Madman's Defence*. The gendered implications of the premise are thus full of ironies. As a self-described scientist of psychology, Axel situates himself in judicial terms as a defendant, but his defence constitutes a series of increasingly vituperative accusations against Maria. These accustions relinquish any pretence of empirical observation or scientific reasoning. He construes her maniacally at the moment of narration as ever-more sexually uninhibited, perverse, irrational, and insane, haunted by pretensions of acting and of seeking to return to the theatre. Those strategies, of course, reflect back on both narrator and narrative. *A Madman's Defence* occupies its critical, modern position because its narrative form is antithetical not only to its content (a supposed impartial retelling of a marriage in crisis), but also to naturalist novelistic conventions: it is a retrospective flashback told in an intimate first-person voice that professes initially to be neutral, rational, and discreet, yet becomes increasingly emotional, redundant, and sensationalist.

Emile Zola's novels about Paris exemplify the genre of the naturalist novel not only for literary scholars, but also for late nineteenth-century Swedish and Scandinavian readers and writers who were familiar with his work in both translation and the original. Based on the objective illusion of third-person omniscient narration in the moment plot events unfold, including extensive details not only about setting (the infamous *milieu*), but also about psychological reactions and hereditary factors, literary naturalism provides a critical context for *A Madman's Defence*. This novel takes an alternate path, however, operating on the assumption that only first-person narration, completely and obviously subjective when construed as part of an autobiographical genre, can purport to represent any form of empirically based, scientific truth-value, an 'enquête … scientifique.' Strindberg's interest in a radical, first-person, private naturalism connects with specific settings, Evert Sprinchorn implies. Strindberg explores, he writes, 'the frontier where jealousy encroaches on madness [and] set[s] up a model of the terrain in his *own home*. That is the scientific method' (introduction to *A Madman's Defence*, xiv, emphasis added). The correlation between psychology, modern science, and the domestic signals the narrative's interest in challenging boundaries between public and private. But home is a highly problematic concept in this novel, which Sprinchorn disregards. Written in the autobiographical genre of private confession – a seemingly non-naturalist, feminized genre explicitly connected to the private and domestic sphere, but originating in a rented room in an anonymous pension – the novel operates on displacements of the public-private paradigm that are critical to transnational literary production at the end of the nineteenth century.

The problems involved with using the first-person in French novelistic prose to explore constructions of sexuality (of which divorce is one social aspect), and particularly same-sex erotic attraction, begin to come into focus at the end of the nineteenth century, as Michael Lucey shows in *Never Say I*. As a French autonomous literary field became constituted through narratives operating on sophisticated versions of third-person narration that aestheticize detachment, like those of Flaubert, the interjection of first-person narration may appear as 'the less rigorous formal path' or as 'aesthetically more demanding to produce – "than the 'I' that in our most common claim to uniqueness we believe ourselves to be"' (Lucey 14, citing Bourdieu). The specific settings and correlating social transgressions of *A Madman's Defence* – the disruption of stable domestic life and a divorce; travelling on the continent; lesbian desire – are relayed by a first-person narrator who proclaims simultaneous rationality and impending insanity, by which his 'I' also becomes part of the narrative's construction of setting. Only from the starting point of a nondescript anonymous pension somewhere in continental Europe, far from identifiable national parameters (Swedish or French), could the two coalesce as a transnational project of scientific inquiry that shares genre characteristics with the journal form. As setting and the use of the first-person pronoun coalesce in *A Madman's Defence*, a public form of novelistic narration (like that of a Bourdieusian-defined autonomous literary field) becomes private. And this seemingly intimate, private, and immediate pronoun (as in our own individual claims to uniqueness) is arguably what allows for Strindberg's first sustained interventions in German and French literary fields: think of the trial of *Die Beichte eines Thoren*, for example. *Die Beichte* is a distinct point of origin for a persistent German (and Swedish) scholarly trend of psycho-pathologizing Strindberg and his work, which Ulf Olsson in a useful term calls the practice of pathography (*Jag blir galen* 94, 169, 179–89). The first person in *A Madman's Defence* partakes when read in this light in a sustained modernist first-person talking cure.

The foreign reception of *A Madman's Defence* fueled Strindberg's sustained notoriety within a Swedish context as well, as the use of the first-person pronoun in French connotes national betrayal. If Strindberg, a Swedish national perspective may imply, had to write about such social transgressions as divorce and lesbian desire, subjecting himself to allegations of insanity, and attempt to deconstruct via transnational travel (even self-construed exile from the Swedish homeland) apparently stable heteronormative paradigms of public and private, why could he at least not have done so from a recognizably aestheticized and detached third-person perspective? Indeed, one crucial aspect that locates *A Madman's Defence* outside established literary convention, and as part of late nineteenth-century modernist experimentation, is that setting and pronoun use disrupt those conventions of genre, linguistics (including monolingualism and national language use), and spatiality that by the end of the nineteenth century were construed as integral to quality, and seen as canonizable, novelistic representation.

The first chapter of *A Madman's Defence* describes a location markedly different from the anonymous European pension of the introduction, while maintaining a temporal immediacy. I quote here from the first paragraph of the first chapter.

> C'est le treize Mai 1875, à Stockholm. *Je me vois d'ici* dans la vaste salle de la Bibliothèque Royale, occupant une aile entière du palais du roi, lambris-sée en hêtre, rembruni par le temps comme de l'écume de mer bien culot-tée. L'immense pièce, ornée de cartouches roccoco, de guirlandes, de chaînes, d'armoiries ... s'ouvre sous mes pieds comme un gouffre sin-geant par ces mille cents volumes qu'elle enferme un cerveau gigantesque où se casent des idées de générations passes ... *Je me vois d'ici* ... en train de classer une charretée de bouquins. (283, emphasis added)

> It was the thirteenth of May 1875 in Stockholm. *I can still see myself* at the Royal Library, which occupies an entire wing of the palace of the King, in the vast hall with its beech wainscoting, brown with age like the meer-schaum of a well-tanned pipe. The immense hall decorated with rococo beadings, garlands, chains, and armorial bearings ... open[s] out, yawning like a chasm beneath my feet, the image of a gigantic brain, with the hun-dred thousand volumes which it h[olds], where the ideas of vanished gen-erations were [are] ranged in cases ... *I can still see myself* ... classifying a collection of old books. (13, with the translation's past tense modified to correspond with the original's present)

The setting's notation, 'the Royal Library of Stockholm on May thir-teenth, 1875,' anchors the narration on the one hand in a verifiably real-istic domain, but on the other signals the narrator's aesthetic strategies of displacement. Zooming in on architectural details (the wainscoting, the beadings, garlands, and chains), the passage immediately discredits attempts of realist, objective spatio-temporal specificity. The passage appears to transition from exteriority to interiority, to a subjective pos-ition, from which Axel can 'see himself' both in the moment and loca-tion of narration, emphasized twice in the opening section.

Strindberg's characteristic use in French of the present tense (often in participial form) to narrate the past reflects the narrative structure. The Royal Library remains etched in the present, while another location, 'ici' (here) is emphasized as the location of narration, which establishes a bilocational present time that is both transnational and bilingual. The setting of the Royal Library is already literalized. The novel's extended flashback begins in a library that resembles a human brain – a site of primary interest for scientific and naturalistic discourse, whose winding sections span a chasm, squarely positioning the supposedly 'true' experience of the narrator's need to defend himself against accusations of insanity as ensconced in the realm of the written word, which is simultaneously an anthropomorphized architectural space. The chasm is also figurative in this passage, since it indicates, by extension, the narrator's displaced location in an anonymous pension in far-away Bavaria, where he has arrived after a stay in Paris. He is dislocated not only from Sweden, but also from one of its primary representatives of national history and culture – the Royal Library. Here he was once classifying the books of a national archive, now he is constructing a modern narrative as a scientific inquiry not only of himself but also of transnational displacements (cf. Olsson, *Levande död* 179–80).

The first two parts of *A Madman's Defence*, set in Stockholm, constitute the most detailed contemporary city description Strindberg ever wrote, far exceeding that of *The Red Room*, which is usually understood as Sweden's first modern city novel. Streets, buildings, apartments, and domestic objects are often described in detail in the French narrative, though there is no pretence at panoramic totality. In contrast to the earlier novel, *A Madman's Defence* offers no panoramic representation of Stockholm on the cusp of large-scale urbanization, industrialization, and rapid migration from the Swedish countryside. A companion description to the famous view from Mosebacke Hill in the opening section of *The Red Room* is in *A Madman's Defence* framed by a window, which Axel opens from the library to take in both the views of the harbour with its ships sporting flags from different nations – Spain, Germany, Denmark, and Russia – and its sounds and smells: horns and bells, machine oil and imported spices (*Le Plaidoyer* 285 [trans. Swerling 15]). Just as in this brief description of a small sliver of Stockholm, locations figure generally as though composed of fragmentary snapshots, culled from an album of memory, or as disparate scenes emerging from under the microscope of the observing, cataloguing naturalist: the flashback description of Stockholm is part of the tension in narrative convention that operates on multiple levels in *A Madman's Defence*.

Some of the narrative's city descriptions appear as fragments influenced not only by the experiences of a narrator-in-exile who has travelled to Paris and on the European continent, but also by having them dislodged from the material circumstances of a still-provincial Stockholm of the mid-1870s. In one passage, for example, the description of a spring market includes merchandise that would have been available much more readily in a market in Paris than in Stockholm, while the descriptive technique emphasizes a temporal bifurcation (the present tense is maintained) that clashes with the enumeration of items: '[A]ux devantures des marchands-fleuristes les azaléas, les rhododendrons et les roses précoces étalent leur pompe criarde; les oranges illuminent les vitres des épiciers, les homards, les radis, les choux-fleurs d'Algier décorent l'exhibition des charcutiers' (362) (In the shop-fronts of the florists the azaleas, the rhododendrons and the early roses offered [offer] their coloured splendour to the eye; the oranges shone [shine] in the windows of the grocers; the lobsters, the radishes and the cauliflowers from Algeria appeared [appear] on the stalls of the greengrocer's [81]). From the produce imported from Algeria (a nod toward France's colonial holdings rather than Swedish trade routes of the 1870s) to fresh roses, such details of the streetscape convey the image of a large, modern city, wherein Stockholm emerges as Parisianized, as part already of the transnational literary framework that the spatio-temporal disjunctures of setting establish in *A Madman's Defence*. The narrative's disjointed fragments of described setting operate on strategies of displacement, which are complemented by temporal disjunctures, in which a past in Stockholm is imagined as a still-present. Such strategies of spatial representation are also part of the deconstruction of the public-private paradigm; the Stockholm of *A Madman's Defence* is a private world, one imagined by a first-person narrator whose understanding of individuality and uniqueness, with subsequent literary output, bridges a 'je' with an 'ici' in the present tense.

Descriptions of Stockholm are explicitly juxtaposed in the novel's first part with nature descriptions. Vaguely nostalgic descriptions of summertime alfresco dining or excursions to the countryside by steamer tie the narrator back to a specific Swedish cultural context. These scenes reflect a late nineteenth-century promise, namely, that summertime predicates for the middle and upper classes an active engagement with rustic (national) nature, including vacationing on a lake or in the archipelago. Later, deciding to break off with Maria, Axel takes a steamer bound for Le Havre, but seeing the rugged Baltic archipelago south of Stockholm gradually disappear in the October mist, he cannot fathom the break it would entail – 'la tension intérieure augmentait; c'était comme le cordon ombilical qui me liait à la terre natale, à la patrie, à la famille et – à elle, était sur le point de rompre' (339) (the interior tension augmented. It was as if the umbilical cord which was linking me to the native land, to my mother country [fatherland], to the family, to Her, was about to be severed [61]). The break is public and private at the same time, and conceived in explicitly national terms. Returning to Stockholm means returning both to Maria as his mistress and to her home as nation. As the narrator begins penning his narrative, however, he is dislocated not only from Stockholm, but also from such a cultural context, living in an anonymous continental pension devoid of connection to home or sentiments of national belonging.

The tension in *A Madman's Defence* between past and present, estrangement and belonging, a scientifically observing 'I' and a subjective one of immediate narration, and city and country, also involves challenges to the public-private paradigm. The narrative repeatedly conjures up examples of how the architectural and gendered conventions of late nineteenth-century urban modernity coincide. The narrator, recalling how he has attempted to break off his illicit love affair with Maria (she is still married), invokes the spatial layout of a busy Stockholm thoroughfare to admonish Maria for her audacity at seeking him out on her own, thus establishing not only the urban landscape as an inherent order of appropriate gender compartmentalization, dictating that women remain stationary in the home while men move about the city, but also that the public domain produces Maria's desire as inappropriate.

Le résultat: la baronne vient par hasard à ma rencontre le midi où je quitte la bibliothèque. Elle s'arrête sur le Pont de Nord, me retient, me conduit à l'écart dans une allée de la place Charles XII. Presqu'en larmes elle me supplie de revenir, de ne demander plus d'explications, d'être à eux comme jadis. Comme elle était charmante ce jour-là! Mais je l'aimais trop haut pour la perdre.

– Laissez-moi, ou vous allez gâter votre renommée! lui infligeai-je, en examinant les promeneurs dont les regards nous embarrassèrent. Allez chez-vous, tout de suite, de ce pas, sinon je vous chasse! (367)

The result was that the Baroness came, as if by chance, to meet me, about midday, when I was leaving the Library. She stopped on North Bridge, held me back and led me aside into an alleyway on Charles XII Square. Almost in tears, she begged me to come back, not to ask any more explanations, to be

simply theirs as before. Ah! How charming she was that day! But I loved
her too much to lose her. 'Leave me, do. You're going to cast a slur on your
reputation,' I repeated to her, examining the pedestrians whose looks em-
barrassed us. 'Return home, at once, or I'll be the one to leave you.' (90)

The street is here the location of social control through the mediation of
the crowd, which, it appears, is one to take gendered divisions of public
space for granted. That confluence of architecture and gender appears on
the one hand as an ideological given, as a marker of the ideological
permanence of the public-private paradigm of social referentiality, and as
a location of narrative control from the present back-projected onto a past
in Stockholm, since the narrator appears to have internalized the norms
of this particular urban space and carries those norms with him to the
moment of narration. The referential markers used to do this – Stockholm
street and place names translated literally into French – are intriguingly
displaced from the social normativization of public and private the narrator otherwise conjures up. '[L]e Pont du Nord' or 'la place Charles XII'
create hybrid linguistic and transnational spaces, which juxtapose recollection with the creation of a new French Stockholm.

The narrator is able to remember and represent in detail both architectural specificities (exactly what merchandise was displayed, in what
particular location Axel and Maria met, and so on) and his own utterances. Just as we may ask whether the speaker's words are his in the
narrating moment (i.e., in the future with respect to the events narrated,
or, as relayed syntactically in the present tense), we may wonder if the
architectural references also belong to the realm of imagination. Is the
Stockholm of *A Madman's Defence* displaced temporally, pulling between a representation that is safely ensconced in the past while being
imagined in the here-and-now of a present inspired by travel on the
continent, and also in Paris? Descriptions like those of the Royal Library,
the market stalls, or the street encounter disrupt understandings of
what is foreign or alien, just as they disrupt conceptions of public and
private. Strindberg's translations of particular Swedish street and place
names create a hybrid space, which is part of how the setting of *A
Madman's Defence* blurs boundaries. Axel tells Maria to return home,
'Allez chez-vous,' while that home is a fictionalized concept. The street
in Stockholm is a public location, but it tells a story that is also private.
In one parallel understanding, Axel and Maria's story cannot be written or published in the private sphere of the nation, but must be inserted
into a form conceptualized as public – the defence speech or scientific

investigation. In another interpretation, Strindberg's manuscript abandons the dual order of native language, relinquishing Sweden's official language (the nation's public form of expression) and his mother tongue (as private and intimate). The narrative is clearly fetischistic about the denial of nation and national language: it maintains it by not acknowledging that Axel is constructing a narrative in a transnational experimental form in a language alien to or acquired by him.

The spatio-temporal disjunctures and their linguistic formalization contribute to *A Madman's Defence*'s hybrid and modernist setting. The narrative's opening section at the Royal Library is also the starting point for a journey, which goes from rootedness in a literalized and literary history of Sweden to an internalization of the experience of travelling on the continent. There, a steam engine unravels him, and 'à chaque coup de piston, je deviens plus mince' (513) (at every stroke of the piston, I grew thinner [225]); later it is 'la locomotive qui m'espouline les boyaux, les lobes de la cervelle, les nerfs, les vaisseaux de sang, toutes les viscères' (514) (the locomotive which unwound [unwinds] my intestines, the lobes of my brain, my nerves, my blood vessels, all my viscera [225]). This is a journey not only toward a cosmopolitan form of literary representation, but eventually also away from such stable conceptions of gender as those inscribed within a nation's public-private paradigm. Those are the questions I will turn to in the following sections.

2 The Apartment, the Railway Station, and the Transnational Rupture of Divorce

The displacements of language use and temporality that form part of the transnational setting in *A Madman's Defence* formulate also a modernist interest in narrative destabilization of a gendered public-private paradigm. This means the literary deconstruction of one of the late nineteenth-century's primary novelistic conventions. As an ideologically restrictive setting, stable domestic apartment living based on heteronormative practices is eventually relinquished, so that the narrative can be written as if outside those restrictions – as if formulating as aesthetic preconditions the social transgressions that caused its shock value at the time, and which situates the novel at a historical moment when divorce and lesbian desire had become emblematic of threats to the nation, to discreet (in both senses of the word) bourgeois subjectivity, to idealist aesthetic philosophy, and to the rupture between naturalism's relaying of social transgressions and modernism's production of those as aesthetic artefacts. For Strindberg to effectuate such a modernist project through a first-person narrator and within what are already transnational, displaced settings (i.e., the very context of *A Madman's Defence*), the constrictions the narrative has to free itself from must at first be established as formal conventions of the text itself. Only as these break down in an impending moment of transnational travel (in a fated scene at Stockholm's train station at the end of the narrative's first part) can the narrative begin to explore alternate paradigms.

A Madman's Defence emerges from conceptions of setting specific to French and European novels at the end of the nineteenth century, as these had come to depend on an 'architectural shifter' as part of a formalized metalanguage for a representational space of literature. Terms like 'structure,' 'composition,' 'framework,' 'point of view,' and so forth, Philippe Hamon argues in *Expositions: Literature and Architecture in Nineteenth-Century France*, illustrate a metaliterary complex. This complex, I argue in an extension of Hamon's work, ties setting to the fundamentals of narrative construction. Novelistic representation increased in popularity in both France and Sweden during a period of tumultuous large-scale architectural urban transformation, exemplified by Haussmann's and Lindhagen's city plans of Paris and Stockholm, respectively. In conjunction with developments such as these, Hamon suggests, it 'is as if the writer henceforth would always have to provide housing for his characters, to make them inhabitants; no longer would he be able to describe any of his heroes' habits ... without also mentioning their habitat' (6). As such, novelistic convention helps architecture, as in *archè* (origin, law), establish itself as an origin of all other arts, Hamon provocatively suggests, by which textual representation of a building not only *is* order, but 'represents an order, and gives orders to its users' (33).

Hamon's understanding of architecture is speculative, but actually quite illustrative of the order (as in the public-private paradigm) that *A Madman's Defence* tries to undo through a modernist and formalized transnationalism. As a form of ur-origin, the *archè* parallels an apparently stable late nineteenth-century heteronormative paradigm. The presence of recognizable architectural objects (of which a bourgeois apartment in Stockholm would be exemplary for Swedish readers, and whose anonymity would be recognizable to continental readers) guarantees the text's connection with 'reality' in ways that can be used by a writer as 'a *privileged shifter*, as an object in which the structural has become concretized or an object that mediates between the text (a semiotic object) and the extra-textual (a nonsemiotic object). Moreover, the building functions as a primary operator of metaphor that allows the real to be rewritten into the text or vice versa' (Hamon 37, emphasis added). The gendered implications are critical here (but completely overlooked by Hamon), since the status of architecture as law and order is in and of itself ambiguous. As always part of a system in which signs are rewriting signs, architecture becomes an iterative practice like that of gender conventions. It is precisely in this relation, which operates by way of narrative setting on formal and social levels, that constructions of gender and architecture correlate, and which modernist representational practices like those in *A Madman's Defence* eventually deconstruct.

The home Maria shares with the baron is a vehicle for the aestheticization and detachment that the private sphere entails. When married to Gustaf and living in their apartment, she is described by Axel in part 1 as a Madonna, as a Virgin Mother, as a Grecian marble sculpture, and as a portrait: beautiful and immobile, distanced and delocalized from actual practices of married life and motherhood. As their affair progresses, Axel's desire for Maria increases when they are together in the home she shares with the baron. Illustrative not only of a distinct homoerotic attraction between two men who desire the same woman in a triangular erotic constellation, as Lönngren has argued, the apartment setting also produces the representation of desire in forms mediated by conventions of the public-private paradigm. In a related argument, Olsson argues that through the aesthetization of Maria, the novel foregrounds a representational crisis of the European novel, which 'anchors *A Madman's Defence* in the *modern*' (*Levande död*, my trans., 172). The 'novel's "crisis" is not a crisis about "masculine consciousness,"' Olsson continues, 'but about the novel as an act in and of itself, i.e., as a crisis of aesthetic representation as such. Naturally it is not a coincidence … that a novel about a woman is a novel about representation' (160–1, my trans.). Olsson argues here convincingly that *A Madman's Defence* makes explicit the gendered structures implicit in European novelistic convention. Locations in the novel similarly produce specific gendered conceptualizations. When Maria's divorce from the baron is immanent, when the private transgression of the adultery is about to be made public, the apartment transforms through imagery marked by death and decay into a haunted house and into a location that transfers from a private home to a public morgue: the apartment 'sente le chloroforme' (382) (was stinking with the smell of chloroform [102]); the location has been tainted: 'ce domicile devasté … cette maison fatale' (393–4) ([this] devastated household again ... that house hounded by fate [114–15]). The apartment setting functions as a shifter to illustrate the problems caused by stifling gender conventions, by which immanent divorce transforms imagery of the domestic to death. These characters need a habitat according to narrative convention, but the habitat produces a public-private problem that can only be resolved by transnational travel.

The blurring of boundaries between public and private in Maria's apartment increases as part of the narrator's strategic rhetoric of self-defence – he is, as we remember, writing his own defence speech in a foreign language to stave off allegations of his insanity. An expedient way in this narrative to maintain order, to appear rational, is to represent one of the causes of his insanity – transgressions of adultery and divorce – as inherent in the setting. Axel's hesitation about Maria's immanent divorce the evening before she is scheduled to leave expresses a spatialized complexity that ties disruptions of kin and nation to architectural ordering: 'L'amitié, la parenté, l'amour, tout est compromis, et l'adultère, tant en règle qu'elle soit dirigée, a mis sa souillure sur les seuils de ce logis' (394) (Friendship, kinship, love, all was compromised, and adultery, despite our care to regularise it, had put its smear on the threshold of that home [115]). The apartment threshold exemplifies the strictures of a public-private paradigm that interlock architecture and gender.

A rhetoric of privacy and domesticity conflicts with the all-too obvious material indications that such are no longer possible, if they ever were: Maria must return home to her apartment at once to prevent a scandal in the street, while a kiss hidden from view behind drawing-room doors makes the conceit of privacy obvious. Similarly, *A Madman's Defence* addresses the conceit of apartment living as private, and this indicates the architectural shifters at play in the narrative's setting. Shoddy building practices of the late nineteenth-century building boom in Stockholm and elsewhere in European cities meant that neighbours could be heard through thin walls, just as entry and exit could be seen by those living below or above. In *A Madman's Defence*, written in 1887–8, events appear to take place about a decade earlier, during an extreme building boom in Stockholm. Like Paris, Berlin, and Vienna, Stockholm's centralized planning favoured apartment building, with housing speculation rampant during the 1870s. In a rush to complete construction, apartment buildings were sometimes erected with faulty materials, insufficient insulation, and occasionally they even collapsed before the move-in date (Johansson, *Stor-Stockholms bebyggelsehistoria*

151–5; Gejvall 42–6). At the same time, debates about and regulations for the healthful design of apartments increased in political and public prominence. In 1877, the national sanitation and public health resolution (Hälsovårdsstadgan) was implemented in Stockholm, which mandated access to drinking water, outhouse facilities, and garbage removal. New rental restrictions meant that apartments could not be leased if they were not safe and clean. These developments complemented earlier directives on healthful apartment building design, such as courtyard size, daylight access, and ceiling height (Gejvall 42–3; on bourgeois ideologies of cleanliness and sanitation in nineteenth-century Sweden, see Frykman and Löfgren).

The material experience of apartment living is one factor in the private-public paradigm that *A Madman's Defence* seeks to rewrite. Another one is how the elusive privacy of modern living is construed as a problem of the commodification of domestic life, correlating implicitly with the rampant housing speculation of Stockholm in the late 1870s and a perception that apartment living had become misguided in terms of its constructions of public and private. Maintaining a large 'salong' (drawing room) as mandatory for middle class apartment design began to be heavily criticized, with the Stockholm Health and Sanitation Organization (Hälsovårdsföreningen) in 1882 arguing sharply against bourgeois practices of designing dwelling space for the public purpose of entertaining one's friends, rather than for one's own comfort (Gejvall 224). The primary social regulations for middle-class apartment dwelling – marriage (and divorce) – are formalized as both private and public economic transactions, while they remain romantic and intimate in an idealistic paradigm that seeks to uphold boundaries between public and private. As Maria is getting ready to leave the home she has shared with the baron, the dialogue turns to financial matters. The impending divorce will cost money; it involves an irreparable break-up of the household that shatters any clear demarcations between boundaries of public and private. In the juxtaposition of objects understood to be intimate (Maria's underwear) with a bourgeois location understood as public ('le salon' [the drawing-room]), this particular setting signifies the trauma at the heart of the first part of *A Madman's Defence*. The narrator recalls (in the present participal form again) the situation retrospectively with fascination as well as rhetorical conditionality:

Dans le salon tout annonce la dissolution du ménage; du linge traînant sur les meubles, des robes, des jupons, des hardes. Là sur le piano les

chemisettes aux dentelles que je sais par coeur; ici sur le bureau les cale-
çons, toute une pile; des bas, naguère mon rêve, maintenant mon dégoût.
Et elle va et vient, remuant plissant, comptant, sans vergogne sans pudeur.
Est-ce moi qui l'a corrumpue en si peu de temps! me dis-je, en contem-
plant cette exhibition des secrets d'une femme honnête. (394)

In the drawing-room everything pointed [points] to the dissolution of the
home. Linen was [is] scattered on the furniture, dresses, underskirts,
clothing. On the piano, there, I noticed [notice] the chemisettes with cleav-
ages [lace] I knew [know] so well. [Here] On the bureau rose [*sic*!] a whole
pile of women's knickers and stockings, once my dream, now my disgust.
She came and went [comes and goes], arranging, folding, counting, without modesty, without shame. 'Was [is] it I who had [have] corrupted her in
so short a time?' I said [say] to myself, contemplating that exhibition of a
decent woman's underclothing. (115)

Underwear spread all over the furniture signals the exposition of the
economic transactions contained in the idea of domesticity in all their
intimate detail – how narrative setting produces a fluctuating paradigm
of public and private, which here appears so confused that even
straightforward verb usage gets interrupted. In the French original,
nouns are piled together without predicate verbs. The parataxis creates
urgency and prepositions, 'there,' 'here' establish a spatio-temporal immediacy. The dissolution of syntax and the fragmentation of grammat-
ical form into single meaning-bearing units is, of course, a well-known
strategy of modernist novelistic form. Here a related technique is used
to overcome the formal problem of representing the transgressions involved in the display of underwear, the egregious concatenation of objects and situations imagined as belonging in separate spheres yoked
together. The syntax helps destabilize the public-private paradigm. At
the same time, the intimate apparel appears to recall a display in a *ma-
gasin de détail* (retail store), a location in which the folding and organizing of underwear indeed would be a perfectly expected activity. The
scene provides a connection with the display of ladies' merchandise,
most strikingly the silken underwear and lace, in Zola's 1883 novel
about a quintessential Parisian department store, *The Ladies Paradise*
(*Au Bonheur des dames*), written a few years before *A Madman's Defence*.
The apartment as department store correlates with divorce as an economic transaction. When displayed, women's underwear becomes
only one of a list of items that indicate the narrator's futile attempt to

maintain the boundaries between domestic space and the market place, between private and public, and between the image of his future wife as both Madonna and whore.

Descriptions like these formulate the modernist setting of *A Madman's Defence* – the realization that boundaries between public and private are gendered, and also that their value as architectural shifters vary depending on which paradigm is construed as primary. The 'dissolution of the home' remarked upon by Axel as he sees Maria's underwear displayed all over the drawing room transcends the apartment, however. It is by traversing the Central Station and travelling to Copenhagen on her own that Maria will be able to attain a divorce; this reflects the historical fact that divorce was for Swedish middle- and upper-class women a transnational enterprise. Leaving one's nation – as an extension of the juridical clause that formalized marital separation, 'förlupa hemmet' (abscond from one's home) – precluded the mandatory one-year of separate habitation between the spouses that was the other way to divorce at the time (Boëthius, *Strindberg och kvinnofrågan* 17). Gendered constructions of private and public were thus implicitly national as well.

The Stockholm Central Station, inaugurated in 1871, stood for the easy transfer of goods, services, and people. Emblematic of modern travel practices, the building and its practices provide one of the many pivotal transnational settings of *A Madman's Defence*. Axel is at the station waiting for Maria, who is to be accompanied to her train's departure by her husband in order to reduce gossip. The baron neglects to appear:

> A six heures le soir je stationne dans la vestibule de la gare centrale. Le train va partir pour Copenhague six heures un quart, et la baronne n'est pas visible, ni le baron non plus … Enfin elle arrive dans un fiacre, mal attelé, s'elançant à brides abattues. – Toujours negligente et en retard! – Affolée, elle accourt à ma rencontre, en se démenant comme une aliénée – Il a manqué à sa parole, le traître! Il n'y sera pas! s'écrie-t-elle assez bruyamment pour attirer l'attention de la foule remuante. (396)

> Six o'clock in the evening. I did sentry-go in [I pace] the large hall of the central station. The train for Copenhagen was [is] to leave at a quarter past six and I could [can] not see the Baron or the Baroness coming … At last, there she was [is]. She came [comes] in a cab drawn by a mare which the coachman drove [drives] at full speed. Always negligent and always late. She dashed [runs] to me, flinging herself about like a madwoman.

'The traitor, he didn't keep his word. He is not coming!' she exclaimed [exclaims] noisily enough to attract the attention of the passers-by who became [become] agitated. (117)

The very location of the Central Station makes the divorce happen by indexing it as a public fact: the baron does not arrive to help them all save face. Axel's pacing indicates stasis in a setting supposedly marked by movement: he moves back and forth, waiting for Maria to arrive and then to leave, fearing a scandal but instrumentalizing the deconstruction of public and private he has sought to maintain before. The presumed anonymity of the train station permits the transgression the narrative has tried to hide: Maria can fling herself on Axel here. This location produces a transition to modernity, which has already been suggested by narrative strategies that blur past and present, juxtapose claims of objectivity with subjective rendition, and cross-cut between locations understood as Swedish and others as foreign. At the impending moment of divorce, the train station is emblematic of both urban modernity and transnational travel. This setting transfers an image of Maria from an aestheticized domestic virgin mother to the social figure of the divorcee. The figuration correlates with an inscription of her insanity – the train station, the implication of transnational travel, and the final relinquishing of a former married life turns her into an 'aliénée' (madwoman); into a character alienated from both home and nation – an alien. Maria will occupy this position during the rest of the novel, while the narrator professes that he wants to free himself from her allegations of his insanity. Madness appears contagious, however, and originates from the location that makes the social transgression of divorce known – Axel's stasis and Maria's flinging herself on him are corporealized gestures of the narrative's frustration with architecturally constituted gendered paradigms of the public and private.

The station crowd's attention leads to an image of immediate gossip flying through the city as if it were communicated by some new form of broadcast technology, moreover: 'Le lendemain du départ toute la capitale est informée sur l'enlèvement de la baronne de X. par un attaché de la bibliothèque royale' (403) (The day after our departure, the whole capital was informed [knows] of the abduction of Baroness X by a librarian at the Royal Library [123]). Certain settings produce certain effects and permit certain actions – the architectural object of a train station reinscribes Maria in the code of 'X.' Divorce (as effected in the train station sequence) becomes a present absence in the text. It reduces the character

Maria from a name and a rational subject into a sign of anonymity, just as the 'X' involves the veritable crossing out of stable married normativity and of national adherence (Maria is travelling to Europe, as unnamed). The production and subsequent cultivation of insanity by way of perceived social transgression is indeed contagious – these are the subject positions Axel will cultivate (albeit in different ways) for both himself and Maria in the remaining part of the narrative.

The episode in the Central Station, and its subsequent effects, tie in with a persistent metarhetorical concern in the novel: the blurring of boundaries between authenticity and performance. This blur is modernity's sign post, but also one of architecture and gender. Maria's hopes of becoming an actress help motivate her divorce from the baron; with Axel, she is promised, she can live the independent life of an artist. Axel repeatedly describes Maria's acting plans, however, in terms of madness, while the act of writing and constructing a narrative is presented by the first-person narrator in the introduction as authentic, honest, and honourable. The narrator's interest in architectural details and his ability to render them with precision in a foreign language, French, illustrates the narrative's interest in juxtaposing authenticity and performance.

French had, in fact, become an intimate and domestic language for Strindberg at this time, Elena Balzamo asserts in marked contrast to much previous scholarship about Strindberg's use of French during the mid-1880s, which has tended to see it as deficient and derivative (see also Olof Eriksson, 'Strindbergs franska: en språklig paradox'). Particularly in the short story collection *Utopias in Reality* (*Utopier i verkligheten*) (1885), written in Swedish while the author was living near Lausanne, can Strindberg's persistent use of Gallicisms be understood to indicate that French was no longer primarily a language of the written, of literature, and of intellectual pursuits – by extension a language of performance, for gaining recognition in Paris, or for situating his work within a context of French as the late nineteenth-century's literary language par excellence (Balzamo 46–7). In everyday spoken language, the short stories represent a Francophone reality through Frenchified words used particularly for household items and objects of domestic architecture (47). Similarly, Strindberg's use of French in *A Madman's Defence* blurs customary understandings of authenticity. As a long narrative that scrupulously translates street and place names, *A Madman's Defence* Frenchifies Stockholm, at least partly for the benefit, it would seem, of a Parisian reading public who arguably knew little about the Stockholm urban landscape.

That *A Madman's Defence* was written in French sheds additional light on the gendered conventions that are part of what makes this novel challenge the public-private paradigm on so many levels. Strindberg's attempt to align Stockholm and Paris on a representational axis is particularly intriguing, not least because it relates to a long tradition of French writing about the capital city that both seeks to uphold and deconstruct boundaries of public and private (Marcus 6; Cohen, 'Panoramic Literature and the Invention of Everyday Genres'). A feminized other haunts the narrative, which heightens the image of Maria as Paris: unreliable, deceptive, vindictive, and unauthentic. Maria's characterization as a piece of art, as a spectacle or fleeting image, also corresponds to the image of Paris, *la cité lumière*, in contemporary cultural parlance, and arguably for Strindberg the author who had only limited and fleeting success there. Paris, for the narrator, as well as for Strindberg and other writers from Europe's margins, represents both a *habitus* of idealized international literary success along the lines defined by Casanova in *The World Republic of Letters* (drawing on Bourdieu), yet functions as an aesthetized location whose corrupted, unattainable status, just like Maria's, aligns it with demonical images of the feminine.

The transnational project of Frenchifying Stockholm in *A Madman's Defence* clearly entails a strategy of making it known to a larger reading public, by which this professed private document becomes a narrative also of transnational literary transfer, of an explicit desire to challenge boundaries of national literatures that at first correlate with adherence to the fictions of a public-private paradigm. In fact, the explicit thematization of divorce as a transnational enterprise in *A Madman's Defence* (Maria leaving both home and nation in the railway station scene) reflects in intriguing ways contested French divorce debates of the mid 1880s. Napoleon's Civil Code had formalized French marriage law restrictively and as reflective of a nationalizing discourse – divorce was hardly possible during most of the nineteenth century. Debates about rights to and practical possibilities of divorce were brought to public awareness in Paris during the 1880s, as Senator Alfred Naquet's well-known 'campaign for divorce' went through a number of iterations before a law was finally implemented in 1884. This law allowed divorce for special reasons only – cruelty, adultery, and serious criminal activity, as Jean Elizabeth Pedersen shows in *Legislating the French Family* (30–5). The Naquet debates occurred exactly at the time when Strindberg was living in France and continental Europe and seeking to become a French writer – the explicit attention in *A Madman's Defence* to the effects of divorce indicate the transnational reach of these issues.

The transgression of divorce in *A Madman's Defence* reflects Swedish and Scandinavian contexts, but the text also glosses specifics of marriage practices in the North presumably for the benefit of a French reader (429 [146]). Such references to marriage and divorce correlate in Strindberg's novel with Maria's aspirations of becoming a professional actress once separated from her first husband. French theatre at the time, Pedersen argues, became a particularly important arena for divorce debates, as 'self-consciously political playwrights sought to persuade their audiences to support social change by producing stories about the effects of particular pieces of French legislation' (1). At the time, the Civil Code maintained its legacy as a symbol of national unity and as a vehicle for creating French identity, particularly in its emphasis on family, marriage, and the domestic. Parisian playwrights Alexandre Dumas fils, Emile Auguier, and Paul Hervieu 'created what they variously called social dramas, thesis plays, or useful theater to dramatize the social injustices associated with various legal structures' (Pedersen 3). Hervieu's play *The Chains* (*Les Tenailles*) is largely unknown today, but after its premiere and successful extended run at the Comédie Française in 1895, it became a focus piece for the Parisian debates on divorce at the end of the 1890s. Compared repeatedly to Ibsen and *A Doll's House*, Hervieu and *The Chains* became yoked with the influence of *A Doll's House*, which had played the year before at the Théâtre de Vaudeville.

With Russian and German authors, Scandinavians like Ibsen and Strindberg became identified by conservative Parisian critics, such as Francisque Sarcey of *Le Temps*, as part of 'The Fog from the North' (Pedersen 50, see also Ahlström, 'Strindbergs erövring' 232–42). *A Doll's House* addressed explicitly intersections between public and private in ways that illustrate divorce not only as a domestic but as a specifically transnational issue. Foreign authors arguably helped French playwrights (like Hervieu) gain traction and influenced the French domestic debates on divorce during the 1890s. As Pedersen puts it, both 'Ibsen's and Hervieu's plays featured rebellious women [both of whom actively argue for marital separation] with conventional husbands, and both provoked similar French debates over whether such women and their sisters were French or foreign,' while, for some observers, Ibsen's success in Paris represented not only 'an international literary phenomenon, but also a serious national political threat' (Pedersen 50–1).

A Madman's Defence was written when the Naquet debates were at their high-point in the mid 1880s. It was published in Paris in 1895, just as theatrical representation about these issues increased in prevalence.

A Madman's Defence's representation of divorce thus correlates with a French late nineteenth-century tradition of coding divorce as dramatically authentic, as worthy of a public form of representation, and as representative of large social problems that tie the domestic to the national. Similarly, French divorce debates and drama contextualize what the architectural settings of *A Madman's Defence* construe as distinctive about late nineteenth-century modernity's frustration with gendered conventions.

These frustrations produce insanity and madness, and they indicate a metaphorical straightjacket that Axel appears to try and write himself out of in his first-person narrative. The reinscription of gendered conventions into architectural objects and identifiable locations signifies the narrative's initial belief in their stability and their materiality, while the divorce transition in the railway station ruptures both gendered conventions and architectural ones. Here space is *not* metaphorical but generates actions that shatter ideologies of domestic and national belonging. These make visible how figurations of apartment setting and domestic dwelling as 'authentic' break down again and again. The railway station reveals that the separation of public and private is a fantasy, and one that is also textually construed. The divorce happens here before its inscription in a legal document. Maria's departure from Stockholm to Copenhagen is transnational; it is part of a modernist conceptualization of subject, nation, and social restrictions, just as it means also a radical departure from the *habitat* (in Hamon's terms) of her old apartment, into a *habitat* not only of travel and displacement, but also of differently gendered positions (as a divorcee and subsequently a lesbian), which the first-person narrative must account for but finds increasingly difficult to describe.

3 Lesbian Desire, Performance, and Transnational Travel

If literary naturalism seeks to provide a habitat (as architectural, gendered, national) that encompasses the public-private paradigm for its characters, that is, to properly house them within late nineteenth-century bourgeois ideology, *A Madman's Defence* illustrates a transition to settings that are modernist. The second half of the novel investigates what happens when a narrative unhouses its characters, when it dedomesticates, and ultimately denationalizes them. The shifters that lock architecture and gender conventions together in the first part of the narrative get disrupted, and any assertions of authenticity as based in references to setting gradually get compromised. This is a critical issue for a narrative that seeks to represent scientifically and authentically the experiences of its first-person narrator, and that has relied on the conceit of exact spatio-temporal specificity to enable that fiction. New living arrangements become increasingly problematic, however, as they challenge a gendered public-private paradigm. This includes searching for new models of marital cohabitation that do not repeat Maria's earlier domestic arrangement, accounting for the fact that their living quarters become increasingly public, not least as the site for dramatic performances, and for the effects of transnational travel and domestic transience.

Axel at first advocates for a utopian domestic living arrangement. After a period of living in separate rented rooms, he wants a thoroughly modern arrangement and proclaims that his interior design will guarantee a continual state of 'le bonheur indécible d'être marié!' (435) (the inexpressible joy of being married! [150]). His and Maria's new apartment in a nondescript modern building consists of a small kitchen and three comfortable rooms that are organized according to gender: 'une reservée à madame, une autre à monsieur et une neutre' (429) (one for the mistress, one for the master, one neuter [146]). The third room is not only neutral as part of a bifurcated gendered division, but also in linguistic terms – the text uses the French term 'neutre,' which denotes both 'neuter' and 'neutral.' The apartment is decorated with Maria's heirloom furniture (a clock, paintings, a writing desk), which gives Axel the impression of being 'greffé sur tronc ... d'être adopté de sa famille'(435) (grafted on to her trunk ... [and] that her family had adopted me [150]); Maria is the 'bienfaîtrice, la donatrice' (435) (the benefactress, the bestower [150]) of the apartment's interior. Axel's vision of married life presupposes both spouses working. Practical arrangements include having food sent from a nearby restaurant, which limits the need for live-in servants. The couple's separate bedrooms prevent anything unsightly with respect to personal hygiene and guarantee a 'bon ménage' (435) (good household [150]), while erotic encounters are made only after mutual consent. This practice puts en end to what the narrator concedes is customary marital rape: 'viols plus ou moins consentis du lit conjugal' (435) (the more or less authorized rape of the double bed [150]).

This new egalitarian marriage model, what Axel calls the 'rêves d'un mariage libre realisés' (435) (dream of free marriage realized [150]), in fact depends on a reorganization of architectural space. Within his own home,

Axel sees a potential for utopia realized, in which happiness in marriage equals challenging conventional demarcations of the public-private paradigm. This dream of the perfect modern marriage comes to a grinding halt, however. The novel's third part devotes only a few paragraphs to it and then turns to a litany of traumatic experiences. The couple's first-born child dies. Maria's lap dog (whom Axel hates) defecates on the living room carpet and by extension spoils the duo's contented coexistence; as Axel's jealousy increases, he threatens repeatedly to kill the pet. He claims he is served only mediocre food (the dog gets the good pieces), and that his wife prefers the dog's company to his. Allegations of mistreatment increase and Axel appears in his first-person retrospective account as increasingly controlling, manipulative, and irrational. Instead of providing a model economical arrangement, the household expenses balloon, superseding both their incomes and dwarfing what according to Axel should be recommended for a household of their size. The radical living arrangement Axel envisioned is revealed as a fantasy, while the blame is placed on Maria's charged sexual interest in others.

Lesbian desire is, in fact, the second social transgression *A Madman's Defence* investigates as constructed through setting. Maria and a maid shut themselves in Maria's private room to keep their sexual relation hidden from him, Axel proclaims; he describes how he walks in on Maria as she is fondling the maid's breasts; how one of her female friends becomes a fixture in the apartment to the extent that he describes his marriage as bigamous (with Maria as the one having two sexual partners); that Maria prefers to spend a summer in the archipelago with her female friend rather than with him, and so on. The threatening spatial implications of lesbian desire, as Judith Halberstam delineates them in *In a Queer Time and Place*, help contextualize Maria's actions and Axel's representations of these. Investigating conditions a century after Strindberg wrote *A Madman's Defence*, Halberstam argues that a queer awareness seeks to 'open up new life narratives and alternative relations to time and space' (particularly reproductive time and spatial parameters for those) and demonstrate the perceived threat of rupturing (hetero)normativity's work, which is to connect the bourgeois 'family to the historical past of the nation' while trying 'to connect the family to the future of both familial and national stability' (2, 5). Maria's lesbian desire in *A Madman's Defence* is disruptive of both domestic and national allegiances, as the family leaves Sweden to escape the supposed stigma of her affairs. The heteronormative paradigm's presumption of authenticity becomes one of performance.

A Madman's Defence, at first explicitly concerned with maintaining boundaries between authenticity and performance, later begins to deconstruct its own paradigm. As a playwright, Axel's self-characterization and the locations in which he writes illustrate the narrative's accelerating deconstruction of a gendered public-private paradigm. He writes, in his own bedroom, the plays Maria performs in, just as he is narrating (from a Bavarian hotel room) in the first person a story about her. But she clearly does not want to follow his script – neither in his characterization as playwright nor as narrator. Even what Axel describes as a star role in a 'women's play,' written explicitly for Maria and to mend fences, is not received with expected gratitude (463 [177]). Maria may be an actress, but she does not perform according to Axel's assumptions. When hired by the Royal Theatre, Maria brings her actor and actress friends to the apartment. There they are, Axel proclaims, always performing; they are imbecilic, vain, and talk only of banalities. He objects to such gatherings in his home, as they become 'conférences d'idiots' (445) (idiotic conferences [160]). The actresses, moreover are lascivious; they entice Maria to kiss and fondle them, while Maria's actions are described as increasingly motivated by performances that cross the gender conventions Axel seeks to uphold. Maria's acting does not respect the boundaries of public theatre performance; she does not stop performing roles, Axel implies, when she comes home. Neither does she respect them when going out: she dresses as a man for the theatre's costume party.

Domestic spaces in *A Madman's Defence* are part of an experimental setting for envisioning a process of performance in narrative, which Axel (as a narrator) seems both to embrace and reject. Such an experiment illustrates the deception inherent in the idea of a naturalistic and scientific project. The elusive goal of making *A Madman's Defence* into an intimate novel of European proportions, i.e., one that as a public document about private content would be guaranteed by scientific inquiry, thus appears increasingly mirrored in Axel's fruitless search for proof about his sanity and Maria's insanity, as these correlate with her acting and same-sex desire (see also Stounbjerg, 'Between Realism and Modernism' 54). Maria's utterances are indeed less and less frequently reported in direct speech. She becomes narrativized as the novel progresses. The novel renounces the dramatic element of dialogue. This is particularly evident in the fourth and last part of the novel, when Maria is repeatedly accused of lesbianism and Axel motivates their travels as a way to escape Maria's ever more flagrant sexual escapades with other women. Concluding as a speeded-up travel narrative through continental Europe, the rapid succession of locations – a dozen or more lodgings in a few years – signals this narrative's modernist flexibility in terms of setting.

References to explicit architectural details and realistic representations of the landscape, however, are almost completely absent in the fourth part of the novel. As the narrative moves closer in time to the present, it abandons its fragmentary but detailed descriptions of recognizable places to centre on Axel's mental and emotional experiences of exile. This establishes an inverted relationship between temporal and spatial distance: the further away in time, the more the narrative relies on architectural details to serve as a referential framework that correlates with a continued use of the present tense. The closer the narrator gets to the moment of narration (and the present time), the fewer the architectural details. One structure supersedes another, and the public-private paradigm becomes increasingly disarticulated. As architectural references break down, irrationality and madness increase.

In a text so concerned with truth and falsehood and acting and narrating, such aspects of authenticity and performance mark the text as addressing, through setting, questions of subjectivity, autobiography, and gendered conventions of literary representation (cf. Olsson, *Levande död* 160–74; Stounbjerg, 'Uro og Urenhed' 214–22). These conventions, and the settings that allow them, indicate that *A Madman's Defence* inscribes itself within important subsets of nineteenth-century French literature. *A Madman's Defence* is arguably Strindberg's most sophisticated, engaging, haunting, and master-piece-like novel and yet, it is written in French, and was never meant to be published or read in Sweden. The two paratexts preceding the introduction indicate this complexity. The 'Author's Preface,' annotated Paris 1894, and the 'Preface,' annotated 'The Author, 1887,' both detach in different ways the name August Strindberg from Axel and from a Swedish national context, as well as from implications of authorial insanity and misogyny (cf. Olsson, *Levande död* 160–5 and Stounbjerg, 'Uro og urenhed' 171–5). Yet *A Madman's Defence* is the narrative that cemented Strindberg's legacy as a misogynist – the rage directed at women in this novel is endlessly and disturbingly fascinating, as its presumed hatred of women is construed explicitly as part of literary forms – narrative, metaphorical, generic, paratextual – that deconstruct any stable demarcations between nineteenth-century ideologies of masculinity and femininity.

For my argument about transnational settings and the ways in which the narrative deconstructs demarcations between public and private, it is significant that the narrative follows several French conventions for the representation of lesbian desire, and departs markedly from others. This hydridity creates a distinctly modernist tension. Representations of lesbian desire in nineteenth-century French literature were generally written by a third-person male narrator. His prototypical 'gaze,' as Jennifer Waelti-Walters argues in *Damned Women*, combines sensationalism and spectacle with denunciation, coding a woman's desire for another as demonizing, irrational, mad, and violent. Balzac's *The Girl with the Golden Eyes* (*La Fille aux yeaux d'or*) (1833) together with Theophile Gautier's *Mademoiselle de Maupin* (1835) set 'the models of lesbian representation for the rest of the nineteenth century,' Waelti-Walters argues, as Balzac [with Gautier] 'is the first to create the lesbian as monster: a mysterious, perverse, jealous, vengeful, and powerful female animal who haunts the decadent male imagination until the end of the Belle Epoque' (20). Both Balzac and Gautier, like Strindberg later, use their male protagonists to reassert a 'heterosexual and hierarchically gendered context' (Waelti-Walters 32). That context is evident in the mid-nineteenth century's most infamous references to monstrous lesbian desire: the scandal surrounding the publication of Baudelaire's *The Flowers of Evil* (*Les Fleurs du mal*) in 1857. Its poem 'Damned Women: Delphine and Hippolyta' (Femmes Damnées: Delphine et Hippolyte) 'gave lesbian desire the damned name' in nineteenth-century cultural parlance, Waelti-Walters argues (33).

During a performance dedicated to the departure of Maria's women friends – described as 'tribades' and known for having attended lesbian cafes in Paris – Axel is struck by the soulful and loving dedication in Maria's dedicated song; there is 'une naivité, une sincérité touchante qui aboulissait tout idée lubique – la femme chantait la femme!' (495) (a touching naïvity and sincerity in her song such that every licentious idea disappeared on hearing that woman sing amorously of woman) [204–5]). Approaching her friend, the 'monstre' (monster) kisses her: 'lui avale les deux lèvres, qu'elle renferme dans sa guelle affreuse' (495) (with wide open mouth, suck[ing] her lips [which she takes in her frightful mouth] [205]). Axel, of course, is both fascinated and revolted. As Dijskstra shows in *Idols of Perversity*, such fantasies of feminine evil was prevalent across national boundaries in fin-de-siècle European culture.

French novelistic representation had by then coded lesbian desire precisely along these lines, as French physician Julien Chevalier writes in his

1885 medical treatise *About Sexual Inversion from a Medical-Legal Perspective*. Written a few years before Strindberg penned *A Madman's Defence*, Chevalier criticizes contemporary novelists less for portraying lesbians as 'violent, jealous, terrible, implacable,' than for their indiscriminating predilection to label lesbian 'vices' as '*neurosis*, an ambiguous and convenient term' to explain 'everything' about their 'unstable, *unhinged*' characters (cited in Waelti-Walters 37–8). Chevalier's medical writing connects explicitly to what the narrator describes as his project in *A Madman's Defence*: protection against allegations of insanity through a scientific and legal process. Lesbian desire is thus not a curious side effect of the narrative, but central to its conceptualization and the transnational settings through which it must be conceived. *A Madman's Defence* makes clear that tropes of French novelistic conventions had travelled into other literary contexts, and could be drawn upon to represent particular forms of transnational modernity in ways that pre-suppose lesbian desire.

One of the ways in which Strindberg construes his narrative's modernity – what makes its explosive content – is the unexpected challenges he puts to codifications of lesbian desire. The interplay between Axel as narrator and the settings he construes for himself and Maria suggest different forms of tensions than late nineteenth-century French conventions for representing lesbian desire. The first-person narrator's authority is destabilized in *A Madman's Defence*. This narrative relinquishes the prototypical third-person sensationalist male gaze that Waelti-Walters traces in favour of an increasingly irrational first-person narrator. This development correlates with Lucey's observations that first-person narration about homosexuality is a later development in French literature and by extension, perhaps, possibly relates more comprehensively to modernist prose developments also in other European contexts (cf. Mesch 42–6). In *A Madman's Defence*, moreover, lesbian desire emerges from a utopian domestic setting in a modern Stockholm apartment, rather than being designated to anonymous locations, rented rooms, parks, and other public locations, which are standard settings of late nineteenth-century French convention. Lesbian desire in *A Madman's Defence* is instead domesticated; the threats it poses to social norms are inscribed within the confines of the home, while those threats are also construed as explicit threats to the nation. As the marriage arrangement fails at the beginning of the narrative's fourth part, the cure is conceived as one of travel, by which the couple leaves Sweden, Axel proclaims, to cure Maria of her transgressive desire and in order for him to regain a firm basis on which to reclaim and maintain his own sanity.

The representation of lesbianism in *A Madman's Defence* offers Strindberg one way to write a transnational modernist narrative that goes counter to both Swedish and French gendered paradigms for challenging boundaries between public and private. As Robin Hackett argues in *Sapphic Primitivism*, literary modernism evolved in explicit tension with the representation of lesbian desire by period sexologists. Drawing on contemporary race science, sexologists helped 'construct symbolic linkages between lesbianism and male homosexuality, blackness, disease, criminality, working-class status, degeneracy, taint, pollution, and prostitution' (21). In *A Madman's Defence* such descriptors – with their spatialized components that connote geographical locations (the non-Western, the urban) – relate explicitly to the male first-person narrator. The narrator proclaims that part of what makes *him* legendary is that such descriptors have attached also to him: 'au cours des années ma personnalité revêt des contoures précises, et au lieu du poëte innocent une figure mythologique se crée, noircie, estompée, cotoyant le type criminel' (479–80) (From year to year my personality was becoming defined in its contours and, instead of the innocent poet, it was a mythological figure which was being sketched, blackened, shaded, verging on the criminal type [192]). A pertinent but overlooked aspect of the first-person speaker in *A Madman's Defence* is that he construes these symbolic linkages so straightforwardly in terms of transitions between different geographical regions and the settings associated with those – from domestic apartment living in Stockholm to boarding rooms in continental Europe.

When Axel and Maria leave the North, they move toward regions that in Sweden as well as other parts of western Europe correlated with those areas that 'Richard Burton defined in 1886 as the "Sotadic Zone." This is an area characterized, Burton claimed, by homosexuality. It includes "Meridional France, the Iberian Peninsula, Italy and Greece, with the coast regions of Africa from Morocco to Egypt"' (cited in Hackett 22). Geographical connotations allowed Victorian sexologists – and implicitly Strindberg as well in *A Madman's Defence* – to 'paint specifics about white middle-class European homosexuality against a backdrop of remarks about ... savages, and primates as well as reference to places frequently outside of Western Europe' (Hackett 22–3). Indeed, as Axel's accusations of Maria's misdeeds increase in rhetorical fervour, metaphors turn specifically to oppositions between Western acculturation and its undeveloped past, as well as to non-Western geographical regions. Maria becomes one of a group of 'sales bêtes' (dirty beasts) representing 'ces intelligences de l'âge de bronze, ces antropo-morphes, demi-singes, cette horde d'animaux malfaisants' (481) (those bronze-age minds, those anthropomorphs, semi-apes, that horde of evil-doing animals [193]). This well-known passage has often been used to exemplify Strindberg's misogyny. The frustration and anger expressed is surprisingly direct.

This extended list of epithets, the paratactic syntax, and the juxtaposition of metaphorical time and space is representative of the intriguing aesthetic strategies of *A Madman's Defence* also in other ways. The descriptors put in relief the delocalized setting of this first-person narration – Axel's accusations are enabled and produced in the absence of narrative architectural markers and of national belonging. Such geographic and linguistic contexts are part of the contemporary transnational threat of lesbianism in *A Madman's Defence*. These code the narrative as in step with continental developments in literary representation and sexology, but also as gesturing toward possible alternatives. Axel and Maria partake in disruptions of the domestic that propel Axel's narrative; their travelling south together formulates a paradigm based on continental travel in which threats to gendered conventions can be narrated, and which conteracts in some ways stereotypical representations of lesbian desire in modernist prose.

As ideologies of private and public clash in the novel, alterations to that paradigm highlight a fundamental instability that marks *A Madman's Defence* at least partially as an attempt at rethinking the form and function of novelistic, first-person narration. The naturalist late nineteenth-century novel runs up against its own formal dissolution in *A Madman's Defence*, as the narrative relinquishes architectural markers. Its formal dissolution must be understood also through the gendering of autobiography at the end of the nineteenth century, when this genre becomes increasingly identified as feminized. Written by and for women (implicitly at home in a stable domestic setting), intimate journaling correlates with the unpublishable, because 'inferior,' literature of late nineteenth-century women writers. Thus, gendered conventions as well as architecture make the defence speech meaningless, as it has already unveiled the impossibility of truthful narration in its dependence on artificial and architectural details of setting. *A Madman's Defence* thus testifies to one of transnational modernism's primary motivators, the realization of the complicated project of encompassing in 'realist' prose what appears to be a fundamentally unrealistic project, namely, the straddling of several distinct spatio-temporal realms that are also interconnected, bridging

Stockholm with continental Europe or writing a private document as a public *plaidoyer*.

4 Modernism and Problems of Transnational Literary History

For scholars and literary historians interested in periodization (a trademark of Swedish literary history as it has been written and promoted during the last century), categorization, and systematicity, Strindberg in general, and his French production, in particular, has provided some serious challenges. Scholars' insistence on biographical interpretation has never seriously engaged with the intriguing questions of translinguistic or transnational production. What does it mean, for example, to write a supposed autobiography in a foreign language? *A Madman's Defence*'s production and reception history is critical in this regard, as it illustrates precisely the complexity that Strindberg was instrumental in both producing and reflecting, with respect to European literature at the end of the nineteenth century. The novel was never published in Swedish in an authorized translation during Strindberg's lifetime. The author did not want it and the characters and plot struck Swedish publishers as too easily recognizable as the story of Strindberg's first marriage and a vindictive portrait of his first wife (see Martin Lamm 192, for example).

The French reception of the German and French versions of *A Madman's Defence* published during the 1890s contrasts sharply with subsequent Swedish reception. The author of *Die Beichte eines Thoren* was prosecuted in Berlin for obscenity, although charges were later dropped, but this event led to attention in Paris. A longer essay in the Parisian journal *La Revue des Deux Mondes* praises Strindberg as one of many Scandinavian authors for whom exile has become a necessary precondition. In the article, Victor Cherbuliez, member of the French Academy, hesitates to read the novel biographically, but positions it as part of a modern 'littérature cruelle' (cited in Rossholm, 'Kommentarer' 572). Contemporary French critic Henri Albert writes in an 1894 article that he finds Axel to be disturbingly and masochistically submissive toward Maria, objecting to the narrative's limited portrayal of women as dominant and perverse monsters, and, as Fahlgren argues, it is clear that Albert finds Strindberg's narrator to be hysterical, weak-minded, and insufficiently masculine (Fahlgren 69). George Loiseau's edited 1895 version had Frenchified Strindberg's manuscript significantly. By removing or softening disturbing passages, Loiseau 'changed raw formulations into an elegant Parisian style' (Stounbjerg, 'Uro og Urenhed' 172, drawing on Engwall, my trans.). But the reception in Paris of this edition indicates that what Scandinavian literature in Paris during the mid 1890s stood for was a particular form of modernity. Negative reviews from the establishment press focused on the perceived danger of succumbing to the program of the Nordic Moderns (also known as 'the Ibsenites'). The novel corresponded with the image of a Northern promulgation of indecency, of sexual explicitness, and of exaggerated interested in so-called women's questions. Content perceived as autobiographical was not deemed a liability but interpreted as a generally Nordic interest in authenticity and portrayal of intense psychological experiences in their social setting, as reflected in the tenets of Georg Brandes, the Danish literary critic most closely associated with the Modern Breakthrough Movement of Scandinavian realism in the 1880s (Rossholm, 'Kommentarer' 588–93).

Strindberg enjoyed a brief period of critical recognition in Paris in the mid-1890s and became understood, fleetingly, as formulating what a Europeanized avant-garde was interested in – the construction of a subjective persona in a self-consciously construed environment of modernity. Swedish reviews in the mid 1890s of the German and French versions were sparse, but generally denounced the work in no uncertain terms. Assuming autobiographical authenticity, reviewers from both conservative and radical camps labelled the work a 'shameless,' 'offensive,' 'vindictive,' 'ruthless,' and 'unfair' report, which thereby should be deemed 'unprintable'; the work inexcusably drags all of 'literature' through the mud, one critic argued, while the Swedish readership was advised to forget all about it (Rossholm, 'Kommentarer' 565–6, my trans.; cf. Olsson, *Jag blir galen* 49, 77; Stounbjerg, 'Between Realism and Modernism' 54).

These comments indicate a general critical stance, in which most of Strindberg's work composed in French or on the European continent was largely dismissed in Sweden, sometimes even characterized exclusively as the result of insanity. A politics of the transnational is clearly evident here. In Sweden at the time, Strindberg's work was caught in a double-bind – published outside of Sweden, in French or in German, it was threateningly alien and ultramodern in its transnational implications. Its content, however, was construed as too personal, too Strindbergesque, and too biographically inflected (critics and readers assumed that the character names Axel and Maria translated directly into August and Siri – the given name of the author's first wife). Thereby, the work became

Swedish, by virtue of its author's nationality, but clearly involved a challenge to national ideology. Even recent critical interpretations of the text that are otherwise illuminating tend to dismiss the intriguing implications of transnational and translinguistic literary production.

The publication and reception history of *A Madman's Defence* as a transnational and translinguistic modern novel tells one story, while Strindberg's own writing about the text another. In two letters written to a relative and a friend during the spring of 1888, Strindberg remarks on the secrets contained in the document, and stresses that those need to be safe-guarded and prevented from public view (Rossholm, 'Kommentarer' 553). But if, as these letters attest, the document is of such intensely private nature, what are the implications of the fact that the text was written exclusively in French? Personal privacy is one, but another is the fact that Strindberg did not want the manuscript labelled as 'Swedish.' If it were, he writes, it could become the legal property of a Swedish publisher and not the author; earlier letters state that he prefers any intimate content to be written in French, so that, for example, his and his wife's relationship would not 'profaneras på Svenska' (Rossholm, 'Kommentarer' 552–3, 526) (be profaned in Swedish, my trans.). Separated from connotations of language as domesticating or nationalizing, neither French nor Swedish provides a home. French operates as a language to capture the modern, just as Europe and France reflect practices of literary production at the time, through which the continent is a way for Scandinavians to become 'modern'; this is also the route Strindberg takes with *A Madman's Defence.* Writing it this way formulates the gesture of becoming modern.

Yet, the curious effect persists. Impoverished and hounded by bills and creditors, residing consecutively in a number of rented dwellings in the Danish countryside, Strindberg seems to relish the linguistic challenge as both intellectually stimulating and as guaranteeing a different form of authenticity and truth-value: 'det knastrar i hjernan när det rätta ordet skall födas på det fremmande språket, men denna ansträngning ger full vision af det upplefvade' (Rossholm, 'Kommentarer' 549; see also Engwall '"Det knastrar"') (the brain is crackling when the correct word is to be born in the alien language, but this exercise gives a complete vision of what has been experienced [my trans.]). *A Madman's Defence* may have been conceived by Strindberg as a private, personal, and intimate document, but it is certainly mediated, and quite explicitly so. The transnational and translinguistic form is critical here because the 'alien language,' Strindberg claims, gives access to a 'complete vision.'

This is of course naturalism's conception of literary narration – as conceived through complete and reliable vision. Yet, as we have seen, *A Madman's Defence* never attempts any strategy of panoramic overview or naturalist painting of a complete social context. Vision – the perception in hindsight of events experienced far away – is clearly subjectively modernist and interiorized.

The tension between private and public that underlies Strindberg's use of French and his focused drive to complete *A Madman's Defence* although it, at the time, was clearly not written to be published for profit, tie this particular first-person novel to the developments in drama Strindberg advocated during the 1880s. What makes this novel modernist is also that it engages explicitly with questions of public and private that were largely formulated in drama at the time. The spatial implications of Strindberg's theory of staged intimacy in the preface to *Miss Julie* involve focusing not only on characters' interiority (e.g., the logic of intense psychological realism for which the naturalist sequence of works is known) but also on the exteriorization of a specific dramatic project, namely, of creating a dominant aesthetic form for the public expression of that which most reviewers at the time and audiences since have thought to be intensely private matters. The private is public, Strindberg's narrative and dramatic production at this time dictates, and he formulates the connection as explicitly spatial, as revealing the logic of architectural and gendered paradigms as inseparable from late nineteenth-century European aesthetics. That the private matter of sexual desire, jealousy, hatred, adultery, and deception, as expressed in Strindberg's naturalist sequence, was to be understood as not abstractly personal, but as explicitly autobiographical, was taken almost for granted by reviewers, audiences, and critics for nearly a century. Such spatial implications of intimacy are at play today as well. Strindberg's sequence of works from the late 1880s – often explicitly conceived for a Parisian audience and, in the case of *A Madman's Defence*, even directly composed in French – seems incongruously localizable to the authorial persona of Strindberg. As seemingly autobiographical documents, they are marred by their own construction of misogyny and invocation of conventions of insanity.

Strindberg with *A Madman's Defence* thus produced a document of infidelity, of treason toward Sweden and Swedish literary history, while a majority of scholars continue treating the work as unproblematically 'Swedish.' Obscuring the challenges *A Madman's Defence* posits with conceptualizations of nation also means overlooking the narrative's interest in expressing its frustration with social conventions, as these are inscribed as part of literary representation. Highlighting its status as fiction, Strindberg also rebels against the gendered conventions that go hand-in-hand with an architectural metalanguage of the time. He is tracing a prison of modernity, one from whose gendered and spatial constraints he cannot escape – whether those constraints localize him as a demented misogynist or as a transnational writer whose location at any given time cannot correspond to an ideology of home or an ideology in which the conventions of gender and architecture may fully coalesce. *A Madman's Defence* is a transnational modernist novel in search of its own territory; it challenges precisely those conventions of the novel genre formulated by the late nineteenth-century ideology of public and private: of nation, of home, of authenticity, of truth, and of the stability of gender demarcations.

2 Rural Modernism: Ethnography, Photography, and Recollection in *Among French Peasants*

It is perhaps curious that one of the major projects August Strindberg sets out to complete in self-proclaimed exile from Sweden is a study of the French peasantry. This work, *Among French Peasants: Subjective Travelogues* (*Bland franska bönder: Subjektiva reseskildringar*) (1889), is rarely read today, although it allows for a fascinating and contrarian reading of European modernity, and gives unexpected insights into emergent literary modernism. In fact, Strindberg's writing on French peasants seeks to rewrite the location of the French countryside in two different ways, through modern ethnography and via aesthetic techniques that draw on impressionistic photography and emphasize subjective recollections of an alien location. One of the main contributions of this non-fictional work is that it presents the French countryside, rather than Paris, as a vehicle for experimentation with modernist techniques of literary representation. Written in Swedish about France around the same time as the novel *A Madman's Defence*, it complements that work's emphasis on travel and displacements as part of a deliberate construction of transnational settings.

Among French Peasants consists of three separate parts, all of which combine personal reflections with observations, interviews, and statistics on French farming and French peasantry, drawn from French and European newspapers, journals, histories, and official documents.[1] It is described as an ethnographic study '*in vivis*' (79), and the subtitle

---

1 See Poulenard for written sources mentioned in the work; see also Robinson, 'Among French Peasants,' for a summary in English of the work's inception; for a retracing of the journeys Strindberg undertakes in writing the book, see Brandell, *På Strindbergs vägar genom Frankrike*; and Ekholm, 'Kommentarer.'

indicates that it is the result of 'subjective' experiences. The introduction, entitled 'Country and City,' is set in Paris. The middle section about peasant life in a country village is set in an unnamed location in Île de France, between Fontainebleau and Nemours, and draws on Strindberg's experiences from the village Grèz-sur-Loing, where he and his family lived as part of a Scandinavian artist colony during parts of 1885 and 1886. The final section describes a trip of three weeks of speedy travel by train, horse, and foot through the majority of France's farming districts, which Strindberg undertook in the fall of 1886. The trip forms a loop from Lucerne in Switzerland, around the Western perimeter of France, to the Mediterranean, up through the Massif Central, and back to its point of departure. The journey is remarkable for its geographical range, the scope of its detail, and the general accuracy of the information provided about geographical features, agricultural practices, and rural customs.

Among French Peasants highlights modern technologies: the speed of train travel is repeatedly invoked as particularly useful for a modern representation of rural practices, and Strindberg had hired an aide to accompany him to photograph landscapes, buildings, people, and practices. The photographic process failed, however, and no plates or prints remain from their travels. In terms of setting, *Among French Peasants* operates within a complex set of representational paradigms, which span national and regional, urban and colonial. The structure decentralizes Paris as an icon of contemporary French culture as it transitions from an introduction marked by stasis to a narrative marked by movement, as the journey around France gradually increases in pace. As the settings move away from Paris, the representational technique also becomes more experimental. The title's inclusionary gesture, 'among,' suggests that its speaker has been immersed in peasant culture and writes from an embedded position that grants him authority. Yet the second part of the title, 'subjective travelogues,' connotes mobility and aestheticized interpretation from a detached and transient perspective. This tension is present continuously in the work.

As written about rural France, in Swedish, by a visiting Swede, *Among French Peasants* hovers, unresolved, in a transnational limbo that is also transcultural, translinguistic, and transgeneric – although it was planned as an illustrated book with documentary photographs, it became a written work only. Similarly, the speaker's position as a migrant in exile, as an outsider and alien, allows for self-reflexive experimental techniques that make *Among French Peasants* such fascinating reading.

The work's peculiarity, or even hybridity, was evident to author, publishers, and critics at the time. Strindberg realized its singularity in a broad European sense and attempted therefore to have translated sections of the work published in Britain, Austria, Germany, Denmark, Finland, and France before the well-known Stockholm publisher Bonnier agreed in 1889 to publish the text in Swedish under the title *Among French Peasants* (see Ekholm, 'Kommentarer' 212–14). Once published, the work garnered little attention by critics and audiences. Although it was arguably dedicated just as much to a French reading public as to a Swedish, *Among French Peasants* was not translated into French until 1988.[2]

Strindberg's work about French peasantry illustrates, however, how important location was to the writer. Strindberg perceives rural landscapes – arguably marginal sites for the construction of late nineteenth-century European cultural modernity and literary modernism – as ways to reach international recognition and experiment with new forms of writing. The author's letters from this time indicate that the work is designed to challenge Paris as an icon of metropolitan modernity, de-emphasize a colonial perspective on locations perceived as marginal to European culture, and counteract romantic and idealizing tendencies of landscape and peasantry portrayal in contemporary visual arts (see also Stounbjerg, 'Ett subjekt intrasslati världen' 38–9) . *Among French Peasants* becomes a study of setting that eventually suggests that a literary figuration construed as alienated from modernity and transnational modernism may in fact be central to its construction: the French peasant and the French countryside.

1 From Paris to the Province: Satire, Subjective Impressions, and Settings of Transnational Cultural Transfer

Among French Peasants is a work about French rural culture and the French countryside, but it begins in Paris. The obviously fictional introduction's first sentence localizes us to Paris in the month of May 'last

---

2 The first French translation, *Parmi les paysans français* was published in 1988; the work has not been published in English. All translations here are my own. Included in a German translation in *Strindbergs Werke, Unter französischen Bauern* (1912), it appears to have garnered more critical traction in German than in Swedish. Wolfgang Schivelbusch, for example, introduces his chapter 'Panoramic Travel' in the German version of *The Railway Journey* with a quote from *Among French Peasants* (Hockenjos, 'Picturing Dissolving Views' 130). Translations of *Brev* are also mine.

year' (in 1885, presumably). The second sentence mentions the speaker's early morning walk, which he directs to the top of Montmartre to drink a cup of coffee and read a newspaper, the Paris-based *Figaro*. The third describes Paris spread out below as 'la cité-mère, världens medelpunkt' (11) (the mother-city, the world's centre point), and the fourth affirms it as 'kulturens underverk, det moderna Babylon' (11) (the wonder of culture, the modern Babylon); a page later it is heralded as 'la cité-lumière' (12) (the city of light). The speaker appears to occupy the position of a jaded *flaneur*, for whom Paris is recognized as a spectacle of modernity. The introduction's enumeration of clichéd Paris attributes is ironic, yet it demonstrates that no study of France, even of its peasants, could begin elsewhere than in the perceived centre of the world, a setting that had also made Paris the ur-origin (the mother of all cities), or the most enlightened place (the city of light). Paris at the end of the nineteenth century constituted a transnational setting, an emblematic location lauded and deconstructed within and for other national literatures.

The second paragraph of the introduction set at Montmartre takes a series of stabs at naturalistic writing, showing in deftly cynical remarks how even the smallest, most insignificant aspect of Parisian everyday practices, even among its workers and servants, had already been described by naturalists like Emile Zola in his novels set in Paris. The introduction is notably set at Buttes Montmartre, the hill famous for its views of Paris in works such as Zola's *The Kill* (*La Curée*) (1872). Strindberg describes how the sun shone on its 'seventy-two thousand buildings,' lighting up its 'four million windows,' while 'forty-three thousand maids' slammed the doors of 'sixty-eight thousand apartment dwellers' in order to serve 'one million twenty-two thousand' cups of coffee, and so on (11). The satirical jabs at the mundane and minutely detailed signal that Strindberg is interested in displacing Paris not only from the centre of France, or of Europe, but also from the centre of literary attention. *Among French Peasants* in a sense begins by demoting Paris as a source of literary inspiration; for the speaker, the French capital can only give rise to derivative and superficial description.

The setting of the first paragraphs of *Among French Peasants* evokes and rewrites as well the introduction to Strindberg's break-through novel about modern Stockholm, *Röda rummet* (*The Red Room*) (1879). As in *The Red Room*, the introduction is set in May at a restaurant with a view over the city. The scene below the narrator's feet is presented like a panorama (indeed, he calls it a painting), the windows and buildings reflect the sun's rays, and even the maid (now a *garçon*) of Stockholm's Mosebacke Tavern is evoked. As the narrator opens his paper, the description turns from visual to intratextual clues that allude to *The Red Room's* protagonist Falk's attempt at joining the newspaper ranks. *Among French Peasants* reappropriates the tension between the rural and the urban that structures *The Red Room* and transfers it to Paris (see also Stenport, 'Making Space'). The introduction to *Among French Peasants* seemingly displaces Stockholm for Paris, while satirizing Zola's naturalist descriptive techniques, while in fact destabilizing Paris as a central point of reference for modern literature. For a migrant Swede like Strindberg, this initial evocation of Paris in *Among French Peasants* signals a continued interest in the aesthetic and cultural displacements involved in the cultural constructions of European cosmopolitan modernity. The work thereby introduces an implicit tension in the construction of setting that is indicative of emergent transnational literary modernism.

Instead of writing about Paris, Strindberg proclaims in the introduction to *Among French Peasants* that he is interested in the lesser-known: in peasants, farmers, and in locations far removed from the metropolis. In a conversation with an old Parisian communard, the speaker in dramatic dialogue lays out his reasons for embarking on a journey to study the practices and customs of the French peasant. He claims that he has wanted for a long time to study the European population of the peasants as a neglected class of citizens (19) and he promotes his knowledge of the debate on the agricultural crisis of the 1880s, which he has derived from reading newspapers, journals, official documents, production and yield statistics, and his 'förträffliga bibliotek' (20) (remarkable library) of scholarly works related to agriculture. Not satisfied, the communard asks what this visitor's real credentials for undertaking the project may be – 'I do not have preconceived opinions,' Strindberg's speaker continues, 'and I want to give you [all Parisians] insights into your country's peasant population, more than I want to learn myself' (20). Along these lines, Strindberg writes in letters about wanting to write *Among French Peasants* as an original story about 'the people and their lives on which all of the city and society rest' (*Brev* 4:60). His missives are explicit about what he wants to do, namely to show 'the French what their country looks like. The rascals only know Paris!' (*Brev* 4:59). Rather than praising an aesthetification of urban modernity, Strindberg attempts to make Paris into the peripheral by emphasizing the rural and provincial. These statements indicate that *Among French Peasants* is conceived as a radical work, as challenging specifically the image of Paris as a cultural icon and a source of literary inspiration.

When Strindberg conceptualized his project on French peasants, he had gained personal experience of both Paris and parts of the French countryside. Arriving from Stockholm in Paris in self-imposed exile in 1883, he settled in Passy and later in Neuilly on the outskirts of a city that had been radically altered during Baron Haussmann's large-scale transformation during the previous decade. City of light, of commerce, of communications, of culture – such were, of course, the myths attached to Paris at the time, as David Harvey shows in *Paris, Capital of Modernity* (see also Higonnet; Prendergast; Stierle). These myths clearly attracted Strindberg and many other Scandinavian writers and artists to France in the mid-1880s. Seeking to identify with the myths and gain access to the Parisian cultural scene, Strindberg presents himself in a letter as a popular French writer of Zola's stature, 'whose novels will sell 50 million copies in France alone!' (cited in Ahlström, *Strindbergs erövring av Paris* 49). In other missives, he complains that Parisians are 'prejudiced and nasty'; Paris itself is insufferable; his expertise is limited to Sweden, and about Paris he knows nothing (*Brev* 3:338, 342). His experiences of Paris, the cultural centre of Europe at the time, are at first negative, but Strindberg quickly rethinks his potential contributions to French culture. He writes home about his role as a Nordic Light, destined to 'attack the false culture in its solid castle, called Paris' (*Brev* 4:169). *Among French Peasants* is part of this attack, by which Strindberg understands his international breakthrough as going via peasants. He is also implicitly reacting against an oblique background of French urban-based early modernism, such as that of Charles Baudelaire's poetry, for example. Strindberg perceives his stance as radical (later readers tend to perceive it as odd), while his self-conceived attack contrasts starkly with predominant late nineteenth-century immigrant attitudes toward their new country. Rather than cherishing, or at least accepting, the conditions in a new country in which he has chosen to settle, Strindberg conceives of his role as critically disruptive, as instrumental in changing both domestic and international perceptions about the French nation.

Visual metaphors are critical to this project, and throughout *Among French Peasants* these metaphors move from realist to impressionist to abstractly modernist, the farther the speaker gets from Paris. In the introduction, the first metaphor invokes a typical nineteenth-century urban panorama. The city of Paris is spread out beneath the feet of the speaker and his interlocutor, the old communard. As they climb the stairs up the windmill at Montmartre to enjoy the view, the speaker describes the city below as already aestheticized, demarcated, and conveniently framed in and by a representational tradition: 'infattad i den svarta ramen visade sig tavlan av Paris ännu härligare än därnere' (13) (now in its black frame the picture of Paris presented itself even more wonderfully than from below). But the visual representation masks real conditions: as the two continue the dramatized dialogue about the contemporary status of the French peasant from their elevated position, the communard expresses an increasingly hostile attitude to the city. He codes it linguistically as a near-vampire, as privileged but decadently wilful, as 'an aristocrat' (14) who lives despondently off the riches of the land. The first-person speaker interjects several times that surely the peasant also receives something valuable in return from the city – culture, ideas, and all the blessings of 'civilization' (14). The communard rejects urban civilization's trickle-down effects by using a particular metonymic object, namely oil paintings (14); indeed, he asserts, peasants need more freedom and fewer oil paintings (18).

The repeated invocation of oil paintings signals that in *Among French Peasants* Strindberg objects not only to metropolitan ignorance about peasant conditions outside Paris, but also to antiquated and deliberately nostalgic aesthetic representations. Such representations were propagated also by painters selling a pastoral idealization of rural life, aimed specifically at the Parisian bourgeoisie. Oil paintings with peasants enjoyed a widespread popularity in France during the 1880s, as R.J. Bezucha and many other art historians have noted, and realist painters like Jules Breton promulgated a harmonious vision of the peasant as poor but humble, which tied into ideologies of peasant imagery that connected rural life with relaxation and repose when marketed to city dwellers (Bezucha 17–19). Not only was oil the dominant medium in French late realistic painting, but landscape painting was the dominant motif as well, as represented both by the volume of paintings sold and by the canonization of imagery as represented by inclusions in the official Paris Salon and purchases by academies, institutions, and benefactors (Bettrell 27). Jules Breton's *The Gleaner* (1877) is exemplary in its simplistic idealization (in both form and content) of rural life as manifest in the figure of a statuesque and solitary peasant woman with her head held high, centrally placed and illuminated against the expanse of an open horizon. French realist rural painting underwent a rapid devaluation in the late 1870s and 1880s, which correlates with *Among*

French Peasants' search for new models for representing rural settings. Bezucha shows that what was once considered a startling effect – the unadorned depiction of rural toil, unencumbered by romantic or mythological symbolism – had lost its edge by the mid-1880s (17). The techniques of popular realist oil painters, like those of Breton and his more famous predecessor Millet, had by the time Strindberg writes *Among French Peasants* come to be associated with a relentless slide into what later critics have called the urban bourgeois fetishization of the 'sentimental, picturesque, and anecdotal' (cited in Bezucha 18).

Among French Peasants is in fact explicit about the ways in which it wants to challenge a fully established set of conventions for investigating, cataloguing, and representing French peasantry in place by the mid-1880s. It is described as a study *'in vivis'* (79), and, as indicated by the second part of the work's title, as a result of 'subjective' travel impressions. One of Strindberg's letters from this time indicates that he does not want to write about French monuments or buildings, but seeks to depict how the French farmer 'lefver och hvad han tänker, hur han har det och hur han och hans landskap [*sic*] hans åkrar och ängar se ut; Jag vill höra hvad han menar om kulturen och framtiden!' (cited in Ekholm, 'Kommentarer' 191) (lives and what he thinks, what his existence is like and what he and his landscape [*sic*] his fields and pastures look like. I want to know his opinions on culture and the future [my trans.]). In terms of genre definition, *Among French Peasants* is largely ethnographic, meaning that it is specifically invested in the 'description of cultures,' as *Webster's Third New International Dictionary* defines 'Ethnography.' Ethnography was a field associated with modern forms of inquiry and representation in Scandinavia at this time, and Strindberg conceived of his own writing as instrumental in developing the genre.

The part of *Among French Peasants* that details Strindberg's travels around France is called 'Autopsies and Interviews' (77). The curious use of the word 'autopsy' here technically means 'self-study,' but it clearly connotes the project's task of resurrecting from oblivion practices of French peasants and the countryside from a figurative death in the modern age. Strindberg affirms that since the English agricultural economist Arthur Young's extensive three-year study tour through France's agricultural regions 1787–90 (published as *Travels in France* in 1792), nobody has studied the French countryside and its population as he intends to do. More significantly, Strindberg's voyage contrasts sharply with Henry James's *A Little Tour in France* (1884), reflecting travel undertaken in 1882. Strindberg does not mention this work, but it provides an implicit point of comparison.

James's *A Little Tour in France* focuses largely on architecture, monuments, parks, and gardens in the provinces, comparing them to landmarks and styles of the capital. James's initial remark in this collection is illustrative; like Strindberg, he objects to the presumption that visitors 'are too apt to think that France is Paris, just as we are accused of being too apt to think that Paris is the celestial city.' James's travels in fact closely follow strategies promoted by France's bourgeoning tourist industry during the late nineteenth century, in which images of the countryside outside Paris, 'la belle France,' quickly became equated also with a presentation of 'la France historique' (Gerson). Travel guides as well as French historians of the late nineteenth century emphasized that what was worth visiting of the French nation outside Paris was largely a matter of architectural sight-seeing, particularly of cathedrals, historical monuments, palaces, or ruins (Bettrell 34). Crammed with information about structures and how to access them through main-line and rural railway lines, French late nineteenth-century travel literature largely ignored the features of the landscape (botany, geology) or demography (peasant and village populations) that are of particular interest to Strindberg's speaker.

Strindberg, like James and fellow contemporary visitors to France's provinces, travels around the country via train. In *Among French Peasants*, however, the medium of railway travel is more than a mode of transportation to access historical or architecturally interesting sites. The question of speed is particularly important for the construction of setting. Strindberg's speaker rushes through the countryside to observe the stationary peasant, a design that formally reproduces dominant discourses of modernity that *Among French Peasants* appears otherwise interested in challenging. In fact, the speed with which Strindberg travels around the country is explicitly invoked as allowing for a new model for ethnographic observation, which leads him to conceive of a modern aesthetic for representing conditions of French peasant and rural life (for an analysis of a related form of description, see Hockenjos, 'Money, Monney, Monet'). A noticeable shift toward metaphors of impressionistic rather than realistic painting occurs between the second and third parts of *Among French Peasants*. These metaphors then evolve into addressing the form and function of photography for the recollection and reinscription of visual impressions in narrative form.

In the third part of *Among French Peasants*, landscapes are described from the railway window as diffused in colour, as if a canvas had variously absorbed pigment, while the sun sets over a mountain range into a chiaroscuro: 'så smälter allt tillsammans i ett outredligt grått' (86) (so it all melts together in undecipherable grayness). In other instances, views of a landscape are described as tableaus being rolled up (92); as views expanding or contracting of '*la belle France*' (94); as colourful blobs of red, yellow, and grey that would make a painter happy (107); as covered with lush greenery, forms, and colours that 'livar upp tavlan' (107) (enliven the picture); as a landscape drawn from 'Rubens tavlor' (108) (paintings by Ruben); as a painting passing quickly by outside the window (116); as a disharmoniously composed motif whose elementary shapes contradict one another (122); as a colourful background against which 'en ensam och kolsvart och kalkvit kvinnofigur' (124) (a solitary female figure, coal-black and chalk-white) emerges in stark relief; as a lively view (130); as providing a desired 'lokalfärg' (140) (local colour); and, as allowing for the inclusion of 'pittoreskt' (150) (picturesque) detail. By focusing on nature imagery, *la belle France*, rather than the monuments and ruins of *la France historique*, Strindberg's prose in *Among French Peasants* seems at first to emulate the largely mundane motifs of French impressionist landscape painting (Bettrell 27–41, 241–72). The speaker presents the river Marne, for example, as best described through a metapainterly reference, as a river 'mycket eftersökt av franska paysageister' (96) (much sought-after by French *paysagistes*).

Among French Peasants initially constructs the setting of rural France according to descriptive techniques associated with impressionist painting of the 1880s. These registers of aesthetic representation are clearly subjective, as Marmus notes: 'Det Frankrike som [Strindberg] presenterar är ett påfund av hans egen blick' (279) (France presented by Strindberg is an invention of his own gaze). This subjectivity, however, is technologically mediated by speedy railway travel. The trip around France must be fast, Strindberg's narrator writes, to facilitate overview and avoid getting bogged down in details (80). Railway travel thereby allows one to quickly 'genomstryka' (80) (paint through) an entire *département*. On the other hand, Strindberg's speaker cautions against trying to capture 'ett främmande land *endast* från kupéfönstret' (81) (an alien country *only* through the window of a railway car). The window of the railway compartment in *Among French Peasants* functions as an aesthetic framing device, as a straightforward reference not only to what is technically called 'cadrage' (the centring of an image), but also to the fact that railway travel becomes a technique that allows for a certain kind of visual composition. Railway travel, as Bettrell and others have noted, facilitated French landscape painting; a day of painting in the country (at least in the countryside around Paris) was easily achieved by Paris-based impressionist painters (see also Hockenjos, 'Picturing Dissolving Views' 132–4). The temporal aspect of impressionist painting thereby correlates with Strindberg's aesthetic project in *Among French Peasants*. The motif or story of a French peasant and a rural region may be quickly or arbitrarily grasped, as one impression of many others that could have been possible, yet the recreation (in painting or prose) of that impression is painstakingly slow and deliberate.

Like many of Pissarro's and Sisley's rural paintings of France from the 1870s, Strindberg's prose appears to portray the French landscape by drawing on a decisively impressionist interplay between light and colour. This interplay is one of 'impressions,' he writes in a letter, and much better suited at presenting an image than scientific generalizations can ever purport to offer (see Marmus 280). The word 'impressions' is highly unusual in Swedish and seems to be a direct reference to French impressionistic painting. *Among French Peasants* provides an important counterpoint to both realist and impressionist renderings of French rural regions, however. The speaker's observations on agricultural practices as well as interviews conducted with peasants and farmers allow the text to counteract impressionist representation of peasant life as a visual surface (Bettrell 41). The speaker's observations also render more complex topographically vague impressionist 'fields,' which eschew specificity, particularly in the representation of agricultural work, including machinery used (Bettrell 241–3). In addition, the text strays from demonization as well as nostalgization of peasant life.

European literary modernism depends not only on the city as a culturally constructed locus for its formal experiments, but also on particular devices and technological inventions, which, literarily constituted, formalize modernism's interest in aestheticized and self-referential challenges to speed and transience, as Thacker argues in *Moving through Modernity*. The contradictions between form and ideology cutting across the representations of late nineteenth-century peasant cultures in *Among French Peasants* emerge in this context not only as intriguing, but also as indicative of formal interests of transnational European modernism around the turn of the century. The formal organization of geographical locations in *Among French Peasants*, which moves from Paris to Île de France and on to outlying regions, leaves Paris and references to older forms of visual representation in order to emphasize, once it reaches the provinces, the complex aesthetic functions of photography.

2 Landscape Photography and Rural Modernism

Setting out on his railway trip around France in the late summer of 1886, Strindberg had hired as an assistant Swedish student Gustaf Steffens to be in charge of a portable camera on a tripod. The camera was equipped to take pictures with a relatively fast shutter speed of 1/25 s (Ekholm, 'Kommentarer' 240). *Among French Peasants* reports that the camera was frequently used to photograph people, landscapes, buildings, and machinery (80, 108, 121, 126, 135, and 148). Sometimes Strindberg and Steffens experimented with snapshot photography through the window of the railway compartment. One such image is described as 'en ögonblicksfotografi' (121), literally a fast-shot photograph as in 'the blink of an eye.' This image, Strindberg writes, shows the farms in the background clearly, whereas the garden in the foreground appears blurry. Telegraph lines, presumably running between the train and the farm, separate the image in long black lines. The effect is described as surprisingly abstract, as geometrical lines cut across the composition and seemingly reflect the rail tracks. The modern manner of composition (travelling by rail and photographing through the window) is replicated in a motif that appears modernist in its abstraction. Although fascinated by this particular exposure and the idea of amateur photography, Strindberg's narrator's attitudes generally reflect the notion that tourist photography had not become a universal given by the mid-1880s. The photographic process was still cumbersome and portable cameras, even if used with newer dry-plate techniques, were highly unreliable (Hockenjos, 'Picturing Dissolving Views' 154–6).

In contrast to realist oil paintings of the 1880s, photography by this time was understood as a scientific medium, particularly useful for ethnographic and anthropological purposes. Describing his project in the beginning of the second part of *Among French Peasants*, Strindberg's speaker refers to his original intention of purchasing portraits of peasants from village photographers, through which 'en etnografisk samling grundas' (80) (an ethnographic collection may be founded). Photographs became 'a major historical form for the late nineteenth' century, as Elizabeth Edwards and many others have argued (5, 131–55; MacDougall 213–17). Photography seemed transparent, instantaneous, and superbly suitable for recording and archival purposes. It could be used in the service of cultural and historical preservation since people did not need to be brought to world expositions or the like to be showcased in reality; objects did not need to gather dust and take up space in museums; and landscapes could be depicted without the baggage of aesthetic conventions associated with painting. Large and sometimes lavishly illustrated volumes of ethnographic research began to appear at this time, created for a readership assumed to be visually literate.

Yet, *Among French Peasants* contains only written references to photographs. Few actual plates remain, since, according to Strindberg's letters, they were mostly destroyed when Steffens tried to develop them after the trip (Hemmingson 89). The potential of *Among French Peasants* to shift the visual representation of French rural life and its inhabitants was thus thwarted, and the work was eventually published without any illustrations at all. Instead, the work begins to theorize the form and function of photography, particularly with respect to the camera's importance as an 'hjälpreda för minnet' (80) (aid for memory).

Reflecting on the form and function of photography as an aesthetic tool for literary representation, the speaker ponders one of the remaining photographs (a landscape motif of Flanders). He compares it to his own sketch of the same motif. Photography, he writes, exaggerates contrasts but leaves out details; it organizes a composition into two-plane opposition (dark earth and light sky), while capturing, it is implied, a more scientific and transparent image. The sketch, on the other hand, triggers memories of three-dimensional fullness, complete with colours, gradations of obscurity, and multiple details (108). The speaker's rhetoric in *Among French Peasants* suggests that even if photographs (whether peasant portraits or landscape images) had been included in the final work, photographs would have ignored the complexity at stake in the ethnographic project of documenting French peasantry. Photographs would have made the work too representative of modernist abstraction. The equation between railway travel and photography seems given, but within the context of this work, it cannot be conceptualized formally. At the same time, the contemporary medium of photography is often alluded to as rhetorically suitable for representing the rural, whereas metaphorical references to painting organize the introduction set in Paris.

A desire to understand what kind of story about French peasants Strindberg seeks to tell must necessarily involve attention to form, and particularly to aspects of literary and visual aesthetic paradigms beginning to be radically reconceived in the mid 1880s. As an ethnographic

work, with social, historical, and political implications for the study of
European modernity, *Among French Peasants* is intimately concerned
with the formal representation not only of the French peasant as an
object, but the context in which that object is encountered and produced. This includes the subjectivity of the depicting agent, as evoked
by its title, as well as constructions of setting. Historical and aesthetic
traditions for the representation of peasants and rural landscapes, particularly in the French tradition, are explicitly connected to a seeing,
experiencing, and sensing subject (*in vivis*) who produces in a first-person narrative a story meant to be different.

In fact, *Among French Peasants* repeatedly refers to the problem of visual
recollection, and of transferring visual stimuli, which, we have been told,
are also experienced *in vivis* and therefore become explicitly subjective.
This complex of problems emerges in several instances in *Among French
Peasants* (see for example 80, 93, 119; and Marmus 283–5). Strindberg refers to the landscape around Tours as an aestheticized and technologically mediated image. It is a picture already composed, yet it remains
crucial for his re-presentation of that experience into prose. 'Det hela
[landskapet] har som totalimpression kvarlämnat i mitt öga minnet av
ett enda stort fruktstycke, målat på en femtio kilometers lång duk som
rullas från väster till öster. Jag refererar ur annotationsboken så som det
då syntes' (120) (The whole [the landscape] has left as a total impression
in my eye the memory of a large piece of fruit, painted on a canvas fifty
kilometres long, which is being rolled from west to east. I refer from my
notebook the way it looked then). In this quote, the eye is not only a
camera, but it seemingly fulfils the potential of cinematic representation.[3] The important aspect, though, is that unlike the belief in naturalistic representation of photography, the image produced is not one with a
realistic likeness to the landscape around Tours, but to a presumably colourful piece of fruit. The image appears as if caught in a spatio-temporal
blender between railway travel and a still-life studio painting.

Strindberg's speaker makes several references to the problematic relationships between observation and recollection, alluding to photography
and the camera as a storage container of imagery. Writing in hindsight,
after having completed the journey around France, Strindberg's speaker

---

3 Hockenjos argues in 'Picturing Dissolving Views' that such descriptions are not proto-
   cinematic, however, but rather reflect the common nineteenth-century device of a
   moving panorama, with a painted image rolled out to present the illusion of movement (130).

draws on a metaphor derived from cameras common at the time to affirm that his visual impressions are collected in 'ögats kassett' (81) (the eye's cassette). His task now is to develop the images from his trip: 'jag vill nu söka framkalla bilderna med alla till buds stående medel, och därvid retuschera upp negativerna' (81) (I want now to develop the pictures with the help of every possible aid, and thereby retouch the negatives). Given the highly aestheticized mode of these descriptions, *Among French Peasants* seems self-reflexively to suggest the fraught premises of ethnographic description. As such, descriptions of the French landscape move from the realist to turn modernist in its challenge of authenticity, sensory experience, and recollection.

Descriptions like these reflect the tensions cutting across Strindberg's speaker's position as an insider-outsider, who, as an interpreting agent, by prioritizing and isolating the function of his eyes as lenses of a camera, seemingly removes himself from the task of *in vivis* study. If the camera produces the scientific, 'accurate' image, how can it be retouched without losing 'authenticity,' he seems to ask. What happens when the visual impressions formerly stored in the human mind (or the human eye) are now stored in a technological device? It is as if he asks, in a self-refexive gesture that signals central concerns of literary modernism, how narrative representation is impacted when a technological device breaks down or fails to reproduce accurately the impressions that were recorded. Or, conversely, what if the impressions recorded by the camera are accurate and the human memory is faulty in recalling these as they never existed? Is the notebook, as a repository of impressions and an aid to memory, more accurate than both the camera and the human brain? Strindberg's narrator seems to ask.

The highly aestheticized language of *Among French Peasants*, drawing explicitly on a wide range of visual methods (photography, realist painting, impressionism), thus paradoxically points to the primacy of text and narrative storytelling for ethnographic purposes. The work initially sets up oppositions between fiction and science, and between impressions of the moment and subsequent recording and recollection of those impressions. Through its ethnographic travels around France, *Among French Peasants* destabilizes formal differences between painting and photography, by which painting correlates with Paris, the old, the nation, and recording. Photography correlates with the countryside, innovation, the transnational, and subjective processes of recollection. This relationship addresses a formal paradox that becomes increasingly important for Strindberg, and aesthetic representation generally, at the end of the nineteenth century: the formulation of representation as an explicit opposition between established conventions (social and aesthetic) and the assumption that in order for a work to be meaningful, it must break with those conventions. As Huyssen argues, one of the foundations of European modernism is that it reacts against bourgeois and authoritarian aesthetic traditions and institutions and 'coincides with [the emergence of new] technologies such as photography' ('Geographies of Modernism' 7). *Among French Peasants* operates simultaneously and manifestly in two distinct aesthetic registers, the textual and the visual, and often these two conflate in interesting ways, while the categories themselves draw on different literary or visual traditions.

Strindberg's speaker in *Among French Peasants* thus presents the French landscape as a literary setting doubly mediated both technologically and transnationally. As an ethnographic traveller and a foreigner, his experiences *in vivis* are immediately revealed as inseparable from a human body's reliance on technological 'aids' of sensory perception, whether framed in the *cadrage* of the railway compartment's window, through a camera, or in the recollections spurred from a notebook with hand-drawn sketches. The setting of the French farmer – the rural landscape and agricultural practices – begins to function as a counterweight not only to the technological, but also to the transnational pull of *Among French Peasants*. Unlike the urban dweller (the communard of the introduction, or Strindberg's own speaker), the French peasant comes to stand for the primacy of the written document – for the maintained primacy of ethnographic description that simultaneously draws on a series of highly aestheticized tropes (impressionist painting and snapshot photography, for example) to challenge convention.

Strindberg's interest in photography around this time and throughout his career has been well documented (see for example Granath; Hockenjos, 'Picturing Dissolving Views'; Hemmingson; and Rugg, *Picturing Ourselves*). Strindberg began photographing himself in a series of autobiographical portraits in the fall of 1886, upon returning from his travelling in France to the village of Gersau in Switzerland where he was living at the time. The Gersau images, described alternately as 'interviews' and 'impressionist-images,' signal that Strindberg was interested in photography also as an ambiguous genre – as naturalistic source material for an 'interview' or as an aestheticized image recalled in a mode reminiscent of impressionism. Photography is perceived as a dynamic and flexible representational form. The ambivalence toward the function of photography as a scientific medium in *Among*

French Peasants correlates with Strindberg's ambivalence toward fiction as a genre. In letters sent during the summer of 1886, just before leaving on his voyage around the French countryside, Strindberg professes to have relinquished for good the falsity of fiction (as in novelistic and dramatic storytelling) to finish his autobiography, framed as non-fictional, and to concentrate in the future on ethnography, history, social commentary, and natural sciences (Ekholm, 'Kommentarer' 190–2). *Among French Peasants* responds, however, not only to Strindberg's professed interest in non-fiction but also to significant aspects of French literary representations of rural conditions and peasant life.

The representational complexity with which *Among French Peasants* treats landscape and rural practices is remarkably modern and experimental. The text's experimental evocation of the function of photography for visual recollection increases as the text moves in larger and larger circles from Paris to the provinces. The text may not initially seem to follow standard definitions for literary modernism; it is not ostensibly about dissolving subjectivity or formalizations of psychological interiority, and its syntax, temporality, and (limited) narrative trajectory are straightforward and logical. Yet *Among French Peasants* can provide us with a different angle on what Pericles Lewis has defined as a distinguishing feature of modernism: its attention to a 'crisis of representation' (1). In its emphasis on a marginalized subject matter – French peasantry and rural practices – *Among French Peasants* also challenges mimeticism and endorses new 'technical innovations' that help reject 'traditional conventions for representing the world' (Lewis 1). In Lewis's formulations, the technical innovations of European modernism include (a) non-objective painting, (b) free verse, (c) stream of consciousness technique in narrative, and (d) breaking down the fourth wall of drama (3). 'In each case,' Lewis continues, 'modernism called attention to the medium of the literary or artistic work, defined itself in contrast to convention, and radically altered the means of representation' (3). *Among French Peasants* does exactly this, as the work challenges representational conventions of ethnographic travel writing. It seeks to present the French countryside and its practices in new ways. Its narrating agent, moreover, is construed as precisely the kind of outsider and marginal figure that has since become emblematic of European literary modernism – the exiled or migrant writer whose perspective from the margin challenges aesthetic and thematic conventions.

Among French Peasants can therefore be seen as at least partly modernist and experimental in that it constitutes a work of cultural intervention that insists on contextualizing culturally, historically, and economically an overlooked collectivity (peasants and farmers) as part of a narrative about modernity. It motivates this intervention and inclusion by a range of formal strategies that make deliberate use of and refer to contemporary practices of representing setting which are, as implied in Lewis's arguments, imperative to later developments in modernism: ethnography, impressionism, abstract figuration in painting, photography, eye-witness accounts, journalistic prose, and documentary enactment in dialogue form.

Literary modernism has been closely associated with urban modernity, industrialization, and mass-market culture, while agrarian practices, and the figure of the farmer, have traditionally been overlooked in modernism. In contrast, 'the idea of joining the terms "modernism" and "colonialism" ... provokes neither alarm nor surprise,' as Begam and Moses suggest (1), since colonialism and constructions of empire have become understood as necessary concepts for understanding literary modernism's relation to nation. 'What these approaches [the urban and the colonial] share is the substantive erasure of the rural as an analytic category,' Maria Farland argues in the context of American modernist poetry (912). In fact, Among French Peasants can help us understand the ways in which European literary modernism assumes an unmarked antithesis: the rural. Read in the context of urban and colonial modernism, we can begin to understand how Among French Peasants helps rewrite the map of transnational European prose modernism. In that capacity, Paris is no longer primarily juxtaposed with or situated in relation to other capitals of literary modernism – Vienna, Berlin, London, New York, or, for that matter, (Strindberg's) Stockholm – but against one of its silenced constitutive others – the French countryside. And that other is being reconsidered by a writer and traveller who positions himself as explicitly alien, other, and marginal and who thereby inscribes himself and his work within transnational modernism's paradigm. Strindberg is thus an ethnographer also of French and Parisian culture, investigating the paradoxes involved in operating on a city-country binary, or one based on colonial discourses of civilization-savagery.

Among French Peasants self-reflexively theorizes its own setting precisely along these lines. The focus on peasants appears to permit close attention to the construction of literary location, as if Strindberg's speaker is operating both within and against aesthetic conventions that link farmers closely to the landscape they are engaged in cultivating. This includes drawing on a colonial rhetoric. In a letter, Strindberg compares himself to Stanley in Africa (*Brev* 4:60). In an early version, the work was to have been called 'Genom de Hvitas Verldsdel' (Through the White Continent) in explicit reference to Stanley's *Through the Dark Continent* (1878) (Ekholm, 'Kommentarer' 193). Strindberg appears to want to turn the colonial paradigm around so that a migrant Swede seeks to understand that which is unknown not only to Paris, but to most of the world – the status and conditions of the French farmer. Strindberg's interest in rectifying the neglect of the countryside also correlates inversely with an established colonial rhetoric in France. City dwellers at the time, in historian Eugen Weber's formulation, 'despised the peasants, exaggerated their savagery,' and 'compared them unfavorably with other colonized people in North Africa and the New World' (11). Weber's history of nationalism and French peasantry, *Peasants into Frenchmen*, in fact begins with a lengthy enumeration of French nineteenth-century sources that show how the French peasant was coded as an uncivilized savage, as a 'cultural and political aboriginal, like to beasts and children' (5–6). Léon Gambetta, a future minister of agriculture, stated in 1871 that French peasants were 'intellectually several centuries behind the enlightened part of the country' (Weber 5). The dominant social and political discourse by the 1880s, Weber argues, had set up a strict city-country opposition, wherein the peasantry had become a drain on the French nation in the wake of defeats in the Franco-Prussian war and France's perceived decline in world politics. The peasant thus 'had to be integrated into the national society, economy, and culture: the culture of the city and of the city par excellence, Paris' (Weber 5).

This cultural context is integral to how *Among French Peasants* addresses and criticizes a Paris-centred view of France's rural regions. Strindberg seeks to make an intervention by showing the French farmer as an agent in his own world to both Paris and other parts of Europe. The project thus relates specifically to dominant late nineteenth-century conceptions of the French nation. *Among French Peasants* reacts specifically against what it argues is a misguided emphasis on scientific and statistical reporting on crop yields, revenue, areas of cultivated land, and so on. Strindberg's speaker states that were one to 'skriva vetenskapligt' (79) (write scientifically) about the French peasant, one might need to spend ninety-nine years researching the ample archives of the nation's agricultural department in Paris. Such an approach, *Among French Peasants* implies, would only strengthen a misconstrued emphasis on Paris for understanding the French countryside, and would only gain a superficial cultural understanding of the French countryside. Rethinking the centre-margin opposition as a matter of setting makes one understand *Among French Peasants* as an unusual work, as engaged in reconceiving transnational literary trends and aesthetic practices. By emphasizing the approach as an *in vivis* study, *Among French Peasants* includes a narrating and experiencing agent who draws on embodied and localized experience to construe alternate understandings of rural setting. First, the opposition between a top-down official view of French agriculture, as based on reports and archival material kept in Paris, is made to contrast with subjective descriptions of peasant experiences and rural locations. Second, the speaker locates as textually constituted the established opposition in French nationalistic discourse between Paris and *la province* (usually understood at this time as the entire land mass between the borders of the rural region adjacent to Paris, Île de France, and the North-African or overseas colonies) as a difference between an immense number of textual sources available in Paris and the relative scarcity of studies undertaken in person and on location outside the city. Third, the use of *in vivis* signals an attention not only to the lived experiences of others, but also to the subjectivity of the observer. In *Among French Peasants* that subjectivity translates into a particularly modern aesthetics that problematizes the transfer of an experiencing subject's visual impressions into media that can impress information upon others.

As is evident in the introduction to *Among French Peasants*, Strindberg was seeking alternate strategies than novelistic naturalism's pretence at scientific observation and propensity for lengthy enumeration of detail. Neither does the work seek to propagate images of the countryside and its population as the site of cruel and self-motivated savagery, along the lines of Zola's depiction of the Fouet family's barbaric attachment to its land in *The Earth* (*La Terre*) (1887). As do many other historians and literary critics, Weber points to the close connection between peasants and savages for many mid-century canonical French writers – Sand, Balzac, and Flaubert, for example (11). In Hippolyte Taine's *Origins of Contemporary France* (*Origines de la France Contemporaine*) (1877), rhetoric on French rural life moves inexorably toward coding peasants as animals (as discussed in Lehning 21). Taine was perhaps the single most important philosopher for the spread of naturalist writing in France and elsewhere in Europe. Zola, the best-known representative of the movement, continues on this path of peasant representation in *The Earth*. Members of the Fouan family of Zola's novel are brutal, greedy, self-serving liars and thieves, not stopping at rape or murder to acquire a parcel of land or maintain a connection to the family home and soil. Although sensationalist in character depiction, the novel describes rural customs and peasant conditions during the late 1860s realistically. The novel draws on Zola's experience of farming growing up near Aix-en-Provence and later in settling near Médon, while revealing extensive research about agricultural politics and reform during the 1880s (Parmée 7–10). Although Zola's interest in including the French peasant figure in the Rougon-Macquart sequence did not arise until well into the 1880s (Parmée 5–6), Strindberg knew about the project and writes in a letter that he fears once again to be accused of copying Zola; the first incident had been upon the publication of *The Red Room* (*Brev* 6:93).

Zola's and Strindberg's near-simultaneous depictions of the French peasant are significantly different, not only in genre (novel vs ethnography, and so on) but also in affective attitude. Naturalism's interest in peasant conditions extends beyond France to include Gerhart Hauptmann's well-known play *Before Sunrise* (*Vor Sonnenaufgang*) (1889), which was inspired not only by Zola but also by Strindberg's naturalist plays *Miss Julie* and *The Father*, as well as Tolstoy's depictions of a Russian countryside in decline in plays like *The Power of Darkness* (1887). Strindberg, despite his proclaimed turn away from fiction, wrote one of his best-known novels shortly after his return from travelling around France. In *The People of Hemsö* (*Hemsöborna*) (1887), he turned his attention to the dire peasant conditions on a small island in the Baltic Sea just east of Stockholm. Peasant characters in this novel are greedy, lustful, self-serving, and brutal; for example, scenes of a midsummer celebration result in extreme alcoholic consumption and sexual licentiousness. The naturalist attention to detail and its coding of peasant practices as near-barbaric in this novel parallel Zola's portrayal of peasants as savages in *The Earth*. Such parallels turn the tables on Strindberg as a transnational writer. On the one hand he is interested during the mid-1880s in presenting facets of French culture to a primarily Parisian audience more familiar with a sentimental view of rural life conveyed in realist oil paintings or the sensationalist strategies of Zola's naturalism; on the other hand, however, he imports not only his interest in the French peasant to write a novel about Swedish peasants, but also seemingly does so with an eye on Zola. This novel was written while Strindberg lived abroad, and, according to one scholar, reflects the author's homesickness (Brandell, *Strindberg – Ett författarliv* 2:178–80). *Among French Peasants* differs from both *The People of Hemsö* and *The*

Earth by not being a novel, but more importantly through its explicit emphasis on new technologies for the conception of rural setting and agricultural practices. The *Hemsö* novel, about Swedish peasants depicted in techniques of French naturalism, thus stands as a remarkable contrast to Strindberg's depiction of French peasants through techniques more commonly associated with early modernism.

Among French Peasants illustrates modernism's difficulty with the rural and the agrarian by offering an alternate model. This work eschews pastoral antiquation, rural idealization, and peasant demonization as part of a national context, while combining multiple representational strategies derived from different technologies and media (ethnography, documentary reportage, travel narrative, historiography, painting, and photography) that justify countryside settings and agrarian practices as integral to representations of European modernity's full complexity.

3 Ethnography and Exile

Literary history, like history in Weber's treatment above, has had difficulties dealing with the rural and the regional as aspects of late nineteenth-century modernity. The period, however, saw an explosion of interest in the study of human practices and customs, reflected in the increasing interest in anthropology, ethnology, and ethnography. Strindberg perceived himself to be instrumental in this process. When reread from such perspectives, *Among French Pesants* emerges as foundational in a European context for charting alternatives to egregiously racist and provincial expressions of (French) anthropology and ethnography. Anthropometrics, defined as the study of 'man's physical character, historical and present geographical distribution, [and] racial classification' (*Webster's Third New International Dictionary*) was strong in the French tradition, due in part to the influence of Paul Broca's physical anthropology, with its 'immense prestige of positive' and 'materialist' approaches to the 'scientific' study of man (Williams 331–2). Weber, along with many others, has remarked that although the French peasant and rural customs may have been well studied by agricultural economists like Adolphe Blanqui or historians like Jules Michelet during the nineteenth century (and since), few of those studies are ethnographic. Few writers, in Weber's intriguingly reproduced colonial rhetoric, have ventured through 'darkest France' (9) to study rural customs. Almost none of France's late nineteenth-century anthropologists and ethnologists were interested in French rural culture, preferring instead to chart distinctions between races or 'exotic cultures' (Weber 8) or to document life and customs in Paris, often published in lavish tableau formats (see Marcus). Exotic cultures and races included not only those of France's colonies, but also the Arctic region of northernmost Scandinavia – Prince Roland Bonaparte (a great-nephew of Napoléon), for example, made extensive forays into Sámi communities during his journey there in 1884. More than 400 photographic negatives remain from this trip, today housed in the Musée de L'Homme in Paris. Bonaparte had a mission to study 'the Lapps [*sic*] from two points of view, anthropometrically and ethnographically' (cited in Edwards 215). It seems that Bonaparte sought at least partially to challenge a French racialist measurement school, which clearly correlates with Strindberg's approach to his studies of the French peasant.

In the Scandinavian countries, ethnographic exploration was often framed as the study of the region's indigenous populations and farming communities. Interest in the native peoples of northernmost Scandinavia, the Sámi, or the Inuit peoples of Greenland, a Danish colony, increased during the late nineteenth century (Bravo and Sörlin, *Narrating the Arctic*). Scandinavian explorers like Adolf Erik Nordenskiöld and Fridtjof Nansen had garnered much attention for their explorations of the Arctic (a later generation of famous world-wide explorers included Sven Hedin and Knut Rasmussen) and chronicled their encounters, which helped establishe the strong Scandinavian interest in ethnography during the late nineteenth century (see Ljungström). A concomitant strong ethnographic interest in farming communities at the end of the nineteenth century, as Mark Sandberg shows in *Living Pictures, Missing Persons*, also led to the establishment of ethnographic museum collections and open-air museums (notably the Nordiska Museet and Skansen, both in Stockholm) that aimed to collect, catalogue, and preserve the indigenous customs and practices of rural Scandinavia as a countermovement to urbanization and industrialization. Strindberg participated in this ethnographic drive while working as a staff librarian at the Royal Library and publishing historical works such as *Gamla Stockholm* (*Old Stockholm*) (1880–2) or *Svenska folket* (*The Swedish People*) (1881–2), explicitly aimed at showcasing Swedish popular history and local customs in a moment of perceived cultural and historical amnesia. *Among French Peasants* thereby relates to Strindberg's earlier ethnographic and popular writing, as part of creating the kind of modern ethnographic works that Strindberg had been pursuing for Swedish audiences just before leaving Stockholm. He seems to assume that his knowledge of Swedish customs and history, attained at least partly through his research at the Royal Library where he worked in the 1870s, and his engaging style of writing popular history in Swedish should translate directly to depictions of contemporary rural France. He also appears to assume in *Among French Peasants* that disclaiming the status of Paris would be a vehicle for gaining international recognition.

Among French Peasants is part of a Scandinavian trend of ethnographic exploration. For a Swede to turn to the French countryside as alike to an unknown continent waiting to be explored by an ethnographic expedition is, however, original in the Swedish tradition. It is also original in the French tradition, keeping in mind the general French anthropological and ethnographic disinterest in its rural regions. Bonaparte's and Strindberg's respective expeditions (both photographic) to 'uncharted' regions of the other's country indicate as well that cultural and international transfer of written and visual representation was part of ethnographic expeditions at the time, which helped shape the field as part of a transnational paradigm of modernity. Turning toward the margins of French culture (the dirty, poor, uneducated, and provincial peasant) points to the need to include the margins of Europe (Sweden, for example) within French cultural awareness. On the other hand, Strindberg's adamant focus on the peasant seems supremely misguided in hindsight – the French (and Swedish) intelligentsia he wanted to impress and educate was completely uninterested in his project of recuperating the status of the French farmer. Similarly, one of Strindberg's few short-stories from this time set in Paris, 'Is This Not Enough?' (Är detta icke nog?) (1887), evokes a highly ambivalent attitude toward becoming a 'European writer' via success in Paris. Rather than addressing a world of arts and letters or *la bohème*, 'Is This Not Enough?' focuses on a peasant trying to sell his produce on the streets of Paris on a hot summer day. Almost succumbing to heat stroke, the man uses his last *sous* to purchase a bottle of poison and dies in the gutter, only to be removed by the police. The farmer who commits suicide in full public view on a hot city street suggests Strindberg's problematic relationship to Paris: as a provincial, his alter ego (the farmer) has no place in the big city. In its hostility to peasant experience, though, the Paris of the story evokes the concurrent practices of removing the peasant from the modernizing Stockholm. This short story and *Among French Peasants* offers a counter-argument to Pascale Casanova's understanding of Paris's centrality for emergent literary modernism in *The World Republic of Letters*.

In this light, *Among French Peasants* takes on a different status; rather than a peculiar oddity, it becomes representative of a general concern in France (and elsewhere in Europe) with the status of farming, agriculture, and peasant practices in a period that has been understood, both by contemporaries and by later critics, as moving relentlessly toward the urban, the central, and the modern. Historian Stephen J. Russell points out that two of the works mentioned by Strindberg in *Among French Peasants* (Laverne's *Economie rurale de la France depuis 1879* and Young's *Travels in France*) 'propagated a history based on delusion [and] misinformation' (Russel 18) that unduly influenced French agricultural research for over a century by presenting small-scale farmers and peasants as almost exclusively reactionary, obstinate, and behind their times (5–7). Weber's adoption of this model, in which peasants became construed as either 'passive victims or willful obstructionists' (Russell 58), or Weber's language inspired by Frantz Fanon's *The Wretched of the Earth*, in which a rural France, 'clothed in colonial garb' (Russell 38), seemingly prevented historians until very recently from recognizing the diversity and adaptability of the small-scale French farmer of the late nineteenth century.

In official, Paris-based, late nineteenth-century discourse, peasants became the black mark on the French nation's reputation; their backwardness and reluctance to embrace a prevalent top-down model of industrial agricultural reform (Russell 15, 32) became a problem for the nation of France in an era of rapidly shifting European and global power dynamics. Perhaps this historical legacy has also precluded literary scholars from including the rural and agrarian as instrumental to literary modernism. *Among French Peasants* clearly gestures to this tension; on the one hand, it is supposed to be a journey *in vivis* with Strindberg comparing his project to that of Stanley's in Africa (as mentioned above), while, on the other hand, the speaker sometimes prefers not to interview peasants because, as he writes, he already knows what they will say, what they think, or what they know: he has read it in books or in newspapers (see *Among French Peasants* 104, 109, 128).

The diversity of farming practices in France at the end of the nineteenth century was significant, however, as Strindberg's *Among French Peasants* shows in ample detail by presenting divergent practices in different regions. Despite the perceived agricultural crisis in the 1880s, farmers enjoyed an unprecedented rise in living conditions and income after 1870, while participating actively in a small-scale market economy that was flexible and dynamic (Russell 5–9); some farmers, for example, catered to the fact that cash crops were worth more than others when exported to cities in other parts of Europe – the Dutch liked one type of asparagus, while the British preferred another (Jonsson 250). The streamlined historiographic view of French agriculture as behind and backwards failed to take into account not only that different regions of the large country grew different crops with highly differentiated yields, but that the farming community in itself was not a homogenous group. The very large majority of farmers, *paysans* and *fermiers*, owned less than ten acres of arable land (many possessed no more than a few acres), whereas the majority of arable land was owned by relatively few landholders. Russell uses the term *les régionaux* to refer to the rural, landowning bourgeoisie, the regional elite, whose interests in crop specialization and agricultural industrialization was often markedly different from the needs and interests relevant for *les villageois*, mostly engaged in small-scale subsistence farming (9–11). Sources show that small-scale farming, the reality for most *paysans*, often diversified its crops heavily, was highly labour intensive, rarely mechanized (the scythe was the preferred tool well into the twentieth century), and resisted crop rotation, fallow periods, and sufficient use of fertilizer, whether chemical, animal, or human (Russell 22; Jonsson 231–46). Diversity meant security for the *villageois*, the small landholder, and large, specialized, and machine-driven agricultural practices were thus never a real alternative in France.

Among French Peasants in fact signals how the heterogeneous, decentralized, and dynamic peasant communities and practices of the late nineteenth century made discrepancies of French nationalistic discourse visible – only a few years before, in 1882, Ernest Renan had in his famous Sorbonne lecture formulated his understanding of national cohesiveness, in which 'a nation is a soul, a spiritual principle.' For peasants toiling individually on small, independently owned parcels of land, the idea of a collective, disembodied, and delocalized nationality may have seemed rather peculiar. The correlation between sentiments of nationalistic belonging and the rise of print capitalism, particularly newspapers, which Benedict Anderson notably traces in *Imagined Communities*, was largely non-existent in the French provinces. As *Among French Peasants* makes clear, peasants and farmers favoured small, regional newspapers to those of national or large circulation. The majority of the regional papers catering to peasants could not even be acquired in Paris, let alone in the next département. Different regional dialects of French also precluded effective communication.

Among French Peasants also obliquely addresses the function of the railroad in nineteenth-century French agricultural history. Eugen Weber, and many historians with him, argues that France's expansive railroad network, which facilitated the transfer of goods and people, was the main transformative reason toward a market economy in French agriculture (cf. Russell 124). This view of the French railway system, as a uniquely transformative wheel with many spokes revolving around the hub of Paris, has been challenged by later historians. In *Among French Peasants* it is accorded relatively little importance for the individual peasant. The railway network, though, serves as a defining but unacknowledged formal device. Strindberg's speaker defines his project in Paris and it is through railway travel that his speaker can engage with rural life in person. *Among French Peasants* responds to a blank spot on the map (the provinces outside Paris) as well as to a cultural blank stare regarding the rural and agrarian, including peasant populations. These aspects show how *Among French Peasants* indicates a range of practices, representational models, and settings and is, in fact, unique not only in the French, but also in a European tradition of depictions of rural regions, peasants, and agricultural practices. This uniqueness involves also Strindberg's narrative representation, which hovers between fictionalization and subjective renderings, to pretences at scientific observation and impartially refereed documentary.

In a book dedicated to the investigation of setting as integral to the construction and reevaluation of early transnational European modernism, the inclusion of Strindberg's *Among French Peasants* may seem to pose some methodological problems. Late nineteenth-century ethnography, travel writing, and reportage (with its inclusion of statistics, political commentary, and catalogues of objects and everyday practices) about rural regions are not the topics, genres, techniques, or settings we customarily associate with literary modernism. If we try to take seriously Strindberg's attempts at rewriting, resisting, and reconstituting myths and mythologies of Paris, while at the same time desiring the benefits he would have had if he were fully incorporated within them, we also run into a problem of the study of modernity per se. Scholars (and readers) like the kinds of studies of modernity that seem to suggest quick, convulsive change and support theories of alienation we know from Marxism and their later development through the Frankfurt School and Walter Benjamin's chronicles on Paris in the *Arcades Project*, that is, they like ever more sophisticated conceptions of mass-market(ed) phantasmagorias of urban modernity – with their necessary natural or original (equally fabricated, of course) counterparts. Holding off on this trajectory for a moment, in a gesture meant to try and understand what Strindberg seeks to do with *Among French Peasants*, and why it appears that the project had such difficulty in gaining traction in the late nineteenth century, I suggest we look at Marx's well-known and strikingly material metaphor on the peasant class. This metaphor also helps us understand why rural regions and agricultural practices have continued to remain a blank for both modernity studies and modernist literary studies.

In the *Eighteenth Brumaire of Louis Bonaparte*, Marx describes the French peasant, *le paysan* (the small landowner and those undertaking mere subsistence farming for their immediate family's survival), as only one of many 'potatoes in a sack'; their 'homologous magnitude' prevents them from relating to one another, and 'admits of no division of labor' (quoted in Russell 19). The peasant in this formulation becomes a figure divested of agency. By insisting on independent land ownership, peasants also become classless, as their stance does not fit a theory of division of labour. Large-scale industrialized, specialized, and mechanized capitalist agricultural enterprises have not yet alienated the peasant from his labour. The figure is therefore insignificant. Marx's simile, the homologous potatoes in a sack, also signals how figurations of peasantry and rural settings have become marginalized from modernist studies. Peasants appear to lack individuality, newness, distinction, and so on, while their alienation is not sufficient with respect to motivations that appear indicative of later literary modernism. That the French peasant valued the idea of individual ownership and saw it as a safety net is hardly a surprising argument in the face of top-down and Paris-based calls for an 'agricultural revolution' (to replicate an industrial revolution), since the yield even of a small plot of land probably seemed a safer way to ensure survival than relying on a wage as a hired farmer in an increasingly mechanized agricultural enterprise. The French peasant in Marx's scheme is easily coded as living an antimodern life in the dark (as a potato in a sack) and as shackled in ignorance to the land.

Among French Peasants seeks to contextualize and challenge this perspective, arguing repeatedly that versions of industrial Marxism are inappropriate for farming communities in France and elsewhere in Europe. *Among French Peasants* does not look nostalgically or sentimentally at farming and rural life, either. Instead, it sheds light on the *crise agricole* of the 1880s as a problem of national and global proportions. In almost every interview, in almost every *département* he visits, Strindberg's speaker hears the same complaints. On the national level, imbalanced tariffs make it prohibitively expensive for farmers interested in small-scale market trade to sell their products in larger cities; sometimes it is even more expensive for a French producer to sell his wares in French cities because of *octroi* (municipal taxes levied on goods brought into the city) and tariffs than it is for foreign producers, particularly of vegetables, to sell to those cities. On the international level, farmers in every region of France, regardless of crop, suffer from imbalanced trade of global proportion. Imports, such as wheat from North America and Russia, frozen meat from South America, wine from California, cork from Spain, and silk from China, are flooding the market (see also Jonsson 251–2). In *Among French Peasants*, the individual small-scale, land-owning farmer appears acutely aware that he acts and is acted upon in a global framework that seems to have rapidly changed from a position where imports had once been a matter of luxury items (coffee, cocoa, sugar cane, and so on) down to the very staples of a subsistence life (wheat and potatoes). Although *Among French Peasants* is clearly in favour of trade protectionism, it also gives several examples of peasants who are engaged in local market trading and have adapted to the changing conditions.

Strindberg's project with *Among French Peasants* thus appears, in hindsight, as remarkably insightful, extreme in some ways, radical in others, and still, as curiously bizarre, not least in its transnational implications. It argues that the French peasant is not backward, but should be understood as the only remaining counterweight to a mainstream drive toward privileging the urban and the industrial as the way of the future. In this context, *Among French Peasants* emerges as innovative, as an ethnographic project *in vivis* about the French peasant that is also methodologically a reaction against positivist and Hegelian/Marxist historicism; as a critical attack on the homogenizing, streamlining idolatry of Paris, of capital, and of ideologies of rapid social transformation. Yet Strindberg, writing from the perspective of a Swedish traveller, as a temporary visitor, clearly desires to be part of the very framework he is criticizing, to show the French what their country (not only Paris) looks like; he does this through construing an extreme position in order to make a mark for himself in a sea of anonymity.

Strindberg came from the educated middle-class of Stockholm and had no personal experience of farming. The impetus for the book has largely been construed as part of Strindberg's fascination with Rousseau and interest in contemporary agrarian socialists, such as Toubeau (Ahlström, *Strindbergs erövring av Paris* 79–83; Kylhammar, *Den tidlöse modernisten* 18–20). But is it not also Strindberg's position in exile that appears to motivate *Among French Peasants*? The ethnographic project and the figuration of its speaker as an outsider (he is a foreigner, scientist, observer, and reporter) can be understood as a perfectly reasonable undertaking for an educated European male of some means, acutely in tune with the colonizing drives of France at the time, or, as an expression of a *flaneur* position transposed to a rural setting. Strindberg's attention to peasant and farming practices were particularly strong during the 1880s, when he lived in self-imposed exile outside Sweden. His interest in agriculture and regional everyday life is not limited to the peasantry of his own nation – with farming coded as a trademark and emblem of Swedish nationalism at the end of the nineteenth century. Rather, it is part of a deliberate project of investigating and reconceiving in new literary and representational forms contemporary Europe for both French and international readers.

Strindberg's decision to write *Among French Peasants* also correlates in specific ways with the history of other Swedish emigrants. Strindberg left Sweden only partly in search of a cultural avant-garde and to become internationally recognized as a best-selling author. He also left for many of the same reasons that more than a million Swedes, primarily peasants and farmers, emigrated to North America during the period 1851–1910: because of economic need and because of repressive social and religious systems. Strindberg had been attacked publicly for writing perceived to denigrate the aristocracy and the royal family in 1883; for the collection of short stories *Giftas I* [*Getting Married*] he was taken to court on a blasphemy charge in 1884. During the peak emigration boom at the end of the 1880s (when Strindberg was living abroad), nearly 35,000 people per year left Sweden for America (Ljungmark 7). As embedded within a collective, 'among' French peasants, the work's title gestures reversely to the problematic status of farmers and emigration in a Swedish context as well. *Among French Peasants* obliquely illustrates the problem of Swedish emigration in a time of increasing nationalism (for a nation not to be able to feed its people is a serious blow to its self-image). The work is arguably a tacit rebuttal of Swedish nationalism, as promoted through ideologies of rural rootedness and farming communities. By writing about French peasants, Strindberg displaces a Swedish national trauma into one that is Frenchified. He is not writing a story of the tribulations of the Swedish farmer in Sweden or a story of emigration to North America, which Norwegian Knut Hamsun, for example, did in his work *The Cultural Life of Modern America* (*Fra det moderne Amerikas aandsliv*), published the same year as *Among French Peasants* in 1889. Like the nearly non-existent scholarship on *Among French Peasants*, the Swedish mass-emigration to North America remained for many years unaddressed by Swedish historians, arguably as it had become viewed as part of a national stigma (the boom in Swedish-American emigration studies began in the 1960s).

Quite rarely do explicit comparisons with Swedish agricultural practices come up in *Among French Peasants*, although the speaker's first-person voice divulges his political preferences for agricultural socialism (built on the premise of small-scale farming rather than industrialized, large-scale operations), denigrates religion (particularly Catholicism), and advocates for the diminution of women's role in the farming family. These are opinions immediately recognizable to a Swedish reader as typical of Strindberg in the 1880s. In the Swedish context, the contemporary and often-represented province of Dalarna carried positive contemporary connotations, as indicative of national independence, the nation's foundation, and cultural conservatism at the end of the nineteenth century (Sörlin, 'Bonden som ideal' 18; Facos 27–71). Strindberg's earlier short story collection set in rural Switzerland, *Utopias in Reality* (*Utopier i verkligheten*) (1885), provides realistic descriptions of the countryside. In this work, as Elena Balzamo argues, descriptions of rural regions and practices function as a Baedeker 'à peine retouché' (39) for Swedish readers (see also Boyer). The more experimental approach and techniques in the third part of *Among French Peasants* suggest that rural settings and agrarian practices become vehicles to challenge the establishment of a Swedish national literature; they help formulate an emergent transnational prose modernism as part of that literary tradition (see also related arguments in Schoolfield, *A Baedeker of Decadence* 43–57).

Among French Peasants is a text, like *A Madman's Defence*, that attempts to relinquish late nineteenth-century nationalist ideologies and write itself out of its own national constrictions. This includes making the French farmer a staunch republican, a free-thinker, and a social radical along the lines of Strindberg's own political preferences (ref Ekholm, 'Kommentarer'). In a Swedish context, agrarian nationalism, when Strindberg wrote *Among French Peasants*, was clearly coded in terms of class. It was a form of social conservatism that contrasted sharply with late nineteenth-century modernization rhetoric, in which representatives of industry *and* labour movements jointly participated (Sörlin, 'Prophets and Deniers'; 'Kylhammar, *Den tidlöse modernisten* 18; see also Battail). Strindberg (and others) called the dominant Marx-derived socialism, as sponsored by the prominent social democratic politician Hjalmar Branting, Industrial Socialism in contrast to Agrarian Socialism. The first strand has subsequently been closely associated with modernity (it is the basis for what most social theory understands as modern) and the construction of modernism's subjects. This rhetoric was also gendered – the Swedish independent farmer was construed as representative of a stable, primordial, and natural ideology of domestic distribution of labour (shared responsibility but different tasks), whereas both modernization and modernist movements in Sweden quickly became associated with ideological challenges of such stable gender constructions. These gendered aspects perhaps made farming culture attractive to Strindberg, while national implications proved harder to reconcile. As such, farming culture illustrates precisely the tensions that Strindberg's own contributions to transnational literary modernism consistently grapple with. This background is implicit not only with respect to the silent period reception and subsequent *non-grata* legacy of *Among French Peasants,* but also with respect to the dearth of scholarship in the Swedish tradition on modernist representation of the rural and agrarian.

To conclude this chapter, we may reiterate how transnational conceptualizations of literary settings, such as those promoted by August Strindberg as he writes about rural regions and agrarian practices in France, Sweden, and elsewhere in Europe at the end of the nineteenth century, challenge exactly those conventions that have made us overlook the rural as an important conceptual category. Strindberg's writing contrasts starkly with both contemporary idealization and demonization of the pastoral. Strindberg's conception of rural settings and agricultural practices illustrates overlooked forms of transnational European modernity at the end of the nineteenth century. *Among French Peasants* destabilizes the centrality of Paris in contemporary European aesthetic formulation and construes rural settings as a vehicle for modernist literary experimentation, in ways that denationalize landscape construction. The work embraces ethnography as a form of modernist project. Although *Among French Peasants* may not wholly embrace a modernist emphasis on photographic technology, it refuses adherence to a realist tradition of painting that draws on the rural as a location for romantic idealism or a naturalist emphasis on scientific observation. Photography and painting are instead both subsumed to text, whereas the narrative becomes a product of railway travel, of locomotion, and self-displacement. This multiplicity helps construe the rural as a possible setting of modernist poetics; it incorporates into the rural precisely the representational and social complexity later studies of modernism have accorded the urban. Strindberg's transnational project of making the French peasant and the French rural landscape a constitutive part of European modernity is thus reflected in the modernist techniques of literary representation upon which *Among French Peasants* relies. A similarly experimental approach is integrated into Strindberg's rewriting of the Parisian cityscape and the Austrian Alps in his French-language novel *Inferno* (1898). That is the text I turn to next.

3 Parisian Streets, Pre-Surrealism, and Pastoral Landscapes in *Inferno*

After his second extended stay in Paris, this time on the left bank near the Montparnasse Cemetery, August Strindberg completed in late spring of 1897 a second long first-person prose narrative in French. He was living in the southern Swedish university town Lund at the time, but left again for Paris in the fall of that year to promote in person the publication of this work, called *Inferno*. It was published in Swedish, Danish, and German translations later that year. In early 1898, La Société de Mercure de France issued it in Paris. It met complete silence in the French press. Composed in the form of an extended flashback consisting mostly of chronological journal entries, the first-person narrator is a Swedish playwright and scientist, whose initials 'A.S.' correspond with the author's. *Inferno's* limited plot focuses on the protagonist's attempts to become a respected scientist and recognized alchemist in Paris, his experiences of paranoia and persecution mania in boarding rooms and hotels, and subsequent religious conversion to Swedenborgian-inspired mysticism. *Inferno* is also a transnational travel narrative, which begins with a reference to Gare du Nord in Paris and whose first half is set in Paris, where it details a foreigner's traumatic experiences of life in the metropolis, marked by poverty, illness, and uncanny revelations and coincidences. The second half charts the protagonist's movements to Dieppe and on to Ystad in southern Sweden, via Berlin, to Klam in the Austrian Alps, and ending in Lund with its protagonist considering a return to Paris to work as a nurse at a hospital, or, alternately, retreat into a Belgian monastery.

Inferno is a bewildering work that has mystified readers and critics since it was first published. Marcel Réja's preface to the 1898 French edition warns in its first sentence that a reader thinking that literature means being entertained by 'd'ingénieuses fictions' (ingenious fictions) or an 'agréable passe-temps de broderies et de fioritures' (an agreeably embroidered and embellished way to pass time) probably will not even consider *Inferno* 'la littérature' (5, my trans.). Though ignored by French critics and readers until a new edition was published in the 1960s, *Inferno* soon became hypercoded in a Scandinavian context. It was indeed initially not read as 'literature' but as a paranoid document of illness, with few redeeming formal aspects, construed as 'the production of a sick brain' and thereby reflecting the author's presumed mental crises (Olsson, *Jag blir galen* 76 and *Levande död* 305–10; Gavel Adams, 'Kommentarer' 330–1). Second, in a gesture indicative of literary history's paradoxical canonization measures, *Inferno* came to define Strindberg's heterogeneous oeuvre, as the one artefact that could possibly help categorize a divergent and sprawling literary universe into an earlier period supposedly marked by naturalism and rationalism and a later one characterized by expressionism and mysticism, or, as a recent work affirms, as transitioning between 'the aesthetics of realism and modernism' (Stounbjerg, 'Uro og urenhed' 323, my trans.). In a third and perhaps even more remarkable strike of codification, *Inferno* was construed as integral to Swedish national literature because, as a presumably biographical document about Sweden's most important modern writer, it could not exist in transnational limbo, even if its author did, and had intended *Inferno* to do so as well. To this day, Swedish editions of *Inferno*, including the *Samlade verk*-edition, are reworked from the text as it was published in Sweden, in a translation by Eugene Fahlstedt, and not from the French original published in Paris in 1898.

The irony of *Inferno's* iconic and overbearing status in a Swedish context, versus its anonymity in the canon of French and European modernism for which it was intended, is critical. In this chapter, I wish to show not only how *Inferno* exemplifies the emergence of transnational European literary prose modernism,[1] but also how *Inferno's* own transnational settings – its marginalization in a literary tradition to which it is actually central, as well as its own construction of material and imagined places that are simultaneously central and marginal to the codification of European literary modernism – sets an ambitious agenda for early

---

1 Per Stounbjerg argues convincingly in the essay 'A Modernist Hell: On Strindberg's *Inferno*' that the prose work is modernist in a European tradition, including the narrative's subversion and disruption of a literary tradition of 'great narratives' (46), even those of religious conversion. Stounbjerg in this article discusses *Inferno's* modernist use of shifting narrative perspectives, invocation of shock, coincidences, and chance, deconstruction of stable allegorical pairs, and so on, but excludes references to setting or to the narrative's transnational implications.

twentieth-century narrative representation, as it negotiates new models for setting's function in literary experimentation. Specifically, *Inferno* shatters a European nineteenth-century paradigm of national literature and organizes a model of transnational modernism through its settings, conception, language of composition, intended audience(s), genre-hybridity, wide-ranging literary references, and incorporation of textual fragments. Strindberg may be using Dante's title and alluding to medieval biblical exegeses about hell and damnation, as well as inaugurating a 'whole line of twentieth-century novels, most famous of which is Joyce's *Ulysses*, which are construed largely on mythic foundations,' as Sprinchorn argues (introduction to *Inferno* 95). But *Inferno* also partakes in a continually shifting experimental literary praxis that shapes Parisian transnational modernism from the mid-nineteenth to the twentieth century. Evoking Nerval's *Aurélia*, Baudelaire's prose poems, and Rimbaud's *A Season in Hell* (*Une saison en enfer*), critical aspects of *Inferno's* Paris setting are reinscribed in Rilke's *The Notebooks of Malte Laurids Brigge* (*Die Aufzeichnungen des Malte Laurids Brigge*) and Breton's *Surrealist Manifesto* (*Le Manifeste du surréalisme*). Read comparatively, *Inferno*, as an overlooked artefact of European literary history, formulates critical implications of setting for European transnational modernism.

Though *Inferno's* protagonist spends plenty of time in Paris, there are hardly any descriptions of the actual cityscape. Public and emblematic locations of Paris are instead conveyed in other ways. One includes multiple references to indexical street and place names, such as La Gare du Nord, Le Jardin des Plantes, and Le Boulevard Saint Michel. Another involves the speaker's reactions to these locations – fear, joy, trepidation, humiliation – and the revelations he perceives as triggered by scrap pieces of paper or dirt in the street. At the same time, Paris is metaphorically construed as full of fragmentary human figurations: pansies that look like children's faces, disembodied hands that chastise and lead the speaker on, household objects that take human shapes, and so on. These mechanisms of fragmentation, displacement, and embodiment also formulate *Inferno's* setting as operating on several levels. On one level, urban representations are explicitly and self-referentially modernist in their short-hand indexicality, their fragmentation, and in the ways they appear to trigger emotional and psychological reactions. On another level, especially in the second half of the narrative, rural descriptions correlate with a pastoral tradition that seeks to uphold nature as a safe and unmediated haven. Nature descriptions at least partially displace modernist fragmentation with an intriguingly conventional recuperative association, so that the pristine landscape of the Austrian Alps or provincial southern Sweden seem to cure the speaker of his madness, even if a sense of persecution and malevolence remains.

Inferno's diegetic setting is transnational; it moves from Paris to peripheral parts of Europe, and then gestures to the possibility that its speaker will return to Paris once more. These geographical coordinates displace the tradition of a cohesive narrative self into one fragmentarily produced by its settings. *Inferno* to most readers, however, seems so insistent on describing psychological interiority – especially the thematization of madness – that the function of its material and imagined setting is edged out of the critical reception. How could a poor, perhaps even mad, foreigner's understanding of Paris, in a work neglected in the French canon while only precariously inserted into the Swedish, say anything about the foundations of transnational literary modernism as it emerges at the end of the nineteenth century? Indeed, what do we do with a text that is all about setting, but refuses to describe setting, at least partly because it is a text seemingly about interiority, as if interiority were not also a question of material spatiality? As Brandell emphasizes, *Inferno* evokes 'concrete reality' and 'exactly observed reality' on every page (*Strindberg in Inferno* 241). But what kind of concretion and observation are we talking about? In *Inferno*, concretion is embodied, fragmentary, and displaced. Its rhetorical strategies emphasize parataxis, ellipses, abrupt transitions, and incorporation of quotations and textual references. The text renounces cohesion in its Paris sections, including observational realist descriptive techniques and symbolist imagery, and flirts with the possibility of coherence as its protagonist leaves the metropolis. *Inferno's* divergent constructions of transnational settings illustrate its self-reflexive interest in a modernist locational politics, which I trace in this chapter. I analyse first the functions of street and place names in relation to the speaker's fragmented body. In the second section, I discuss how *Inferno's* settings relate particularly to Breton's formulations of surrealist experimentation in place narration. In the third, I turn to the construction of nation and history in *Inferno* and *The Notebooks of Malte Laurids Brigge*.

1 Streets and Corporeality

A text that is so explicitly about the experience of location (a foreigner who seeks to become an insider in Paris), but refuses to describe that place, poses intriguing conceptual problems. There are over five dozen street and place names in *Inferno*'s Paris sections. These are indexical markers rather than representative of novelistic descriptive techniques. Ranging from La Gare du Nord and Le Café de la Régence on the first page, to small streets in the Quartier Latin that appear in the text just before the protagonist leaves the city, the text expresses a desire schematically to map the city in indexical form. Thanks to the proliferation of street and place names, we know the whereabouts of the speaker at all times. This explicit attention to geographical coordinates makes it possible to locate his exact movements for a reader familiar with the map of Paris. (see also Briens 281–92) *Inferno*'s intended Parisian reader at the end of the nineteenth century could easily have followed the speaker around to construct his or her own fantasy of immersion. For a reader without that intimate knowledge, such as most of Strindberg's Swedish readers then and now, this indexicality is deliberately disorienting. The strategy establishes Paris as a composite of scattered fragments. The Swedish *Samlade verk*-edition indeed includes a pull-out map with selected street addresses indicated. That map, however, corresponds to Strindberg's movements in Paris at the time, and not explicitly to *Inferno*'s speaker's movements. The biographical rationale for the map's inclusion is problematic but also highly illustrative in that it actually does not matter, for *Inferno* as a textual artefact, whether a peripatetic cartography could be accurately drawn from this one visual representation of Paris or not.

Inferno instead develops an explicit strategy of urban modernism, in which the metropolis is a prerequisite, but whose cartographic details are denied representational value. The experience of Paris equals an inability to describe it. The setting of *Inferno*'s Paris sections is in its indexicality, but it is refused referentiality and this is indicative of the fragmentation that the narrative fosters on all levels. Street and place names may index Paris, but as synecdoches, as *pars pro toto*, they are also figurations of displacements that tear apart a fantasy of totality. *Inferno*'s speaker seeks to represent the subjective complexity of his experiences in Paris, but simultaneously reveals that project as a phantasmagoria of narrative. But *Inferno* needs to deal with Paris as a location and as a literary trope. As such, *Inferno* correlates inversely with what Eric Bulson argues, drawing on Benjamin's interest in the 'peculiar voluptuousness in the naming of streets,' namely that street names 'have a sensuous quality and possess that unique power to conjure up images of entire cities' (1). Instead, *Inferno*'s many dozens of street and place names starkly contrast with its professed interest in its speaker's interiority. This paradox creates a vacuum, which appears to posit materiality, the urban environment, against interiority, the narrator's psychological experiences.

To overcome a narrative impasse that seems to juxtapose interiority with exteriority, *Inferno* turns to its speaker's body. This strategy is established in several interrelated ways in the first chapter of *Inferno*. His hands aching and with arms symptomatic of blood-poisoning, the speaker is nearly overwhelmed by his own physicality before he is admitted to a charity hospital, the Saint-Louis in northeastern Paris, to have his hands treated. Any references to what this place looks like are laconic – 'une chambre abstraite, nue' (*Inferno* 18) (a bare, unadorned room) (*Inferno*, Sprinchorn trans. 125). The protagonist, his hands bandaged, encounters a curious set of characters in the hospital's dining room: '[J]e me trouve dans une société macâbre. Des têtes de morts et mourants; ici il manque le nez, là un œil, là la lèvre est fendue la joue pourrie' (18) (I found [find] myself in macabre company. [There are skulls and] faces of dead and dying men. [There, a nose is] missing, [there] an eye, [there a lip hangs] loose, [there is a] rotting cheek [125]). The illness, poverty, and destitution not only of *Inferno*'s speaker, but also of a group of outcasts perishing in the anonymous care of the convent charity institution, produce the experience of Paris. The present tense used in the French original connotes a spatialized immediacy – the scene is materially present at the speaker's recollection, which contrasts with the simultaneous coding of the scene as an allegorical *dance macabre*. Without appetite, with its hands bound, in captivity, the body participates in a dance of death, as the doomed clink glasses with personified, but fragmented, figures of death. As an expressionistic metaphor of modern alienation, in which the present clashes with conventions of the past, the scene concludes with an ironic celebration: 'Dans ma coupe d'arsenic je trinque avec une tête de mort qui me salue en digitaline' (18) (I clinked [clink] glasses with death's head [a living skull], and we drank [drink] each other's healths, I in arsenic, he in strychnine [125]).[2] For *Inferno*'s speaker, Paris is a site that propels increasing corporeal fragmentation. Hands, nose, eyes, heads disassemble. Mutilated, dehumanized bodies surround the narrator, who, unable to use his

---

2 Strindberg's French tends to use the present tense liberally, and occasionally inconsistently. Sprinchorn's translation, however, uses the past tense even when the original has present tense. Verb tense translations have been modified in the following to correspond to the author's original use of the present tense. The *Samlade verk* edition generally uses present-tense Swedish when the French does.

own hands, becomes himself construed as a displaced fragment. One of the narrator's few extended encounters with other poor Parisians, the patients and criminals housed at the charity hospital, is displaced into aesthetic, fragmented, figures ('death's head'/skull). The text formalizes an experience of a location by embodying and fragmenting it.

Street and place names are numerous in *Inferno* and the narrative accounts for its protagonist's whereabouts at any given time. But the speaker's experience of Paris includes also that of getting lost, despite the text's cartographic insistence. Upon his release from the Saint-Louis Hospital, he takes an evening walk through the working class and industrialized area of Saint-Martin in northeastern Paris, symbolically and materially another universe from *les grands boulevards* of western Paris, where *la flânerie* would be an expected as well as aestheticized activity. This walk, like his stay at the hospital, takes on hellish qualities, and setting is construed in terms of embodied sensory experience rather than verifiable descriptions of buildings. Warehouses stink of raw meat and rotten vegetables, and blind alleys are full of 'ordures, le vice, le crime' (26) (garbage, vice and crime [129]). The speaker constructs his displacement from known coordinates by literalizing them as embodied: 'Je cesse de lire écritaux; m'égare, retourne sur mes pas que je ne trouve plus' (26) (I stopped [stop] reading the street signs, I lost [lose] my way and turned [turn] back without being able to find my way again [129]). In Arne Melberg's formulation, the passage functions as a 'counter-*flanerie*' and offers an image of Paris as an aestheticized labyrinth ('Strindberg stiger ner: *Inferno*' 234). Setting, though, is construed less in terms of visual cues (the traditional strategy for description) and more in terms of displacement onto other aspects of embodied experience. It is olfactory (smelling raw meat), distinctly tactile, and disturbingly auditory. The speaker stumbles, while 'Des individus suspects me frôlent, lançant des mots grossiers … j'ai peur de l'inconnu, tourne à droite, tourne à gauche, tombe dans une ruelle sordide […] Des filles me barrent le chemin, des voyous me ricanent …' (26) (Suspicious-looking individuals brushed [brush] against me, hurling foul words after me … I was [am] afraid, of [the unknown]. I turned [turn] to the right, then to the left, and stumbled [stumble] into a sordid street […] Prostitutes barred [bar] my way, apaches [hoodlums] jeered [jeer] at me … [129]). As the speaker stops reading street signs, their indexical prevalence remains while the number of ellipses increases. Seven sets of ellipses in square brackets, in one short passage, indicate the gaps in spatial description, yet also tie the construction together as a matter of formalized fragmentation. This particular setting cannot be described in the narrative, but that indescribability must be indicated. Gaps that string the fragments together become identified as a matter of personal discomfort (getting lost), as well as on a syntactical level that formalizes displacement. Ellipses are, of course, place markers for that which cannot be described. They indicate a gap filled with meaning, stringing separate clauses together without explicitly connecting them, just as the speaker's descriptions of Paris formulate an aggregate that refuses coherence as well as causality.

Inferno displaces the trope of a confident Parisian *flaneur* from the centre of its inscription of Paris in a modernist frame of reference. When the narrator associates for an evening with an alluring woman, she, as a femme fatale, invites painful insults on the street that hurt both of them. Setting is again coded here as a mix between cartographic indexicality (they are walking along Rue de Raspail and Rue de la Gâité) and the corporeal and fragmented. His body feels as if it is bent under a whip, pelted, lashed, beaten on the street: 'les souteneurs et les cocottes nous giflaient par des injures outrageantes' (40) (pimps and prostitutes pelted our cheeks with their outrageous insults [138]); it felt like 'une pluie fine agaçante comme des verges' (42) (a harrying shower of rain that lashed us like so many slender rods [138]). Arriving at a restaurant, he remembers he is broke, a realization which 'me frappe sur le crâne comme un coup de marteau' (42) (felt as though I had been hit on the head with a hammer [138]) and 'la rue noire et boueuse me créva le coeur' (46) (black, mud-filled streets made my heart ache [141]). Being lost is also a sexualized experience on the streets of Paris, in which the protagonist's self-professed 'pureté psychique' (purity of [his] soul) and 'virginalité mâle' (10) (male virginity [121]) is turned from a fantasy of wholesomeness and purity to one that is fragmentary and painful.

The posited illegibility of the city – the way the speaker seems unable to grasp the clues with which the setting appears to be brimming – occurs, however, only on one level in this scene, as it is tied to the speaker's body: the sense of physical discomfort, when stumbling, being nauseated, sick, or sexually repressed. In other respects, this kind of city experience is transparently legible as a modernist tale of confusion, but one that reinserts its protagonist into a recognizable pattern of late nineteenth-century urban narration. When leaving behind the hellish back streets around Porte Saint-Martin, the narrator composes himself and transforms the experience into one that adopts the position of a Parisian *flâneur*. 'Deux pas me conduisent aux grands boulevards, que je descends. L'horloge du Théâtre [*sic*] indique six heures et quart. L'heure juste de l'apéritif, et mes amis attendent au café Napolitain comme d'habitude' (26) (Two steps and I was [am] back on the grand boulevards and walking back towards the center. The clock on the theater said [says] a quarter past six. Exactly that hour of day when my friends were [are] waiting for me as usual at the Café Napolitain [131]). The city is legible, safe, and walkable again, as soon as the narrator leaves the quarters east of Porte Saint-Martin. Reinscribing himself within a quintessential and immediately recognizable model of urban modernity, a Haussmannian boulevard comes to resemble a theatre stage, where setting is momentarily visually construed: 'au fond se dresse la colonne de David comme une borne' (32) (At the far end, like a goal post, rose [rises] the Colonne de David [133]). No longer lost or hurting, the speaker appears to relish the construction of such a quintessential Parisian sign; he is 'râvi du spectacle symbolique' (34) (ravished by the symbolic sight [133]). Such gestures, Pricilla Parkhurst Ferguson argues, are part of the *flaneur*'s appropriation of the city, through which he 'desires the city as whole, not a particular part of it ... The flâneur domesticates the potentially disruptive urban environment' (quoted in Ishikawa 107). In *Inferno*, that connection is both a pose and the foundation for the text's experimental drive, which juxtaposes belonging with estrangement.

Drawing on such a recognizable and familiar setting, visually construed, is a matter of reaffirming conventions, just as the protagonist confirms that he belongs in Paris as well as in its textual production. Like the street names listed in *Inferno*, his name is indexed in *Tout-Paris* and he is a registered member of The Society for Dramatic Authors in Paris (76 [155]). He is a denizen of Montparnasse, becomes homesick for the Left Bank when traversing the Boulevard des Italiens on the Right Bank, and his nerves are so well attuned to the city, he affirms, that he can feel the vibrations from carriages passing over Pont du Carousel oscillate all the way to the Quai Voltaire and the Cour des Tuileries (112 [180]). The fragmentation of Paris into smaller and smaller pieces, such as street names, neighbourhoods, or geological vibrations, as well as its registers and catalogues, indicate both familiarity and detachment. His points of reference are also demarcated synecdoches (his name as one part of *Tout-Paris*) that seek to construct a fantasy of embodied belonging that is always fragmentary, like nerves deciphering signals from the ground of Paris.

The embodied fragmentation so critical to the construction of setting in *Inferno* is also integral to its narrative construction. As a recurring thematic and rhetorical device, disembodied or damaged hands provide structure for the first part of the text. *Inferno's* first chapter is called 'La main de l'Invisible' (The Hand of the Invisible) and references to an 'invisible hand' occur many times in the first chapters of the Paris sections (e.g., 16, 32, 38 [124, 132, 136]). This fragmentary, disembodied, immaterial hand – a rhetorical device – is initially presented as a metaphysical, extranarrative, and allegorized entity of occult proportions governing the narrator's thoughts and actions. Yet the device's origins are physical and material in different ways that bridge setting and embodiment – the occult is always material for Strindberg. The narrator's hand is composing the journal in retrospect, since the moment of narration is May of 1897 and the narrative begins in November of 1894. This gap immediately indicates how a narrative written in journal form (in longhand, one assumes) in fact operates in two temporal registers at the same time, a past and a present separated by nearly three years, as well as in multiple spatial registers, including Paris and Lund (the location of composition). The actual narrative is prefigured by several textual excerpts from other sources, which emphasize corporeal and spiritual suffering, repentance, and chastisement. A short mystery play was included as an introduction to *Inferno* when it was published in Paris in 1898, followed by an extended quote by Louis Claude de Saint Martin, a writer of the French early nineteenth-century Illuminist movement, sometimes called the 'Luther of Occultism.' Two excerpts from the Bible (Ezekiel 14:8 and I Timothy 1:20) and one from St Rémy were chosen to preface the Swedish edition. These textual fragments function much like the ellipses and paratactic constructions of *Inferno*, as they are displaced from their original setting and not explicitly connected to one another, or to the description of Paris and the narrator's experiences of it. It thus seems that all examples of fragmentation are posited as on the same level, with none subordinated to others. All levels of materiality are equal, which indicates Strindberg's understanding of a modernist materiality.

Inferno's initial emphasis on disembodied hands ties the narrative's montage of disparate textual sources to an aesthetic of physical discomfort and corporeal fragmentation. After the narrator's first chemical experiments, the skin of his hands, 'cuite devant le grand feu, tombe en écailles' (10) (roasted by the intense heat of the fire, was [is] peeling off, falling in flakes [121]). Infected, 'le sang suinte et les douleurs sont insupportables' (12) (the blood oozed [oozes] out, and the pain became [becomes] unbearable [121]). Soon his hands are 'noires et sanglantes' (16) (black and bleeding [124]) and 'il se déclare un gonflement des veines brachiales indiquant une intoxication du sang' (16) (swelling of the veins of one arm set [sets] in, symptomatic of blood-poisoning [124]). His hands, 'liées' (22) (bound and bandaged [128]), indicate the futility of his scientific experiments. Like the setting of Paris, which is so rarely described in *Inferno*, descriptions of painful bodily experiences (bleeding hands, blood poisoning) must be suppressed. Abstract and disembodied references to sensory experience instead take precedence, as indicated by the chapter heading, 'The Hand of the Invisible.' In this way, the material body's suppression correlates with the suppression of setting in ways indicative of European modernism's complex relationship to the subject's experience of the modern city.

Separated from home and family, the speaker is alone in a foreign city and country. The railway station mentioned in the narrative's first sentence indicates the speaker's transient and impermanent status in Paris, as well as his displacement from a national context. Like the text's introductory quotes, he is a fragment. He has just bid farewell to his wife who will return to their sick child in an unspecified and denationalized 'pays lointain' (8) (distant country [119]). The concept of home appears negated, as the two Parisian place names introduced in the first paragraph, La Gare du Nord and Le Café de la Régence, are locations of transience. Sickness and isolation become constitutive of an experience of the metropolis. Along those lines, the speaker's emotions are described as 'savage' and his body as fragmented – his heart contains no more love, while his soul dislodges itself after a glass of absinthe, so that he is sent soaring high 'au dessus des petitesses de la grande Ville' (8) (above the pettiness of the great city [119]). Paris is, in the first pages of *Inferno*, not construed as a bustling metropolis of industrial and cultural production, nor as a spectacle of consumption already mythologized by the end of the nineteenth-century, but as an intriguing formal amalgamation that combines late nineteenth-century transnational and displaced mythologies about urban modernity, occultism, and literary aesthetics with subversive defiance.

Paris is also introduced as a metaphorical theatre set, as a 'théâtre des combats intellectuels' (8) (an arena of intellctual combats [19]), where the speaker has reaped some success and has had a play performed. As such it is meta-literarily inscribed in *Inferno* as one of the points of origin of literary modernism, as a location in which European literature stages and performs itself as *literary*, as a centre in a wheel of cultural exchange that turns geographical marginality into aestheticized centrality, as Pascale Casanova argues in *The World Republic of Letters*. The setting of *Inferno* provides for its speaker a different kind of 'home' along the lines of Casanova's argument. Strindberg describes conflicted relationships to Paris in many texts, as I demonstrate in my discussion of *Among French Peasants* in the previous chapter. The experimental essay 'Deranged Sensations' [Sensations detraquées] indicates another stance. This essay was published in three installments in *Le Figaro Littéraire* during the winter of 1894–5, when Strindberg had just arrived in Paris. Its protagonist arrives by train not to Gare du Nord, but to the city of Versailles, where he fantasizes about what his experience of arriving in Paris will entail. Having travelled on a metaphor of modernity (a steam train) through 'les époques de la vapeur et de l'éléctricité' (the age of steam and electricity) he is now thoroughly 'nerveux' (nervous) and inquisitively giddy – 'Suis-je sur le point de devenir moderne?' (n.p.) (Am I about to become a man of today [modern]? [trans. Robinson 128]). The speaker immediately inserts himself into a framework thematically shaped by industrialization, speed, and technological progress. He recognizes that his physical reactions are caused by travelling from a geographical periphery, 'des monts et des vallées' (n.p.) (the mountains and the valleys [122]), to the proximity of the metropolis. The rail travels displace logical faculties, as they have 'remué la pulpe de mon cerveau. Si bien que j'ai perdu la faculté de suivre mes pensées' (n.p.) (so thoroughly jumbled my brain tissue about that I have lost the ability to keep my thoughts in a sequential order [123]); soon he perceives that 'divisé en deux, mon cerveau entre en lutte contre lui-même, et je m'attends à voir se promener la moitié de mon corps sur la place d'Armes tandis que l'autre moitié restera là' (n.p.) (my brain divides into two parts and joins battle with itself, and I expect to see half my body stroll across the Place d'Armes while the other half remains by the lamp post [125]).

Approaching Paris means an immediate fragmentation of both body and essayistic syntax, as indicative of modernism's figurative split mind. Ellipses and question marks increase in prevalence in the essay. In contrast to *Inferno*, the speaker in this essay, however, still posits that a systematic appraisal of the city in its entirety is possible, and from the grounds of the Versailles Palace he reinscribes the mythic modernity of Paris in terms that are not only aggrandizing, but explicit in their search to conceive of the city as an abstract totality. Paris is 'la grande ville, la foire et l'usine des cerveaux combattants' (n.p.) (the great city, the market-place and workshop [factory] of embattled minds [122]); it is *la cité lumière*, a 'Heliopolis ... la Ville, la grande ville, la plus grande ville du monde' (n.p.) (Heliopolis ... the City, the great city, the greatest in the world [134]). This essay conforms to a paradigm of how to write modernity, Olsson argues in *Levande död*, in which Strindberg tells his 'future audience [in Paris] that he knows the language and the literary tradition of its fiction, making himself readable ... Every new attempt to write the world [however], to write "Paris," must formulate itself as a commentary to an already written book' (301, my trans.; see also Melberg, 'Barbaren i Paris' 74–8). Strindberg's hyperbolic mythification of Paris in 'Deranged Sensations' ties in, as well, with its representation in *Among French Peasants*, where it is coded as a location of derivation, stasis, and decline.

The desire to describe, formulate, and encompass Paris is so intense it is nearly palpable in 'Deranged Sensations.' Yet the essay may actually be more radical in its formal conception of urban modernity than it first appears. Its middle section, namely, is clearly also comical and ironic. So in awe is the speaker of the presence of Paris, that his increasingly elegiac invocations to the greatness of Paris reads more like hyperbolic statements suitable for a provincial visitor than an aspiring member of the avant-garde. The speaker, confused by the perspectival illusions of the Versailles Palace gets so frightened he frets, starts climbing lamp posts, invokes God's presence, clasps his hands, and as a consequence emerges as not only high-strung, but quite ridiculous (see also Olsson, *Jag blir galen* 268). Furthermore, a text so indebted to apostrophizing Paris actually never makes it to the city proper. This essay presents, on the one hand, a hypersensitive subject whose body's fragmentation process begins as soon as he comes near Paris, and, on the other, a subject intent on totalizing the image of Paris as 'la grande ville.' Yet, that totalizing gesture is quickly deconstructed, as Paris itself becomes a communicating body that appears to send him a message: 'c'est Paris que j'entends bruire du haut de cette chaîne de collines' (n.p.) (it is Paris that I can hear murmuring along this chain of hills [127]). Conveyed through the auditory canal of the Sèvres valley, he hears 'des foules qui gémissent, des cœurs esseulés dont les battements pompent un sang épuisé, des nerfs qui se brisent avec un petit craquement sec, des sanglots, des rires et des soupirs!' (n.p.) (the wailing of crowds, abandoned hearts, whose beats pump up an exhausted blood, nerves which break with a tiny dull thud, sobs, laughter and sighs! [127]). The intense material connection between *Inferno*'s speaker and the city, conveyed in fragmented form through his body or embodied objects, is thus prefigured in 'Sensations détraquées.' That connection is also made explicit in the essay, since the speaker asks himself whether his embodied connection with Paris is not a matter of 'des sensations subjectives? ... *N'est-ce point moi, moi-même que j'entends*? (n.p.) (subjective sensory impressions, *if it is not myself I hear* [?] [127]). Although the speaker negates the question, the transnational and modernist project of both 'Deranged Sensations' and *Inferno* of course stipulates that this is exactly the connection worth investigating in experimental prose, and particularly as a bridge between interiority and material spatiality.

By seeking to write about Paris, in French, in explicitly experimental ways, Strindberg presents himself as a modern author, partaking in the myth-making strategies of Parisian representation, which are also indicative of his own attempt to become, like Paris, one of the meaningful embodied fragments produced by the literature of modernity. Strindberg establishes himself in relation to major Parisian writers of the nineteenth century, attempting to become 'Ockultismens Zola' (The Zola of Occultism) and calling *Inferno* 'ett poem på prosa' (a poem in prose) (Gavel Adams, 'Kommentarer' 350). Anne Bourguignon situates *Inferno* as representative of an early 1890s *crise du roman*. Drawing on Michel Raimond's argument on French literature's explicit renunciation of realism and naturalism, Bourguignon emphasizes that *Inferno*'s interest in 'le surnaturel' (the supernatural) and similarities with Huysmans' *En Route* indicate Strindberg's general awareness of French literary trends (263–4). *Inferno*'s 'generic ambiguity' – Gavel Adams's useful term – has led to lengthy discussion on whether *Inferno* is autobiography or fiction, and if fictional in nature, what kind of fiction (occultist, decadent, experimental, autobiographical, religious).[3] Olsson argues in *Levande död*, moreover, that *Inferno* is a novel that partakes in explicit allegorical figurations of modernity. As a modern

---

3 For the most significant works on *Inferno's* ambiguous generic definition available in English, see Brandell, *Strindberg in Inferno*; Eric Johannesson, *The Novels of August Strindberg*, esp. 173–91; Sprinchorn, 'Introduction: Strindberg from 1892 to 1897,' esp. 80–96; and Gavel Adams, 'The Generic Ambiguity,' in which she argues that *Inferno* changes gears in chapter 10 and moves toward an autobiographical account, incorporating the scattered pieces of Swedenborgian philosophy that Strindberg had started accumulating. Although Strindberg claimed that *Inferno* was an autobiographical text, based on his diary *Ockulta dagboken* (*The Occult Diary*), Gavel Adams and others have relayed in detail the fictional impetus of this text; see also Stounbjerg 'A Modernist Hell' 54–6; 'Uro og Urenhed' 278–84; Olsson, *Levande död* 305–97; and Teilmann, 'Generiske interferenser.'

religious allegory, Olsson argues, *Inferno* reveals what Adorno calls the negative dialectic of modern art forms: the literary object's commodity form is inscribed in a system dependant on exchange value, which it simultaneously rebels against. *Inferno*'s author occupies a similarly fraught position, I contend. He wants to stake out his own, extreme field of modern literature, while desiring to occupy a central position among the many Scandinavian authors who sought to establish themselves as European modern writers. Among them, Strindberg knew best the pull of Paris. He moves there and adopts its language, he writes for its publications and rewrites its literary topoi and tropes, he seeks to 'erövra världsstaden' (conquer the metropolis) (cited in Ahlström, *Strindbergs erövring av Paris* 222).[4] He intervenes in a transnational modernist paradigm that nevertheless depends on the central metaphor of Paris, seeking to shatter and displace the mythology on which his writing relies.

In *Inferno*, Paris is a location of fragmentation. And *Inferno* is a fragment in search of a whole, but which simultaneously rejects a literary tradition of Parisian urban narrative representation, as exported around

---

4 The research on Strindberg's period in Paris from 1894 to 1898 is vast (for a brief introduction in English, see Sprinchorn's introduction; Lagercrantz 258–87; and Lamm 291–304). Ahlström, *Strindbergs erövring av Paris*, provides a thorough contextualization of the period. During most of the twentieth century, literary scholarship in Sweden and internationally tended to discuss *Inferno* and other works from a biographical and psychologizing standpoint, tracing Strindberg's mental instability and alleged insanity as directly influencing his prose at the time. For a representative example, see Brandell, *Strindberg in Inferno* 66–97. Lars Gustafson, however, argues that 'Strindberg's *Inferno* does not need psychiatry to any greater extent than does Dante's' (132); Weinstein takes a similar approach and classifies *Inferno* as 'a radical text' in which 'the customary anchors of time, space, and ego have been lifted' (113). Recent critical efforts have unveiled the mythos surrounding Strindberg's 'autobiographies' and self-construction of madness during this period. Exemplary for their critical insights are Olsson's book about Strindberg, *Levande död* (esp. 305–14, which also offers a thorough literature review on scholarly interpretations of *Inferno*; see also Lindvåg) and *Jag blir galen* (esp. 245–72). *Levande död's* discussion of Strindberg's French-language essays, such as 'Sensations détraquées,' and *Inferno* provides a major break with earlier criticism. Critical inquiries that provide supplemental important background to my arguments include Melberg, 'Barbaren i Paris' and 'Strindberg stiger ner: Inferno'; Gavel Adams 'The Generic Ambiguity,' 'Strindberg and Paris 1894–1898,' and 'Strindberg's Inferno and Rimbaldian Poetics'; Brandell, *Strindberg in Inferno* 237–51; and Carlson's *Out of Inferno*, 173–222, 284–97. Strindberg's French language writing in *Inferno* has been discussed in detail by Sophie Grimal, 'The Alchemy of Writing.' For more on Strindberg's French, see my previous references in this book; Engwall, *Strindberg et la France*; and Eriksson, *Strindberg och det franska språket*.

Europe by Flaubert or Zola, Huysmans or Maupassant, or, for that matter, travel guide books, the manifold popular non-fictional prose pieces described as 'panoramic' (Cohen, *Profane* 82, drawing on Benjamin), or the glossy reports on the Parisian fashion scene readily available in many illustrated weeklies. *Inferno's* formal fragmentation charts its own setting to claim its own modernist stakes. Neither is the text like anything published in Sweden at the time. *Inferno's* disjointed construction of Paris makes of Paris also a fragment of a modern avant-garde, which it displaces from its perceived centrality. Perhaps this is part of the reason why *Inferno* quickly became such a problematic text for Swedish (and French) readers and Scandinavian critics to engage with. Negating the centrality of Paris by refusing to describe that setting, *Inferno* also disrupts identification with Swedish versions of early metropolitan modernism, understood as influenced particularly by French models, such as the polished, detached, stylized *flaneur* literature by Hjalmar Söderberg, whose novel *Doctor Glas* (1905) has become a classic example of early twentieth-century Swedish urban literature (see Kjellén for a thorough discussion on Paris and Swedish *flanörlitteratur* around 1900).

2 Surrealism and Setting

Fragmentation ties form and content together in *Inferno* and locates it as part of a modernist revision of the legacy of Paris. This strategy also situates the text as a central artefact in the many revisions to a literary praxis of modernism that constantly seeks to recodify, reformulate, and reinterpret Paris. Most strikingly, *Inferno* formulates problems of setting that some of the best known surrealist prose works address in the 1920s, that is, how to reveal the power and function of setting without resorting to realist or panoramic description (see also Cohen, *Profane* 82–4; Ishikawa 103–7). *Inferno's* multivalent genre status subverts established forms of the nineteenth-century novel, just as Breton's *Surrealist Manifesto* denounced the descriptive tradition of the French novel form and its 'attitude réaliste ... faite de médiocrité, de haine et de plate suffisance' (*Oeuvres Complètes* 1:313) (realistic attitude ... made up of mediocrity, hate, and dull conceit' [Breton, 'Manifesto of Surrealism' 6, trans. Seaver and Lane]). Breton lambasts the novel form for its formulaic plots, its emphasis on temporal progression, its dependence on character types, and its trite spatial description (*OC* 1:309–16). Breton in the *Surrealist Manifesto* defies descriptions of interiority, whether of location or psychology. He asks to be spared from yet one more description of a bedroom; from a conventional postcard landscape description; and from supercilious analyses of psychological interiority, which '[make] l'inconnu au connu, au classable, berce les cerveaux' (OC 1:315) (make the unknown known, classifiable [and dull our brains] [9]). For Breton, psychological interiority, like setting, can no longer be described in ways inherited from the realist or naturalist novel but must become material (for a discussion of connections between Strindberg and Breton, see Abolgassemi).

Breton's disdain for spatial description, whose facile mimeticism had been made redundant by photography, he argued, became a foundational tenet of surrealism. The extensive elaboration on setting in Louis Aragon's A Peasant in Paris (Un Paysan à Paris), for example, provoked a 'torrent of indignant words' in a surprising 'outburst,' the author himself has reported (cited in Taylor). Breton, like Strindberg in Inferno, however, relies on the indexicality of street and place names to represent Paris; material artefacts and cartographically verifiable place names are quintessential to surrealism's project. Just as Strindberg investigated the potential of experimental photography, and had his famed 'Celestographs' exhibited in Paris in 1894, Breton included multiple photographs in his prose work Nadja (1928), which displace literary spatial description in favour of visual montages that juxtapose narration with pasted-in photos of locations in Paris. This novel also juxtaposes material aspects of the urban landscape with an interiority that cannot be described: Nadja's confusion increases with the number of photographs. Unlike for Inferno's protagonist, no recuperative trajectory is offered her, as she languishes in a mental institution at the end of the novel. Models for spatial representation that could make prose the location in which the marvellous, 'le merveilleux' is formulated – as Breton argued in his first manifesto – actually includes an unexpected transnational prose connection that ties Paris to the northern margins of Europe As Breton writes, 'Il peut paraître arbitrare que je propose ce modèle, lorsqu'il s'agit du merveilleux, aux-quelles les littératures du Nord et les littératures orientales ont fait emp-runt sur emprunt' (OC 1:320) (It may seem arbitrary on my part, when discussing the marvellous, to propose this model, from which both the Nordic literatures and Oriental literatures have borrowed time and time again [15]). Breton most notably posits Hamsun's Hunger (1890) as an important forerunner of the surrealist movement. Whether or not Breton was aware of it, there are critical similarities in the city descriptions between Hunger and Inferno, including the weight that these two narratives place on peripatetic ambulating and fortuitous coincidences derived from everyday experiences, similar to the *objet trouvés* and *le hasard objectif* (a chance encounter) the surrealists find in the streets of Paris. For a later critic like Evert Sprinchorn, *Inferno* creates 'poetry out of life's trivia, in much the same way as the surrealists made art out of *objets trouvés*' ('Introduction' 94). The specific connection is one of setting – and, as I have argued in this book, location is not 'trivia,' but rather integral to narrative construction and European literary modernism.

Réja contextualizes *Inferno*'s reliance on coincidences in his 1898 preface: 'La théorie des coïncidences, la législation du hasard, voilà ce qu'il [Strindberg] vient offrir à nos esprits éduqués dans un déterminisme rigoreux' (8) (A theory of coincidences, a legislation of chance, that is what [Strindberg] offers to our senses educated by a rigorous determinism [my trans.]). Though Strindberg was inspired by Swedenborgian theosophy and its emphasis on earthly and celestial correlations, as well as by a medieval conception of nature as a chain of being, *Inferno*'s setting is actually determined by material coincidences. Street scenes repeatedly juxtapose the random and the material, without giving any rational explanation, which also prefigures surrealism's interest in the perception of signs and objects in the streetscape. Letters written in coal on a wall assure *Inferno*'s narrator of imminent successes in his chemical experiments (68 [151]), noticing the number on a child's playing card prevents him from seeing a certain friend (100 [172]), tree branches on the street form linguistic signs that warn him about imagined enemies (104 [173]), and icons on scraps of paper in the gutter bear meaning that he should immediately leave Paris (120 [191]). Strindberg's speaker may seek order in the universe, but the vehicle for interpreting the world is always a material object.

In *Nadja*, too, Breton mentions the occult and a belief in *le hasard*. Breton's use of the occult, Madame Sacco, *la voyante*, and so on, may appear more secular than *Inferno*'s, but the two uses combine in their material triggers – without objects, there are no coincidences. Chance encounters and found objects in Paris are specifically associated with the narrator's chemical experiments, suggesting that *Inferno* uses the streets of Paris to promote, along the lines of later surrealists, unexpected juxtapositions which challenge the supposed rationality of scientific experimentation as well as the implied setting of such experimentation – a laboratory, a university, or the like. Savouring the limited success he has just reaped as a chemist, for example, the speaker takes an evening walk in a gloomy neighbourhood. He stops at a street corner, amazed: 'Je m'arrête au coin de la rue Alibert. Pourquoi Alibert? Qui ca? N'est-ce pas que le graphite trouvé par le chimiste dans mon soufre se nommait graphite Alibert. – Et puis après? Drôle, mais l'impression d'une chose inexplicable me reste à l'esprit' (24) (I stopped [stop] at the corner of Rue Alibert. [Why] Alibert? Who was he [is that]? The graphite the chemist found in my sulfur, was that called Alibert graphite? So what? It was [this is] bizarre, but the impression of something inexplicable was [is] lodged in my mind [129]). The indexical street name Rue Alibert formulates a fortuitous coincidence, since the seemingly random street name becomes associated not only with a person – 'Who is that?' (emphasis added) – but with a chemical compound. The radically incompatible – a street sign, a personal name, and a chemical experiment – are juxtaposed and construed as indicative of the power of Parisian space, and the French language, in Inferno.

Inferno's Paris section formulates connections between material objects that are never explained as part of any system, whether natural, scientific, or mystical. Instead, the chance encounter is corporeally internalized in a gesture indicative of Inferno's modernism: the impression of the Alibert chance encounter '[lui] reste à l'esprit' ([is] lodged in [his] mind]. As Kiyoko Ishikawa argues, it is precisely the fragmentation of the urban landscape that sets Breton's spatial imagination apart from the long tradition of Paris representation he draws on, as he introduces 'une optique fragmentaire' to formulate 'une géographie intérieure' (107). The same technique is used in Inferno to affirm the materiality of random chance encounters in the city. Upon returning from a laboratory at the Sorbonne, for example, the narrator passes by the initials A.S. printed above a shop window. For him, this is a 'vision d'une réalité indéniable. Peinte sur le carreau de la boutique je trouve les lettres intiales de mon nom: A.S. flottant sur un nuage blanc argent et au dessus un arc-en-ciel' (34) (Ah! A vision of undeniable reality. Painted on the wooden square over the shop were [are] my initials A.S. floating on a silver white cloud and hooped over with a rainbow [133]). This fortuitous coincidence signals for the speaker the immanent success of his chemical experiments, at the same time as two fragmented letters from the alphabet are displaced signs that indicate the random aspects of signs in the streetscape (see also Olsson, Levande död 362–6). This internalized chance encounter, a result of objets trouvés (the verb trouver, to find, is often used in the French original of Inferno) sets the stage for a sequence of similar revelations. Stopping by a bouquiniste outside the Odéon Arcade a few moments later, the narrator randomly, 'sans préméditation' (34) (quite without thinking [134]) picks up a tattered copy of Orfila's chemistry book. He opens it up 'au hasard' (34) (at random [134]) and finds that in addition to oxygen and hydrogen, the chemical substance he is currently investigating (sulfur) contains a third component. He returns to his hotel room at the Hotel Orfila, reads Balzac's *Séraphita*, and through it encounters Swedenborg, and subsequently proceeds with attempts to make gold. This connection is later repeated as another instance of graffiti. He arrives 'sans préméditation' (68) (by chance [151]) at Meudon, where he notices the letters F and S scribbled on a wall, which fortuitously 'se dédouble étalant devant mes yeux le secret de l'or' (68) (double in front of my eyes to reveal the secret of gold [151]). The displaced and random letters are noticed first because they connect the speaker's last name with the first initial of his estranged wife's – F. This juxtaposition propels his imagination into a surrealist *rapprochement* of two separate realities, expressed as 'une vive impression de quelque chose miraculeuse' (68) (I had witnessed something like a miracle [151]). Similarly, after attempting a repeat experiment on making gold, the speaker's morning walk in L'Avenue de l'Observatoire reveals two pieces of cardboard that he interprets as good omens for his experiments (88 [165]).

Aspects of setting link these chance encounters. The *objets trouvés* of the street (signs, shop window, a book for resale at a *boquiniste*, graffiti) connect with the letters of personal names (Alibert, A.S., Orfila, F.). These help motivate the speaker's chemical experiments. *Inferno* juxtaposes several different interpretive registers here. The speaker's burnt, aching hands have sent him one kind of message; the inconclusive chemical results another, and the visual images and random objects of the chance encounter in the streets yet one more. The coincidences for *Inferno*'s speaker are always material and explicitly connected to an urban setting – street signs, books, letters by a window, a chemical compound, graffiti. As such, Stounbjerg argues, *Inferno* conveys Aragon's surrealist conception of the city's 'vertige du moderne' ('Uro og Urenhed' 302). In this process, the narrator trusts the random chance encounter in the street more than rational argumentation by other chemists, which is indicative not only of the surrealist belief in the power of the visual chance encounters and unexpected juxtaposition of material artefacts, but also specifically in Breton's understanding of scientific method as integral to the surrealist project (Adamson 270–2). Breton in the *Surrealist Manifesto* famously revolts against positivism and realism, while lamenting that logical processes 's'appliquent à la résolution de problèmes d'intérêt secondaire' (316) (are applicable only to solving problems of secondary interest [9]).

What Breton in the *Surrealist Manifesto* calls the marvellous, 'le merveilleux' (*OC* 1:320–1), derives from Gérard de Nerval's concept of 'supernaturalism' (*OC* 1:327). Breton refers explicitly to Nerval's *Aurélia, où le rêve et la vie* (1855) as an early model for the movement in the *Second Manifesto of Surrealism* (1930). Nerval's importance for the surrealists is in fact suggestively prefigured also through a lesser-known point of connection. Strindberg appears to situate his proto-surrealist narratives of Parisian displacement in a direct line from *Aurélia's* tales of uncanny revelations, which bridge materiality and non-materiality. Like *Inferno's*, *Aurélia's* speaker moves, mostly on foot, to, around, and within Paris, and he as well affirms the streetscape's importance for dreaming. *Aurélia's* first sentence asserts, 'La rêve est une seconde vie' (Our dreams are a second life), in which 'une clarté nouvelle illumine et fait jouer ces apparations bizarre' (2) (a new brightness illumines these strange apparitions and gives them movement [3], trans. Geoffrey Wagner). Nerval begins the second paragraph with a reference to Swedenborg and many plot events seem echoed in *Inferno*. In descriptions of Paris in the second section of *Aurélia*, for example, its speaker finds scrap paper filled with meaningful but random letters, perceives human figuration in pebbles, and distinguishes how electricity travels through the atmosphere. Taken to the Hospice de la Charité (a charity hospital housed next to an insane asylum) to recuperate, he acquires a level of 'force invisible' (invincible strength) that allows him to perceive how 'tout dans la nature prenait des aspects nouveaux, et des voix secrètes sortaient de la plante, de l'arbre, des animaux' (98) (everything in Nature took on a new aspect and secret voices ... came from plants, trees, animals [56–7]).

Rimbaud's *A Season in Hell* is another important early inspiration for the Parisian surrealists, as Matthews explores in his article 'Du surnaturalisme au surrealisme.' Strindberg was living in Paris when Rimbaud's notorious collection of poetry was reissued by Verlaine in 1895 (it was originally published in 1873; see also Brandell, *Strindberg in Inferno* 240–1; Gavel Adams, 'Strindberg's *Inferno* and Rimbaldian Poetics'). *Inferno's* implicit references to *Aurélia* and *A Season in Hell* affirm that the emblematic elements of Parisian literary modernity so important for the surrealists – displacements, fragmentation, inexplicable correlations – also rework aesthetic traditions both geographically and linguistically marginal, such as those written by a transnational, displaced writer like Strindberg about Paris. As such, *Inferno* functions as an overlooked transitional text between these better known artefacts. *Inferno* becomes an unexpected chance encounter, spatio-temporally dislodged, which bridges the tradition of Parisian modernism from Nerval to Breton. These kinds of connections help us understand how transnational literary prose modernism evolves in ways that both thematize and exemplify the function of setting.

Strindberg was just as little interested in a symbolical formalization of experience as he was in promoting art for art's sake. Instead, a chance encounter allows for the possibility of becoming, 'pourquoi pas – illuminé!' (39) (why not? – illuminated! [136]), prefiguring the kind of rhetoric that the surrealists would later employ. Coincidences and chance encounters emerge for surrealists in the city, which also transfers the psychological into a spatial and material realm – the *objets trouvés* upon which the art form relies are found on the streets of Paris in Breton's novel *Nadja* and in other canonical texts of the movement. The chance encounter in the street evokes a non-symbolist 'image' that corresponds to the chance meeting of words in automatic writing, which ultimately produces 'une sorte de réalité absolue, de *surréalité*' (*OC* 1:319) (a kind of absolute reality, a *surreality* [14]), Breton writes in the *Surrealist Manifesto*, or as a necessary juxtaposition between setting and psychological interiority. Like Strindberg, Breton depends on Paris for the production of a surrealist aesthetic framework, but seeks to subvert the narrative conventions that *are* this setting. Simultaneously, the representation of psychological interiority is equated with scrap pieces of paper found in the gutter. The one cannot be narratively conveyed without the other.

Whether Breton had personal knowledge of *Inferno* when he wrote his manifestos or the narrative *Nadja* is unclear. It is more likely that his knowledge of Strindberg's writing referred to drama, which was better known in France at the time. Breton's colleague Antonin Artaud famously staged *A Dream Play* in 1928 (and sought, without success, to have *Ghost Sonata* produced). This production caused a scandal and the definitive rupture between Artaud and Breton, since Breton and other surrealists reportedly attempted to sabotage the performance with the rationale that drama was no longer surrealist, i.e., spontaneous or unscripted (see Swerling, *Strindberg's Impact in France* 68–71; Tidström chapter 3, section 3.2). *A Dream Play* is ironically the dramatic work by Strindberg that most closely approximates the surrealist understanding of the power of dreaming, of association, and of the unconscious.

The critical points of connection between *Inferno* and the later surrealist imagination of Paris are instead formal, as I have suggested above. These connections in representations of Paris stretch in unexpected transnational constellations from the mid-nineteenth century to the 1920s. They help code Parisian literary settings into recognizable entities, and this paradoxically allows Breton and other surrealists to construct this city as a space where coincidences easily happen, or rather, where chance encounters are immediately recognized for their 'coincidental' qualities. Strindberg arguably helps establish the foundation for such an interpretation, which correlates with Margaret Cohen's argument that what Breton presents as 'chance encounters' are actually structured according to both historiographical and gendered trajectories, in which Paris emerges as an overdetermined context (*Profane* 77–119; see also Collier; Burgin; and Caws, *Metapoetics*). Breton's *Nadja*, Cohen argues, refuses any 'monumental vision of Parisian historical grandeur' (79), but instead incorporates recent aspects of social violence that challenge the popular notion of Paris as an accessible and glorious repository of the nation's history, otherwise promoted in travel guides and panoramic literature well into the 1920s. That *Inferno* lacks references to Paris's and France's historical past is perhaps less surprising, given its author's active construction of a transnational authorial persona not mired in centuries of historiographic or literary practice. The reluctance to embrace official history links both texts as resolutely displaced from a national paradigm. Surrealism, moreover, despite its close connections with Paris, has been construed as a transnational, if not 'global' (Chénieux-Gendron 2), or even 'galactic' (Shattuck 12) movement, later critics affirm with some hyperbole.

French surrealism as a form engages aesthetic concerns of transience and fragmentation in the wake of the First World War. This is reflected not only by the fact that many of its most important contributors in Paris lived lives marked by displacement after the war, but also by the movement's emphasis in literary and visual arts on discarded objects and unexpected juxtapositions of items and genres of representation. As a transnational writer, Strindberg's own writing in *Inferno* is clearly marked by transience and displacements – the work was better understood in Germany, Bourguignon argues, and arguably had stronger impact there (274). Kafka recognized the protosurrealist and modernist qualities of *Inferno*, Bourgignon shows, and according to one of his contemporaries, reading *Inferno* promoted 'une sensation de déjà-lu' (275) (a sensation of the already-read [my trans.]; see also Gravier). Another prominent German-language modernist of the twentieth century, Thomas Mann, saw connections between the surrealists and Strindberg's writing in French about Paris. Mann describes Strindberg's writing as spanning a range of literary movements, including prefiguring Surrealism: 'Standing outside and above schools and movements, he [Strindberg] unites them all. A Naturalist as well as a neo-Romantic, he anticipates Expressionism ... At the same time, he is the first Surrealist – the first in every sense!' (trans. and citation from Rugg, 'August Strindberg' 6).

Breton's project of rewriting a surrealist Paris according to the practices of le hasard objectif and des objets trouvés echoes the contradictions and possibilities suggested by Strindberg in *Inferno*. Rather than searching actively for the chance encounter, as the surrealists arguably do despite their insistence on its spontaneous and random quality, *Inferno's* speaker occupies a liminal position in the urban landscape, yet objects found on the street and signs posted on buildings not only allow him to interpret the city, but also lead him to situate himself as concretely part of the landscape. The materiality of the city produces his interiority; without artefacts or street signs, the fragmentation of his psyche becomes illegible as a narrative trope. This strategy momentarily turns a bewildered outsider, *Inferno's* lonely, sick, and poor narrator, into a Parisian 'insider,' into an active agent who internalizes the random images offered by the city. Like Breton's and Aragon's surrealist city tales from the 1920s, *Inferno* depends on Paris as a material location, while simultaneously challenging, and thereby offering alternative models for, a transnational, displaced understanding of the French capital around the turn of the century. *Inferno* presents its speaker as engaged in making Parisian urban space into an extension of its marginalized speaker, as part of the text's corporeal construction of urban fragmentation

Strindberg's importance for surrealist visual experimentation has been addressed during the past few decades. The official website to a large exhibition of his painting and photography at London's Tate Modern in 2005 affirms the connection, emphasizing that Strindberg believed 'that chance played a vital role in the creative process' and that his approach 'later became central to the theory of major artistic movements such as Surrealism' (Tate Modern website). Paul Wescher emphasizes that Strindberg helped shape 'modern thought and vision where it finally led to Surrealism' and formulated a 'first organized effort of grasping the significance of the reality-behind-reality, of guiding the chance element into the channels of visibility, tangibility' (94, 99).

Neither Artaud nor Breton fully acknowledged Strindberg's influence until much later, however. Relating Strindberg to Nietzsche and Rimbaud in the essay 'Arcane 17' (1944), Breton evokes a long-standing general fascination with the writer, but it is upon viewing Strindberg's paintings at the Musée d'Art Moderne in Paris in 1962 that he makes the connection more concrete. After that show, Breton is reported to have read aloud to a group of surrealist sympathizers Strindberg's 1894 essay 'Des Arts nouveaux! Ou le Hasard dans la production artistique' (The New Arts! Or the Role of Chance in Artistic Creation'). Breton's synthesis was then, 'Il a tout vu avant nous' (He saw it all before us) (F. Arrabal, cited in Swerling, *Strindberg's Impact* 187).

It is true that Strindberg attempted to create new art forms which challenge both the nineteenth century's belief in linear progress and rationalism's prerogative to formulate art as reflecting reality; he also sought to challenge an aesthetics of simplistic symbolism without material components. Narrative prose settings, like *Inferno*'s, are indeed a privileged locus of this materiality and provide an explicit connection with surrealism's challenges to urban description, which has previously been overlooked. *Inferno*'s settings and the transnational context in which they are conceived and received emphasize how the investigation of human interiority is a matter of objects in space. Setting is thus not simplistically reflective but productive of aesthetics and formal experimentation.

Inferno's conceptions of materiality are prevalent not only in the Parisian cityscape but also in the anonymous and generic dwellings in which the speaker resides. These dwellings formulate an experimental aesthetics highly reminiscent of surrealism, although the movement's best-known texts generally eschew dwelling spaces in favour of those that are understood as public – restaurants, streets, theatres, arcades. Dwelling locations in *Inferno*'s Paris sections are nevertheless important. They are named and identified, but rarely described in any detail. They are always transitory – a pension, a hospital, hotels. Only once does the speaker enter a family's apartment, during a Christmas celebration, and he immediately feels uncomfortable, reminded of his estranged wife and daughter; he soon leaves for a walk in the street. Dwellings, like streets and public places, are also intimately connected to bodily functions. At Hôtel Orfila, his window faces an alley with a row of outhouses whose sounds and smells drift into his own room and juxtapose the image of a cloister with an outhouse. When a lunch tray with food is left on his table next to an unemptied chamber pot – juxtaposing the body's input and output – the narrator formulates dwelling as an 'enfer excré-mentiel' (66) (excrementitious hell [150]). The body's refuse foregrounds the speaker's status as a displaced fragment in the city, for which ideologies of home and belonging are not only an illusion, but a prerequisite for storytelling about transnational existence that is at the core of *Inferno*.

The Paris boarding rooms are both laboratories and studios. Transient aspects of dwelling become prerequisites for new expressions of visual art. Again, both chemical and aesthetic experiments depend on corporeal expressions. Lumps of coal, commonplace objects valuable as a source of fuel for the narrator's scientific experiments, are reinterpreted as anthropomorphized humans or replicas of creatures that are also aestheticized objects: a lump of coal looks like 'le tronc plutôt humain' ([the torso] more than a human body than anything else); another lump resembles a gnome, and a third is 'une madone avec l'enfant, style Byzantin, incomparable comme ligne' (70) (a Madonna and child, modeled in the Byzantine style, with an incomparably beautiful line [152]). He affirms that 'des objets réels se revêtirent de formes humaines souvent d'un effet grandiose' (88) (real objects did often appear to me as being endowed with human shapes [166]). Pillows on his bed look like a sculptural figuration in marble, which transforms into an animation of Zeus: 'Plus on regarde et plus vivant, plus terrible l'apparition prend corps' (90) (The longer we stood gazing, the more real, alive, and awesome became the apparition [167]). Thomas Götselius argues that Strindberg's dynamic visual imagery, like the transformation of a pillow into a figurative Zeus head, relates to photographic practices of the late nineteenth century, by which photography challenges the relationship between sign and image, or suggests a 'photographic mode of seeing, in which phenomena of the world cannot be trusted and the gap between perception and knowledge is both palpable and decisive' (129, my trans.). Götselius's understanding of the technical mediation of Strindberg's imagery is significant, as it also helps illustrate *Inferno*'s deliberate inscription of itself in a modernist literary framework.

But chance encounters are also explicitly embodied in Strindberg's text, as *Inferno* formulates a montage of unexpectedly juxtaposed materials, motifs, and settings. It proposes '[u]n nouvel art révélé et d'après nature!' (90) (a new art revealed, an art taken from Nature herself! [167]). Strindberg seems to echo implications of Nerval's term 'supernaturalism,' developed later into Breton's term 'surrealism.' The reconception of the form and function of a laboratory transfers in *Inferno* into aesthetic experimentation, as Anna Balakian argues it did also for

Breton (173). *Inferno's* emphasis on fragmentary or distorted bodily shapes, displaced from their customary meaning and use, is one important contributing aspect of this, while the narrative's interest in discarded objects, refuse, and garbage indicates how objects produce meaning in *Inferno* most explicitly when they are displaced from their contexts. As such, they replicate the speaker's status in unfamiliar boarding rooms in Paris.

Several of *Inferno's* strategies for representing setting, corporeality, and material objects are expressed in the groundbreaking essay 'The New Arts,' which Breton later affirmed as prefiguring the surrealist movement. First published in the Paris journal *Revue des Revues* on 5 November 1894, this essay by Strindberg delineates a new aesthetic theory designed explicitly for the avant-garde. Materiality, chance, and corporeality are evoked as counterarguments to both biographical and symbolical models of aesthetic production and interpretation (see also Balakian's assessment of Breton's aesthetic criticism of the early 1920s [172–7]). In his emphasis on the arbitrariness of artistic production, Strindberg writes that as he paints, his 'main manie la spatule à l'aventure' (58) (hand manipulates the spatula at random [99]) and 'l'ensemble se révèle comme ce charmant pêle-mêle d'inconscient et de conscient' (58) (the result reveals itself as a charming mixture of the unconscious and the conscious [99], trans. Albert Bermel). The process of aesthetic production, especially when formulated in an essay designed to be modern and Parisian, notably turns the medium inward, rather than the other way around. It is not human interiority (the mix between conscious and unconscious) that produces new art forms. Experimental art reveals, instead, interiority as corporeal and material. The essay criticizes quite explicitly the contemporary Parisian impressionists and symbolists, while suggesting a 'théorie pour l'art automatique' (64) (theory of automatic art [101]). This theory of an 'automatic art' signals important connections to later surrealist explorations of the artistic 'automatic' method, and also the movement's interest in mixing genres of narrative, pictorial, and object representation (see also Håkansson 63).

As a painter of seascapes working from memory in a Parisian apartment he had borrowed from friends during the fall of 1894, Strindberg produced canvases that emulate his aesthetic theory of displacement and fragmentation. The technique is innovative – he relinquishes the brush in favour of the spatula. Motifs are neither naturalist nor impressionist depictions of the urban environment outside his window. Neither are they explicitly expressionist, in the sense of evoking a state of mind or aggregate of emotions. The irony of Strindberg's painting during the fall of 1894, Söderström argues, is that despite Strindberg's apparently quite sophisticated knowledge of contemporary aesthetic trends in Paris (such as impressionism, symbolism, synaesthecism), his art, like his prose in *Inferno*, was little appreciated at the time. His '"expressive" yet "contentless" paintings were simply not "modern,"' Söderström claims (264; cf. Carlson, *Out of Inferno* 269–71).

Transitory dwelling locations like the ones in *Inferno* are aesthetically productive. They are also sites that make constructions of interiority problematic, especially in terms of *Inferno*'s oft-repeated allegations by its speaker that he is going mad. In interiors, madness is made material and conveyed through discrete sensory impressions; the speaker hears hammers banging, electrical cables are hauled, mysterious persons appear, a hotel proprietor is spying, an infernal machine torments the speaker, a wheel is turning around and around in the room above his, and an electrical storage battery produces a shower of electricity (142, 144, 150 [197–9, 201]). Olsson traces in *Jag blir galen* this kind of rhetoric as part of an established late nineteenth-century convention of coding madness, not least in a French tradition, in ways that replicate the favoured treatment methods for mental illness – isolation, electrotheropy, strapping down, and so on (138–42; see also Björklin, cited in Weinstein 476). It is clear that *Inferno*'s speaker shares similar experiences of Paris with many other migrants and exiles – Breton's character in the eponymous novel *Nadja* is one, while Rilke links transitory dwelling spaces, hospitals, electrical machines and madness closely in the first Paris sections of *The Notebooks of Malte Laurids Brigge*. *Inferno* constructs the city as a problem of materiality and interiority in which setting is critical, but descriptions of it are always sublimated, so that experiences of dwelling also produce 'Un état d'âme plus tôt [*sic*] qu'une opinion fondée sur des théories; un pêle-mêle de sensations plus ou moins condensées en idées' (50) (a state of soul rather than a view based on theories; a disordered chaos of sensations more or less condensed into ideas [142]). This state is spatial, since the result is 'une expansion inouïe de mes sens intérieurs' (56) (an unprecedented expansion of my inner senses [145]). Such experiences of setting formulate the modernist connection between materiality and interiority upon which *Inferno* relies, echoing Breton's admonition of facile and formulaic psychologization of novel characters.

Transitory and temporary dwellings in *Inferno* also signal an eradication of geographical difference that is part of the myth of European modernity. For *Inferno*'s speaker, interiors in different locations – Paris, Dieppe, Ystad, Klam, and Lund – are described in strikingly similar corporeal terms. In his room in Dieppe, 'L'idée d'être persécuté par les ennemis éléctriciens [*sic*] m'obsède de nouveau' (154) (the idea that I was [am] being persecuted by enemies with electrical devices began [begins] to obsess me once more [203]). In Ystad he imagines that a giant machine that generates electricty and an enormous battery are hidden near his room (164 [208]). His friend the doctor asserts that 'les mémoriaux des maisons d'aliénés connaissent à fond ces histoires des électriciens!' (166) (the Insane Asylum records are full of detailed accounts of enemies with electrical machines! [209]). Likewise, the protagonist's room at his mother-in-law's, the beautiful and quiet Rose Room in Klam, Austria, is soon described as a torture chamber, replete with electrical machines (218 [234]). The world of dwellings looks and feels the same, so that a transnational experience is one coded not by geographical specificity in domestic interior, but in uniformity. Confirming this trend, the speaker is approached at the end of *Inferno* by an acquaintance who mysteriously loathes his transitory dwelling space, and has 'pri[t] en horreur [s]a chambre à coucher' (302) (conceived a horror of [his] bedroom [276]). The protagonist says he volunteers a remedy, but those words are not represented in the text. Clues to his own interiority and that of others remain a blank. This use of temporary dwellings correlates with the protagonist's state of mind – interiority is always emphasized, but never symbolized or expressed in ways other than those that are material and embodied. Similarly, the transnational that is always part of *Inferno*, the setting that produces this narrative but that can rarely be described, engages these questions as it leaves Paris and proposes that a literary codification of rural landscapes produces material and spatial consequences.

3 Landscapes

Leaving Paris via Dieppe in Normandy for Ystad in southern Sweden and then Klam in Austria means transitioning from a quintessential urban centre of literary modernity to locations that are not only more marginal to the themes of interiority and spatiality in European modernism, but which express aspects of transnational complexity in different ways. Normandy relates explicitly to one of the ways Strindberg positions himself as a proud latter-day Normand in his essay 'A Barbarian in Paris' (Un barbare à Paris) published in *Revue des Deux*

Mondes in Paris in December of 1894. In this essay, Strindberg argues against the French press's negative portrayal of Scandinavian literature. The essay was part of an intense debate about the form and social function of Scandinavian literature – particularly in works written by Ibsen, Björnsen, and Strindberg – which concerned Parisian journals in the mid 1890s. Strindberg uses the term 'barbarian' in the essay title in explicit reference to its use by Parisian critics as a derogatory label for writers understood as 'Germanic' (Ahlström, *Strindbergs erövring* 237–45; Gavel Adams, 'Strindberg and Paris 1894–98' 92–6). Strindberg's response to this debate emphasizes the historically significant and long-standing close cultural associations between Sweden and France. As a Normand, rather than a 'barbarian,' Strindberg affirms a proud heritage of Norse culture (which he at other times rarely evokes) and compares the Notre Dame cathedral with the graceful lines of a Viking ship and a northern forest (see also Olsson, 'En nordlig Strindberg'). A similar transnational and transhistorical metaphor codes the *Inferno*'s speaker's impressions of Ystad, a town in the southern Swedish landscape of Scania that maintains close connections with Denmark, of which it was a part until 1658. Rather than naming a traditional Danish-looking Scanian farm house, the friend of *Inferno*'s speaker is described as residing in an exotic-looking 'monastère Bouddhique' (160) (Buddhist monastery [206]), which juxtaposes architectural styles from different parts of the world. Such a building would perhaps entice a Parisian readership interested in positioning the North as a site for the exotic, mystical, and possibly dangerously barbarian.

The rural setting of the Austrian Alps at Klam is coded in ways that bridge literary codification of landscape representation with the transnational. As a part of the Habsburg empire, Austria at the end of the nineteenth century had become a location explicitly connected to the instability of national representation in Europe. At the same time, features of the alpine landscape gain explicit meaning in *Inferno* as correlating to the protagonist's posited religious conversion. The rural landscape, more anonymous and less coded as a signifier of modernity, allows for the gradual ordering of the protagonist's psyche, its move from disordered complexity to a Swedenborgian correspondence theory that neatly aligns exterior with interior in a theological frame. In *Inferno*'s twelfth chapter, a noticeable shift occurs. Here, setting and location are made interpretable through a landscape overview. Climbing a mountain on his last day in Klam, the speaker takes in 'une vue superbe sur la vallée du Danube et sur les Alpes Styeriennes. Je respire pour la première fois, ayant quitté les sombres entonnoirs là bas ... C'est beau comme le ciel!' (268) (the superb view over the Danube valley and the Styrian Alps. The dark hollows below were all behind me and I found [find] myself breathing again for the first time ... It was [is] as beautiful as paradise! [259]). This landscape makes the world intelligible, and one in which opposites can safely co-exist: 'Est-ce que la terre renferme le ciel et l'enfer [?]' (268) (Does this earth perhaps contain both heaven and hell? [259]). Through a panoramic view over nature, the speaker is cured of the madness induced in the city and in the Scanian farm that looks like a Buddhist monastery.

The Klam section of *Inferno* has been interpreted by Ulf Olsson as evoking an 'an allegorical landscape, shaped in accordance with Christian stereotype' (*Levande död* 326, my trans.) Though this is accurate, there are other equally significant interpretive trajectories available. One includes a conceptual system based on the pastoral. In the Klam section, descriptions of pristine nature help transfer the narratives of Catholicism and Swedenborgianism (as relayed by the speaker's mother-in-law and her sister) into a material landscape, just as *Inferno's* stories of fragmentation and displacement are rooted explicitly in an experience of Paris. Through the narrative of a landscape pastoral, or later through the small-town environment of Lund, the noise, dirt, and excrement of Paris are made to make sense in retrospect. The location of Paris and its modernity is reinterpreted through the idea of pristine nature in the Alps. From this perspective, the speaker sees Swedenborg's theosophy inscribed in the landscape. Swedenborg helps him interpret the meaning of locations and frees him from being haunted by 'des electriciens [sic], des magistes noirs, des envoûteurs, des jaloux faisers d'or et de la folie' (292) (the [electricians], the black magicians, the sorcerers, the envious foes of the gold maker, and from madness [268]). *Inferno* experiments with strategies that are meant to code experiences as 'authentic' and thereby as restorative and curative, so that the path to mental stability is marked by walks in the fresh air. Displaced from Paris, the narrative cannot maintain the gestures of fragmentation that at first define it.

Inferno's setting once it leaves Paris hovers explicitly over a non-urban transnational terrain that is a significant but often over-looked aspect of experimental European prose modernism, particularly starkly so as literature negotiates, participates in, and reacts against increasingly prevalent discourses of nationalism. The fragmented and displaced body parts so prevalent in the Paris sections of *Inferno* diminish in prevalence in the rural settings. The departure from the city is a construction of making the disparate whole; the speaker's body heals, as the rural landscape produces a monistic correspondence theory. This is a fiction also constitutive of transnational European modernism, and without which we cannot understand the power of urban myths. In Sweden, for example, the rise of the prominent literary and aesthetic movement *nationalromantik* (neo-Romanticism) during the 1890s was explicitly connected to socially and politically progressive rhetoric. The movement rejected empty idealism or trite nature imagery to convey instead images of the North as strongly rooted in and explicitly referential to a long-established cohesive and just past. This very rootedness allowed it to be formally experimental and politically progressive, as Facos has explored in *Nationalism and the Nordic Imagination* with respect to the innovative pictorial art of Sweden at the end of the nineteenth-century. Strindberg in *Inferno* evokes, however, an expressly denationalized and delocalized landscape tradition. Nature in *Inferno* is displaced from current ideological uses of pristine landscape. Nature heals, but not according to the discourses prevalent in the 1890s generation that tied nature specifically to nation; the 'healing' that *Inferno* proposes is actually also a matter of displacement.

The juxtaposition of *Inferno*'s disparate settings – Paris, the small towns of Dieppe, Ystad, and Lund, the pristine alpine landscape of Klam – has, as I have emphasized in this chapter, repeatedly established close links between material spatiality and a bodily fragmentation that rarely indulges in representations of psychological interiority. These relationships of setting are construed as predicated on a transnational existence. Such aspects of *Inferno* are part of another persistent literary praxis when it comes to renditions of Parisian modernity, such as those in Rilke's *The Notebooks of Malte Laurids Brigge* (1910). This text construes Malte's experiences of Paris as bodily constituted, and almost always as fragmentarily so (see Huyssen, 'Paris/Childhood'). *The Notebooks* famously emphasizes how its first-person protagonist, Malte, in Paris learns 'to see,' a formulation repeated and reworked in the first five notebook entries. Similarly, *Inferno*'s narrator finds his sense of vision heightened and, with his artist friend, he emphasizes how '[n]ous faisons des progrès comme voyants' (92) ([w]e were [are] making progress as seers [168]). Like *Inferno*'s protagonist's stay at the Saint Louis hospital, one of Malte's most formative experiences in Paris is in a hospital, where fragmented, seemingly dehumanized patients endure an endless wait. Parisian buildings in *The Notebooks* are also famously corporealized, and material objects take on human shapes, while humans are objectified and fragmented.

References to hands are common throughout *The Notebooks*, where they evoke an explicitly modernist rhetoric of bodily fragmentation and illness that *Inferno* also construes as critical for its description of setting. Hands seem to be increasingly disembodied, moving of their own accord as well as dismembering themselves from a corporeal totality (see for example entries 7, 56, 61, 90, and 103 of *The Notebooks*). In a famous section of the fifth entry, a woman's face is described as dislodging itself to rest in her hand. In entry number 20, during Malte's long wait at the Salpêtrière hospital, he remarks on the proliferation and use of bandages, how they cover whole heads, leaving only an eye open or a hand exposed: 'viele Verbände gab es … Verbände, die verbargen, und Verbände, die zeigten, was darunter war' (cited at Project Gutenberg) (there were many bandages … Bandages that hid, and bandages that revealed, what was under them [56], trans. S. Mitchell). In this passage, a noun or verb form of 'verband' (bandage) is repeated six times in a few short lines, covering up rhetorically the gaps in perception, which Malte so often otherwise remarks on. The thematic similarities between the hospital visits in *The Notebooks* and *Inferno* are clear, but Rilke's use of repetition contrasts starkly with Strindberg's ellipses, so that the bandages in *The Notebooks* become visibly symbolical, hiding the human body beneath them, and seeming linguistically to cause the fragmentation of the body they should be helping to heal or unify.

Representations that seem to echo explicitly *Inferno's* speaker's displaced position are remarkably striking in *The Notebooks*. References to these connections are largely absent in both Rilke and Strindberg scholarship, however. Taking stock of his time in Paris, Malte itemizes an experience that could thematically have been part of *Inferno*. Linguistically, the passage is very different from *Inferno*. Its use of subordinating clauses and adverbial connections constructs a metonymical chain that contrasts with *Inferno's* linguistic fragmentation: '*Selbst* in der Zeit, *da* die Armut ihn täglich mit neuen Härten erschreckte, *da* sein Kopf das Lieblingsding des Elends war und ganz abgegriffen, *da* sich überall an seinem Leibe Geschwüre aufschlugen wie Notaugen gegen die Schwärze der Heimsuchung, *da* ihm graute vor dem Unrat, auf dem man ihn verlassen hatte, *weil* er seinesgleichen war:selbst *da* noch, wenn er sich besann, war es sein größestes Entsetzen, erwidert worden zu sein' (Project Gutenberg, emphasis added) (*Even* during the time when poverty terrified him every day with new hardships, *when* his head was the favorite toy of misery, and utterly worn ragged by it, *when* ulcers broke out all over his body like emergency eyes against the blackness of tribulation, *when* he shuddered at the filth to which he had been abandoned because he was just as foul himself: *even then*, when he thought about it, his greatest terror was that someone would respond to him [225], emphasis added). Rilke's inscription of Malte's experiences in Paris, as one long chain of logically linked events, temporally marked, is thematically similar but quite differently expressed. Rilke's description of Paris, in fact, has in its temporal, rather than spatial, emphasis, a lot to do with the formulation of Paris's supposed antithesis in *The Notebooks* – the nostalgic Danish past.

Both *Inferno* and *The Notebooks* spend less and less time in Paris – the Paris presence is remarkably diminished in the second half of *The Notebooks*, as it turns from 'Death' to 'Love' after the central tapestry scene at the Cluny Museum that separates the narrative's first and second halves. Geographical displacements gesture to *Inferno*'s and *The Notebooks*'s complexity, as these depend in both texts on a geographical Other that is clearly juxtaposed with Paris. In *Inferno*, it is most explicitly the alpine landscape of Klam; in *The Notebooks*, it is the Danish countryside. These locations provide both texts with complementary explanatory narratives, which seem to lead to ambiguous religious conversions. In *Inferno*, it is one of recuperation and denationalized authenticity that becomes coupled with a mystical Swedenborgianism (later at least partly renounced); in *The Notebooks* it is a childhood history that is also a national imaginary and leads to ruminations on the Avignon papacy and extended discussion on the prodigal son. *The Notebooks*, as Linda Rugg argues, 'is an experiment in autobiography, intentionally iconoclastic, intentionally troubling and troubled,' which also reflects 'Rilke's own extreme difficulty with his experiment' and how it 'backfired, with far-reaching impact upon its author' ('A Self at Large' 44). *Inferno* clearly shares similar features, in terms of its status as a textual artefact as well as repercussions for its author.

Both protagonists are 'fleeing' from a wife and child at the beginning of the text: in *Inferno* this new sense of freedom is explicitly stated, while *The Notebooks* never directly engages it. Both texts claim to be reworked from other genres: *Inferno* professes to be a journal, which is turned into a novel (of a kind); *The Notebooks* began as a series of personal letters and was reworked into a novel (of a kind) that claims to be a journal (*The Notebooks of Malte Laurids Brigge*). The transnational biographies of their respective authors engage with questions about rewriting Paris from a migrant's perspective, in which Rilke constructs an entire national history to accommodate Malte's reconfiguration of Paris, while Strindberg largely relinquishes any national or historical suppositions for *Inferno's* protagonist. The past, whether in terms of national or personal history, is no source of comfort or fodder for nostalgia for Strindberg's speaker. *Inferno* is written by a Swede as if he were French and who reconnects with himself in the alien landscape of Klam; *The Notebooks* by a Czech author whose first language is German and posits a Danish history for his protagonist to filter the sense of alienation in Paris. The incomprehensibility of the city, the fear, loneliness, and illness it produces, the frustration and poverty, are, in both narratives, reworked through the stories produced in the rural setting. The denationalized aspect of *Inferno* clashes with an overinscription of an imagined nation and an imagined national history that is also personal in *The Notebooks*. The death of the nobility in Denmark fosters the representation of a transient impoverished modern writer in *The Notebooks*. Denmark is like a frozen historical and material place, in which many of the 'historical' references are anachronistic, but which is seemingly recovered, thawed, and inserted into modernity in Paris. This juxtaposition of experiences in the moment – we know very little of *Inferno's* speaker's background, childhood, upbringing, or personal history – for example, dislodges nature not only from nation, but also from ideologies of domestic belonging. The speaker's temporary dwellings are as uncomfortable in the country as they are in the city.

Both texts are documents of a modernist fragmentation in genre, geographical instability, and in juxtapositions of psychological interiority and material exteriority, and both texts insist on corporeal fragmentation as a stylistic strategy. Transnational aspects have also begun to figure more prominently in scholarly criticism about *The Notebooks*, whereas traditionally both Strindberg and Rilke scholars have tended to focus on the Paris sections of the respective works. Huyssen's essay 'Paris/Childhood' is a case in point, since it downplays any section of *The Notebooks* not explicitly set in Paris. Yet, *The Notebooks*, like *Inferno*, constructs an image of the experience of Paris that is filtered through imagined Nordic constructions, in different ways (see also Allen 178–217). The reconstruction of a Nordic past in *The Notebooks* is part of an overlooked aspect of transnational European modernism, as it is also a project of literary recuperation. In a section entitled 'Bibliothèque Nationale,' Malte is described as identifying with a northern poet (usually understood as Obstfelder) whose project he recuperates in the French national library (see Ekner). Rilke inserts Scandinavia into a narrative about Paris, as he does with references to Ibsen. Strindberg is never mentioned in *The Notebooks*, and critics have not previously concentrated on possible connections between this work and *Inferno*. Multiple other transnational connections that triangulate Rilke, Paris, and Scandinavia are often brought forward in the criticism, however. It is well known that Rilke corresponded with and admired Georg Brandes and was profoundly influenced by J.P. Jacobsen's novel *Niels Lyhne* (1880). Rilke got to know Sweden and Denmark during the time he was writing *The Notebooks*, particularly as a visitor to Ellen Key and other intellectuals associated with the *nationalromantisk* movement in Swedish arts, literature, and social reform (Unglaub; Schoolfield, 'Rilke and the Fall of the House of Schulin'). Rilke's constructions of Malte and Danishness also rework one of the most famous transnational Danish figurations, Shakespeare's *Hamlet*; both protagonists, to point to just one aspect in common, leave as orphans a ghost-filled Danish past for new beginnings in Paris. Melberg argues, moreover, that *The Notebooks* illustrates a lesser-known trajectory of Danish writers, like Sophus Claussen, who published prose poems about Paris in the Copenhagen daily paper *Politiken* during the 1890s (Melberg, 'Rilkes Malte: Ännu en skandinav i Paris' 46–9).

In the case of *Inferno*'s legacy, a small national literary tradition (the Swedish) seems to have had difficulties negotiating such an expansive, complex figure as the authorial persona conveyed by *Inferno*'s first-person speaker. The text fits neither Swedish nor French paradigms of city and embodied representation at the time. Rilke negotiates similarly complex questions in *The Notebooks* by displacing his protagonist and first-person narrator more explicitly from his own biographical persona and formulating an aesthetics of city representation that perhaps more successfully operates on different registers of embodiment, fragmentation, and displacement. But the results within a transnational paradigm of literary modernism are strikingly different – *Inferno*'s explicit self-referential references to its own materiality and the setting it construes for itself has instead largely been understood as an autobiographical gesture. This has positioned *Inferno* as a Swedish text not by virtue of its language of composition or a national setting, but because it appears to construct an image of interiority that could only correspond to its author's – Strindberg's own professed madness after his stay in Paris in the mid 1890s. It has been overlooked that *Inferno* refuses most such assertions of psychological interiority but instead emphasizes materiality and spatiality in narrative construction. Rilke's *The Notebooks*, on the other hand, has become exemplary of European prose modernism.

In fact, the highly ambiguous and ironic ending of *Inferno* refuses national, generic, linguistic, or subjective closure, just like Rilke's narrative about Malte. *Inferno* suggests the immanence of a supranational state, formulated as an idea of 'des États-Unis occidentaux' (306) (The United States of the Occident [278]). Unlike Malte's vague but firm final affirmation of the power of Love, proclaimed in a non-specified setting, *Inferno*'s speaker in the final pages of the novel wavers between different religious affiliations, different political movements, and different geographical trajectories. Leaving Sweden is necessary, although it is never affirmed whether he will serve as a male nurse at the hospital of Frères Saint Jean de Dieu in Paris, or await an answer to join a Belgian monastery. The ending displaces material setting into abstract, literary, and cartographic realms, reversing a trajectory that began with specifics and indexicality of setting and transfered to embodied experience. The fragmentation that is indicative of *Inferno* is maintained to the end, as the narrative refuses to close on itself. Strindberg refused at the end to call *Inferno* a novel – and his French editor Réja concurs with this understanding of its ambivalent form (is it even literature? he asks in the preface). *Inferno*'s settings in fact operate explicitly on multiple levels of the transnational, as it becomes a paramount consideration for European literary modernism at the end of the nineteenth century. The ways in which this narrative gestures to and is echoed in other literary representations explicitly concerned with displacements and transience – from those of Nerval and Rimbaud to Mann, Kafka, and Rilke – indicate on many levels the narrative's explicit intervention in constructions of modernity. These questions, of how literary setting correlates with contemporary literary movements, are of central concern in the long prose narrative Strindberg composes just after *Inferno*. Written in Swedish in Sweden, but detailing experiences of Berlin and of transnational European travel in the early 1890s, this novel, *The Cloister*, takes up problems of possibilities of transnational existence in different ways. I turn to these questions in the following chapter.

4 Speed, Displacements, and Berlin Modernity in *The Cloister*

As I argue in this book, many of Strindberg's prose texts formulate and illustrate an intriguing logic of multilingual and transnational relationships, particularly in relation to France and French-language culture. Late nineteenth-century Sweden's and Scandinavia's multifaceted relationship with Germany come to the forefront in one of Strindberg's few texts set in Berlin. In *The Cloister* (*Klostret*), a deliberate conceptualization of transnational literary modernism as predicated on speed, transience, and displacement is advocated as an explicit rejection not only of the aesthetics and epistemology of realism and naturalism, but also of symbolism and decadence. Composed in Swedish in Sweden in 1898 after Strindberg's third sojourn in Paris and only posthumously published in 1966, the production and reception circumstances of *The Cloister* indicate the narrative's transnational aspects. Like *Among French Peasants*, *A Madman's Defence*, and *Inferno*, the text begins in a city and ends as a travel narrative. *The Cloister* is also metaliterary in terms of setting, drawing on both the Scandinavian presence in Berlin's cultural life in the early 1890s and on emergent strategies of modernist urban representation, in which technological mediation and subjective experience combine to challenge contemporary panoramic representations of Berlin and to suggest new narrative techniques for European city writing. In conjunction with this, *The Cloister* presents intriguingly fluid and unstable gender relations and paradigms of sexual desire as part of its construction of a different literary Berlin, while emphasizing ambivalent attitudes toward Prussian power in the modern *Großstadt*.

The Cloister directly addresses the absence of a renaissance in German prose literature during the 1890s. The original setting of Berlin is significant, as *The Cloister* appears to search for formal strategies to reinvigorate contemporary representations of Berlin in German and European prose, seeking to take Berlin out of the bourgeois realism and philosophical idealism of Theodor Fontane or Friedrich Spielhagen or the naturalism of Gerhart Hauptmann, Arno Holz, or Julius Hart. *The Cloister* obliquely offers alternative models by emphasizing the profound impact of life in the big city by experimenting with gradations of dispassion, such as a detached third-person narrative perspective, hovering ironically between the metatextual and the biographical, and articulating interconnections between novelistic prose and urban experience that have since become constitutive of European modernism, including fragmentation and spatio-temporal compression. *The Cloister* is clearly conceived in a form different from naturalist drama, the genre most often associated with Scandinavian modernism as it pertains to Berlin, and different from the subjective or material immediacy attempted in Strindberg's previous novels written in French, *A Madman's Defence* and *Inferno*. Part of what I seek to do in this chapter is to take *The Cloister* out of obscurity and position it as part of a burgeoning European canon of transnational literary modernism, in which Berlin's urban modernity is constructed not from perceptions of its own centrality, but through the tension established by an artefact and a perspective seemingly marginal or alien to it. I thus situate the text less as an autobiographical record of Strindberg's time in Berlin and more as an explicit intervention in literary representation of, and cultural commentary on, late nineteenth-century Berlin. These aspects are obliquely reflected in *The Cloister's* thwarted publication trajectory.

Although Strindberg understood *The Cloister* as an autobiographical text, and critics have generally concurred with that opinion (Ståhle Sjönell, 'Kommentarer' *Klostret* 285–6), these so-called autobiographical texts are literary works filled with ambiguities and formal complexities that indicate their fictional status. *The Cloister*, however, exists only as a fragment, most likely lacking its final section, and has been published in different versions (Ståhle Sjönell, 'Kommentarer' *Klostret* 290, 292). Although Strindberg (short of cash in the fall of 1898) quickly pitched *The Cloister* manuscript to the Stockholm publisher Gernandt, who enthusiastically accepted it with an advance payment and scheduled it to reappear in the spring of 1899, the novel was not actually published until nearly seventy years later, in 1966. A German translation by Walter Brendsohn appeared a year later. The delayed publication date parallels the delay in composition in intriguing ways.

The Cloister was written in Swedish in the fall of 1898, six years after Strindberg had left Berlin and upon his return to Sweden from a stay in Paris, where he had been involved in the publication of *Inferno* at Mercure de France in early 1898. The parts of *Inferno* set in Paris present a protagonist displaced into an urban space where fragmentation and confusion mark his experiences as increasingly corporeal or represented by material correlations between random objects. Different in content, tone, and style, *The Cloister's* descriptions of its protagonist's experiences of Berlin may initially be understood as filtered through *Inferno's* Paris, thanks to the six-year delay in composition. The narrative, told in the third-person perspective, is original as it transforms its verifiable spatial coordinates into a fictionalized form that draws on modernism's interest in spatio-temporal displacements as a formal strategy. *The Cloister's* complex relationship between urban settings (Berlin, Paris, and to some extent Stockholm), languages of composition (Swedish and French), and time period (1892–8) negotiates the kind of experiences of transnational modernity that have later become hallmarks of European modernism. In part 1 of this chapter, I address along these lines how modes of transience and displacement inform the narrative construction of setting. In part 2, I investigate the spatial implications of *The Cloister's* alternative gender constructions. In part 3, I conclude with a historically contextualized argument about the text's metaliterary and cultural implications for the possibility of Strindberg's intervention in early Berlin-based transnational literary modernism.

1 Transience and Displacement

Set in the early 1890s, *The Cloister* moves in expanding circles from its point of origin in Berlin to the Baltic Sea, Hamburg, London, and Austria, to gesture in its final sequence that the protagonist is bound for Paris. The novel's transnational plot and themes of transience also displaces Berlin by leaving the city for other parts of Europe. *The Cloister* addresses both literally and metaphorically the ambivalent status of Berlin in European culture at the time. The Berlin sections concentrate on a group of artists and writers, loosely modelled on Strindberg's own experiences in 1892–3 with the *Friedrichshagener Kreis*. This was a group of international migrant artists, writers, and philosophers associated with the restaurant Zum Schwarzen Ferkel, located on the corner of Unter den Linden and Neue Wilhelmstrasse in central Berlin.

As an unpublished, largely forgotten novel about a sustained experience with a European metropolis, *The Cloister* is more than a parenthesis or an illustration of the Ferkel circle. It complements Strindberg's city narration about Paris and Stockholm and offers alternate conceptualizations of Berlin as a modern urban aggregate, and how this complexity is negotiated by a first-time visitor to the city. The plot is perfunctory and only about half of the novel is set in Berlin, where the protagonist Axel associates with a group of other Scandinavian writers and artists. *The Cloister*'s narrative structure seems formulated as a reaction against the naturalism of Berlin writers by initially establishing the big city as its point of origin and centre, then quickly moving on to rural areas and other regions of Europe. In Berlin, Axel meets the young writer and at first unnamed New Woman figure Maria (the names of the main characters in this novel repeat the names of many other Strindberg novels, notably *A Madman's Defence*). He later has a brief affair with another woman, Laïs, but Maria and Axel marry shortly thereafter. Axel and Maria travel, then separate while Axel stays with Maria's wealthy family in Austria, and they reunite briefly in Berlin before Axel leaves on his own for Paris.

The Cloister's diegetic events centre on movement, travel, visits, and isolated meetings. Told in the third-person, the text focuses on Axel exclusively but rarely gestures toward psychological complexity or emotional intensity. The novel combines limited spatial description with rapid plot progression. This swiftness in description combines with the protagonist's extreme mobility – he is generally on the move either within locations in Berlin or travelling through other parts of Europe. His mobility translates into neither established parameters of travel writing or *flaneur*-literature, nor to detailed descriptions like those of Berlin essayists like Conrad Alberti in the late 1880s or the impressionistic vignettes of popular press writers like those of Alfred Kerr in the late 1890s. The writings of Alberti and Kerr combine travel and movement with extensive descriptions of the land- or cityscape (see Kerr; Schutte and Sprengel). *The Cloister* also differs from the textual genre most closely associated with Berlin's transition to modernity at the end of the nineteenth century: newspaper prose (see Fritzsche, *Reading Berlin 1900*). Instead, *The Cloister* spends little time on spatial descriptions, a recognizable feature of naturalistic city writing, or on subjective experiences of a particular location, a feature of symbolism. The protagonist's experience of time and place as out of sync in Berlin creates a dynamic context. He is dislodged from conventional social frames of reference, and also displaced from calendar and clock time and recognizable physical locations.

Introduced laconically as 'The Swede,' the protagonist is metonymically linked not only to his presumed home country, but also to a social context in which geographical coordinates are generalized to an epithet. When the novel begins, Axel has changed boarding rooms five times in three months, his possessions fit comfortably in a suitcase, and he demonstrates his pride in 'att icke vara mantalsskriven utan bara äga ett pass' (*Klostret* 10) (not to be on any [resident] register, to own nothing but a passport [*The Cloister*, Sandbach trans., 11]). The image of the transient European exile is thus immediately established. The first chapter is short, but introduces a flashback to the comfortable apartment with 'sex rum och kök' (10) (six rooms plus kitchen [11]) that Axel has left behind in his home country. This reference to a stable domestic life in the past contrasts sharply with the five different Berlin locations described in *The Cloister's* first chapter: a small boarding room, a party in a villa in the wealthy Tiergarten district, a ball, a late-night drinking establishment, and a restaurant called 'The Cloister.' The quick succession of swiftly described places manifests the text's rhetoric of transience and mobility in different ways. The suppression of domesticity, of a seemingly deliberate renunciation of the comforts of (a) home, locates *The Cloister* as an early example of the many works of European modernism that thematize the problematics of domestic belonging – including *The Notebooks of Malte Laurids Brigge* and Kafka's *Metamorphosis* and *The Process*, for example.

Waking up in the first paragraph of the novel and noticing his feet on a pillow in the second, Axel is immediately introduced in the form of spatial asymmetry and confusion. He turns around to get his bearings and notices that his new boarding room 'sålunda fått två fönster sedan igår' (9) (must have acquired two windows since the previous day [9]). He wonders why hens cackle outside his window and no carriages can be heard on the street outside. He has trouble remembering what day of the week it is, since 'han höll aldrig reda på dagarne ... kunde skriva 1891 i stället för 1890 och ... kunde datera ett brev Fettisdagen eller Rötmånaden emedan han icke kände datum' (11) (he kept no count of the days ... was perfectly capable of writing 1891 instead of 1890, and ... of heading a letter Shrove Tuesday or The Dog Days, simply because he did not know the date [12]). Thus confused about the spatio-temporal coordinates of the present, he recalls from his bed the previous evening's events, which included a visit to a rich patron of the arts at his villa in the Tiergarten district and long conversations at the less respectable late-night establishment National near Friedrichstrasse. Beginning a story in daybreak, with the main character waking up, is an age-old convention that *The Cloister* turns on its head. Instead of pointing forward in chronological time, a flashback ensues about previous events and a discussion of time as out of joint, in which events are also recalled in reverse chronological order.

The novel's title, *The Cloister*, is salient in this respect. It connotes references to seclusion, isolation, and interiors characteristic of a monastic building, which contrasts sharply with gestures to cosmopolitanism and spatio-temporal dissolution. The title, however, refers more specifically to the restaurant and bar where Axel congregates with his Scandinavian compatriots – nicknamed in the novel 'The Cloister.' The mimicry offered by the irreverent, idiosyncratic juxtapositions of stylistic levels and references between the title and the locations of the first chapter is not only intrinsic to *The Cloister*'s project but also signals the ambivalence with which Berlin is consistently portrayed in the narrative. In the first chapter, the remarkably sparse descriptions of Berlin locations emphasize the city's entropy – it is cold, stark, and dirty. Interiors are contrasted with streets covered in wet snow where 'hjulspåren drogo upp svarta linjer, så att snön syntes ännu vitare och smutsen ännu svartare' (15) (wheels cut dark lines, which made the snow look even whiter and the mud blacker [16]). Filth and dirt are inseparable from descriptions of north-central Berlin; the crowding, poverty and high mortality rates of the working-class districts were infamous at the time (Richie 161–7; see also Forsell). These scattered remarks about the Berlin landscape are part of a limited number in *The Cloister* that gesture even remotely to a realistic description of life in large parts of the city during the early 1890s. Yet, this gesture is turned immediately to metaphor. Berlin appears deathly pale and sick: 'Staden liksom stod lik ... himlen sjuk i färgen' (15) (The city was like a corpse in its winding sheet ... the sky had a sickly hue [16]). The descriptions then turn inward, first to a detailed description of 'The Cloister' restaurant and then to Axel's subjective experiences.

Registers of the hyperbolic, mythic, and symbolical are used to describe the restaurant. In contrast to the street outside, the establishment's brightly coloured stained-glass windows 'visade alltid vackert väder' (15) (always made the weather appear fine [16]) and the indoor space is warm and welcoming. The description moves between references to health and sickness, life and death, idealism and religious revolution, aestheticism and entropy. Mention of religious paraphernalia, juxtaposed with descriptions of an interior fashioned in decadent style, furthers the deliberate contradictions invoked by *The Cloister*'s first chapter. As a 'kyrksal' (church-like room) with a 'tabernakel' (tabernacle) or 'baptiserium med en förgylld kolonn i jesuiterstil' (baptistery, with one gilded column in the Jesuit style), 'ett kapell' (a chapel), the establishment seems appropriately, on the one hand, named 'The Cloister' (15–16 [17]). On the other hand, the disparate locations, time periods, and locations are connected in a montage of secular irreverence – the establishment looks alternately like a theatre stage, an arcade, a pagoda, and a 'riddarsal' (Knights' Hall), while travel posters from different tourist spots around Europe (Nice, Dieppe, the Alps, and Helgoland) cover the walls of the entrance (15–16 [17]). This idiosyncratic mix illustrates late nineteenth-century trends in interior decoration, and also presents different locations and styles as if in a miniature curiosity cabinet, filled with eclectic samplings juxtaposed without inherent rationale, yet signalling the inclusion of a transnational Europe shrunk and distorted to fit into one location.

The eclectically designed space is described as distorted in other technologically mediated terms, since it gives the impression of functioning as 'en optisk illusion ... en ändlös labyrint, i vilken man ofta gick vilse emedan man misstog sig på vänster och höger' (16) by means of an optical illusion the premises gave the impression of being a never-ending labyrinth, in which you lost your way because you confused right and left) (18); there are no clocks on the wall there and 'man glömde tiden' (16) (you forgot about time [18]). The protagonist and his friends 'var som hemma där' (16) (felt at home [18]) while the bar functions as a complete network central for artists and writers, who find more than food, drink, and shelter there. This is a space that caters to them as professionals, providing opportunities to meet with editors and directors, access to telephones, writing material, and assistance with running errands. Transience and impermanence become the reason for being in the montage of spatial references narrated in *The Cloister*. The eponymous establishment not only reflects but also construes a location where conventional coordinates of time and place are irrelevant. The setting functions as part of an optical illusion, and the function of this labyrinthine space is not to find a way out, but to learn to feel at home in a location shaped as a montage of idiosyncratic cultural references and transform those into aestheticized experiences.

The Cloister construes experiences of Berlin not only as part of an optical illusion but also as technologically mediated. As a writer, Axel processes experiences as if they were photographs and stores them as if in a bank vault: 'Genom att på detta sätt ligga och idissla sina upplevelser omsatte han dem dikteriskt och de inpräglades eller fixerades genom denna procedyr så, att han kunde disponera dem för kommande bruk lika säkert som medel insatta i en bank' (13) (By lying and ruminating over his experiences in this way he reconstructed them in a literary form and thus engraved or [fixed] riveted them on his mind, so that they were available for future use as surely as savings deposited in a bank [15]). Literary creation is not only technologically mediated, but in these Berlin sequences explicitly associated with making money, with the conditions of being a professional writer. Memory is also photographically construed. Axel recalls past events in ways that 'framkalla gårdagens händelser och personer' (27) (reconstruct [develop] the people and events of the previous day [33]), and often, he continues, 'utfördes denna psykiska operation av sig själv, så att när han sökte erinra den nya okände, bilden av en äldre bekant trädde fram och täckte mer eller mindre av den nya' (27–8) (this psychic operation happened of itself, so that as he was trying to recall the new person, the image of some old friend would emerge and more or less cover the new one [33]). *The Cloister's* descriptions of events and locations contrast with naturalism's photographic mode of capturing the whole picture, and instead focus on the subjective and delimited, as well as on the process rather than the final result (see also Rugg, *Picturing Ourselves* 112–13). Interpersonal relations become mediated, as psychology and technology appear to conjoin in Berlin: '[Axel] brukade säga i sällskapet när man ville skicka efter någon frånvarande: ska vi telepatera efter honom? '(42) (if at a party they wanted to send for some absent friend he would say: 'Shall we send for him telepathically?' [51]).

The Cloister moves between interiors that appear technologically mediated, whether in a psychological or material way. In contrast, the text refrains from any realistic or naturalistic descriptions, including referring to indexical markers like street or place names, used so prevalently in *Inferno's* Paris sections (they number more than five dozen there). References to real locations are sparse and brief. The names of the Schöneberger embankment, the Lützow Bridge, Tiergarten, Neues Museum, Schifferbaudamm, Courbière-strasse, and Pankow glide by, without any description. Setting is constructed in similar ways as the protagonist leaves Berlin to travel around Europe. In contrast to the enticing picture on 'The Cloister's' travel poster, Helgoland is just 'den lilla ön i havet' (45) (the little sea-girt island [57]); Hamburg, a location that prompts thoughts of quick departure and indicates how travelling quickly through the continent has become a perceptual given, 'när han kom ner till järnvägsstationen föll som en blixt den tanken i honom: om jag reser nu är jag på Klostret om sex timmar' (54) (and at the railway station he was suddenly struck by the thought: 'Shall I go now? In six hours I could be at the Cloister' [66]); London is hot, filthy, and disturbing, as in 'Westminster där gatorna vimlade av de besynnerligaste figurer, vilka liknade de hamnar man ser i skräckdrömmar (58) (There [in Westminster] the back streets were teeming with the strangest people, who resembled the terrifying figures [ports] one sees in a nightmare [71]). Transnational displacements are part of how *The Cloister* construes its detached perspective on setting in Berlin and in Europe. This perspective, moreover, correlates with formal experimentation and strategies that question established gender paradigms.

2 Gendered Alternatives

The skewing of spatial coordinates brought up in the first paragraph of *The Cloister* (when the protagonist wakes up with his feet on the pillow) continues in the recollection of events from the previous night. The evening included, as the protagonist retells, a visit 'som åskådare' (11) (as onlooker [12]) to a so-called Wiener-Ball – a dance event frequented by both male and female homosexuals. *The Cloister's* description is unusually candid in the context of contemporary German literature, but the narrator oscillates between reporting and interpreting the ball in a pattern of ambivalence. According to Neil Miller, Strindberg's Wiener Ball description has 'features of a documentary account' that combines 'shock and sympathy,' and is, Miller proclaims, 'the first description of a homosexual ball ever published' (118). The latter is most likely an overstatement (given *The Cloister's* 1966 first publication date), but the novel's description of the event merits an extended quote:

> Huvudstadens perversa typer hade nämligen för bättre uppsikts skull fått tillstånd att hålla kostymbal. I början av balen gick det högtidligt till nästan som på ett dårhus. Män dansade med män, melankoliska, strängt allvarliga som om de utfört en handling på någons befallning, utan nöje, utan ett leende. Mellan danserna sutto paren och sågo varandra i ögonen som om de läst sitt öde. (11)

In order that a better check might be kept on them the perverts of the capital had been given permission to hold a fancy-dress ball. When it opened
everyone behaved ceremoniously, almost as if they were in a madhouse.
Men danced with men, mournfully, with deadly seriousness, as if they
were doing something they had been ordered to do, without pleasure,
without a smile. Between the dances the couples sat gazing into each
other's eyes, as if in them they could read their fate. (12)

The public costume ball under police supervision that Strindberg
calls 'Wiener Ball' went under the names 'Puppenbälle' (doll balls) or
'Urningsbälle' as early as 1868; by 1886 they had become a regular feature of Berlin night life; and, by 1900, such costume balls had become a
'Berlin specialty' drawing significant foreign audiences (Theis and
Sternweiler 61). Although brief and clearly ambivalently conceived, the
ball scene will continue to resonate on several different levels of *The
Cloister*, as I will discuss shortly. During the early 1890s, when *The Cloister*
is set, Berlin was known as the European city where homosexual culture could be most openly engaged with. This was the case despite an
increasingly oppressive and authoritarian *Kaiser*-kult, the large Prussian
army stationed in and near the capital, and the well-known and restrictive paragraph 175 of German law that had made in 1871 male homosexual interaction illegal. Few arrests or persecutions actually occurred
for the officially termed crime of pederasty, however. The bars, restaurants, clubs, dance halls, bath houses, and accommodation venues that
catered to male and female homosexuals had, in fact, made Berlin a gay
tourist destination by the late 1880s (Theis and Sternweiler 48–62;
Bleibtreu-Ehrenberg; Hogan and Hudson 246; Robb 166). Several other
factors also contributed to this development.

While the gay scene of the upper classes and circles associated with
Wilhelm II congregated in private clubs and establishments, homosexuals in the rapidly increasing working class population of Berlin frequented other kinds of establishments. As historian Alexandra Richie
shows, housing and economic conditions, particularly in the heavily
industrialized and slum-like working class areas of North Central
Berlin during the 1880s, were abominable, which also lead to the proliferation of drinking establishments, *Kneipen*, and to increased crime and
prostitution (163–7, 184). This was the time that Berlin became known
as 'the fount of perversion, criminality and evil' (Döblin quoted in
Richie 166). Arno Holz's *The Book of Times* (*Das Buch der Zeit*) (1886) and
Gerhart Hauptmann's naturalist play *Hannele* (*Hanneles Himmelfahrt*)

(1896) document the social destitution. Of Berlin's two million inhabitants in 1891, fifty thousand were estimated to be engaged in prostitution (Richie 160, 166). By the end of the century, 20 per cent of those were homosexual male prostitutes and another 20 per cent were lesbian prostitutes (*The Cloister* refers openly to homosexual prostitution), which provided another reason the city had become a destination of gay tourism (Theis and Sternweiler 52–3; Robb 157).

Strindberg's constructions of homosexual and same-sex desire has only relatively recently begun to be critically investigated by scholars such as Roy, Borgström, and Lönngren. I discuss Strindberg's constructions of lesbian desire and deconstructions of a gendered public-private paradigm in a transnational context in a previous chapter about *A Madman's Defence*. As both Borgström and Roy have noted, Strindberg composed an earlier version of *The Cloister*'s Wiener Ball scene. This French-language piece, called 'The Perverts' (Les Pervers) (1894), aimed for publication in Paris, constructs a complex picture of homosexual culture as part of transnational modernity. Strindberg writes in essayistic first person about a ball he has attended in Berlin, frequented by barbers, waiters, and bath masters, who, he writes, belong to the under class, 'la basse classe' (164). Male same-sex attraction is described in this piece as a vocational illness, 'une maladie professionelle' (164), caused by the proximity between professional and client, or customer and waiter. Female same-sex attraction is understood as a result of heterosexual prostitution. This essay, in contrast to sections of *The Cloister*, generally shuns any moralizing. 'The Perverts,' like other pieces written in French during the summer of 1894, was described by Strindberg as a sensational and utilitarian article aimed for Paris publications like *Le Journal*, *L'Echo de Paris*, or *L'éclair*, which he aspired to have published by the time he arrived in Paris in 1894 (Eklund, 'Kommentarer' 195). Some of those essays were indeed published in Paris in 1894–5, but 'The Perverts' does not seem to have been one of them.

In an article aimed for a Parisian audience, the inclusion of a description of a Berlin homosexual ball appears to be a deliberate strategy. Its shock value would attach to its author a legacy of contemporary cosmopolitanism. It would also strengthen an image befitting the modern and morally uninhibited writer that Strindberg had, although in other contexts, already become known as in Europe through the sexually explicit *Miss Julie* and the much-noted 1894 indecency trial in Berlin of the German translation of *A Madman's Defence* (*Die Beichte eines Thoren*). The protagonist of *Inferno* – a novel written in French and largely set in

Paris which I discuss in the previous chapter – is chaste and virginal, devoted to science, and, yet he is poor, sick, in pain, and yearning for an accepting community of male intellectuals. The contrast posited between Berlin and Paris in Strindberg's writing at this time will be explored in some detail later, but it is clearly conceived as near-oppositional. Thereby it illustrates from an unexpected perspective the French-German animosity in the wake of the war of 1871, which includes German Kaiser Wilhelm II's interest in strengthening pan-Germanic nationalism (including relations with Sweden) and the nationalistic cult of the virile, strong, heterosexual Germanic male.

The homosexual ball described in *The Cloister* also reflects Germany's, and in particular, Berlin's status as a centre for continental studies of sexology and same-sex attraction in the late nineteenth century. These studies widely influenced discourses on sexuality, morality, pathology, and sociology all over Europe – even though they reached Sweden in Swedish translation somewhat later (Fjelkestam 98–103). Seminal Berlin sexology studies include Karl Heinrich Ulrichs's *Forschungen über das Rätsel der mannmännlichen Liebe* (1864–79), Gustav Jaeger's *Entdeckung der Seele* (1879), Richard von Krafft-Ebing's *Psychopatia Sexualis* (1886), Albert Moll's *Die konträre Sexualempfindung* (1891), and Magnus Hirschfeld's *Sappho und Sokrates* (1896). The theories and terms used to classify and describe same-sex attraction advocated by these German physicians and sexologists ranged widely in scope and perspective, but were largely conceived from scientific and social perspectives, rather than religious and moral ones (see in particular Jones 43–92). This was a significant shift, and allowed both for the beginning of a wider social acceptance and a strengthened pathologization of same-sex attraction. By 1897 Ulrichs, whose term 'Urning' for a male homosexual had become standardized, Hirschfeld, whose 'third sex theory' became particularly influential, and the publisher Adolf Brand were known through their organizations and publications as the leaders of an emerging 'homophile emancipation' movement in Berlin (Hogan and Hudson 245). Strindberg's interest in these questions arguably stems at least partly from the fact that he had lived in and associated with avant-garde Berliners at the time when some of these works were being written.

By the time Strindberg composed the essay 'The Perverts' (1894) and the novel *The Cloister* (1898), he had moved from the German capital via Paris to rural Austria and the small town of Lund in Sweden. The texts clearly reflect, however, that Berlin was known as the uncontested European capital of homosexual culture. Although other terms, such as urning, sodomite, pederast, bugger, or contrarian were generally used to describe homosexuals in Europe at the time (Strindberg, for example, never used the term 'homosexual,' Roy notes), the cultural presence and growing visibility of such marginalized groups became closely associated with the status of Berlin as a modern city. The brief and condensed description of the Wiener Ball in *The Cloister* makes manifest that aspect of Berlin culture. Yet, as I suggested above, the novel's ambivalent depiction of this scene is important for several reasons. Although early in its representation of what we today may call urban queer culture, *The Cloister* by no means offers a wholesale endorsement. Indeed, the description of Axel's disgust is immediate and intense: 'Det var det hemskaste han någonsin sett' (11) (It was the most horrible thing he had ever seen. [12]). Later, the narrator comments on the appearance of the participants; they appear marked, different, and plagued: 'Gudarne ha slagit dem med vansinne … Det är ett straff för okända synder … Pandemonium, helvetets sjunde avdelning' (12) (The gods have struck them mad … It was punishment for unknown sins … Pandemonium, the Seventh circle of Hell [13]). The connection between homosexuality and insanity is part of an established late nineteenth century-medical convention explored not least by Carl Westphal during the 1880s in his treatment of Berlin homosexuals as the 'Professor für Geistes- und Nervenkrankheiten' at the city's Charité Hospital. Westphal emphasized homosexuality as a congenital and physical illness of the nervous system (Jones 54–6). In *The Cloister*, homosexuals are described as 'olyckliga, själslytta' (12) (the wretched, the mentally sick [13]), but also as religiously condemned, whereas in 'The Perverts' the condition is construed as social and contextual, as a professional malady. The inclusion of homosexual culture is important within the textual universe of *The Cloister*, however, as it supplements the rudimentary spatial descriptions of Berlin to construct an alternate setting, namely the inclusion of a subculture that is part of a distinctly transnational conceptualization of modernity that denationalizes Berlin and turns it cosmopolitan.

Strindberg's attitudes toward homosexuality are generally understood as measured in a period context; some scholars argue that his descriptions played a role in the gradual destigmatization of European homosexual culture (see for example Roy). This worked in two ways. During the late 1870s and early 1880s, Strindberg became known in Sweden through different publications as the foremost public conveyor of modern European (particularly French and German) thoughts on homosexuality, helping to shift the rhetoric about homosexuality in Scandinavia from one based solely on religious morality to one that could also include scientific and social theories (Roy 5, 17). The short story 'Nature the Criminal' in *Getting Married II* (*Giftas II*) (1885) is known to gay historians, also outside Sweden, as one which sought social explanations and a decriminalization of same-sex attraction (Miller 118). *The Cloister* conveys clearly that a cross-dressing ball is innocuous entertainment and that police supervision is unwarranted, objecting that participants are unduly treated as 'brottslingar' (12) (criminals [13]).

The narrator recognizes the Wiener Ball scene and the particular Berlin setting as paradoxical on several levels. Not only is the event described as surprisingly solemn and emotionally gripping, but also as explicitly parallel to Axel's own experiences of intense love but failed relationships: 'Martyrium även där, självuppoffring, trohet, alla dygder mitt i lasten' (12) (Martyrdom here too, self-sacrifice, faithfulness, all the virtues in the midst of vice! [13]) Axel remarks on the inconclusive social implications, in which the gendered conventions of a dance event leave the impression of 'något oförklarligt som varken patologi eller psykiatri kunde lösa, och det ohyggliga fann han ligga däri: att det gick så allvarligt till – och att det var så anständigt!' (12) (something inexplicable, which neither pathology nor psychiatry could explain. It seemed to him that the most horrible thing of all was that everything was done so seriously, and that it was all so respectable! [13]). Axel's reactions to the scene run a full range between moral condemnation, social consternation, emotional empathy, and intellectual confusion. The event is not easily classifiable to the narrator because the scene perhaps seems uncannily reminiscent of Axel's own situation.

Like Axel, the dancers at the ball are displaced from known coordinates, temporarily allowed a seemingly sanctioned existence in Berlin, yet one which is clearly demarcated not only by the law (the police in attendance) but also by the fact that they are observed as curio-spectacles by apparently heterosexual visitors, like Axel. Axel is a traveller with no permanent address who woke up with his feet on the pillow in a seemingly alien boarding room. It is an intriguing but unlikely possibility that he could be a temporary visitor specifically interested in Berlin as a gay tourist destination. The passage conjoins instead with other strategies of spatio-temporal displacements in *The Cloister's* first chapter and presents another facet of Strindberg's city writing – this is a detached description of an aspect of modernity that, although parallel to Axel's own experiences, is also marked as a literary construct, as a gesture to relations and locations made possible by the diversity and size of a city like Berlin, in which Axel, a traveller, can occupy a position as an anonymous and detached spectator, as a modern artist in exile. The mythification of Scandinavian influence in Berlin culture at the time suggests that the modernity, the light, and the critical perspectives supposedly brought by the Northerners to conservative Berlin carry over in this passage to sexual paradigms. The passage gestures to the possibility that *The Cloister* seeks to construe its main character as a cosmopolitan man of the world, who, although a visitor to the city, can express his experiences not only with some sophistication, but in fact write of them as constitutive of a burgeoning literary modernism that presupposes Berlin as a necessary setting.

The Wiener Ball section is composed in short hand, moving quickly through a scene that could have been developed more fully. Indeed, the dearth of realistic details is particularly striking and the speed with which the scene is presented connects to the rapid succession of locations in *The Cloister*'s first chapter. On the one hand, the speed emphasizes ideologies of urban modernity, and is reminiscent of later European modernist novels describing city life as a dichotomous pile of isolated, disconnected, and symbolic locations and events. As such, the first chapter ties into an emerging aesthetics of modern city literature. On the other hand, the first chapter consists of a succession of interiors that largely disregard the urban environment outside. These interiors function like a set of miniatures in explicit reaction to naturalism's attempts at panoramic representation of a society; the disparity of these interior settings contributes to the modernist representation of Berlin in *The Cloister*.

Relationships marked by transience and displacement allude as well to the personal situation of the characters who frequent 'The Cloister' – not only are they visitors to Berlin, but they are also removed from their countries and conventional domestic living arrangements; the restaurant becomes a different form of home. 'The Cloister' in *The Cloister* functions as a narrative mise-en-abyme to indicate as well the construction of modern Scandinavian literature in a European context. Several of Scandinavia's 'mest bemärkta män' (16) (most remarkable ... men [18]) in Berlin are divorced, the narrator notes in the first chapter. Challenging a cornerstone of bourgeois society – the social contract of marriage – characters are construed as literarily related to protagonists in Ibsen's *A Doll's House* or Strindberg's *A Madman's Defence*. Two primary observations are made about marriage and divorce in *The Cloister*.

The first illustrates a tenet of the Scandinavian breakthrough movement, namely that divorce is treated not as a moral but as a social issue, problematic but to be expected. This observation correlates with the description of characters, as outsiders, disruptive of heterosexual normativity and harbingers of chaos, which is just the kind of image fostered by and about Scandinavian avant-garde writers in Berlin at the time. The second observation, however, is more intriguing: by marrying or cohabiting with divorced women, men demonstrate an unusually 'ren och stark' (pure and strong) love, foregoing innocent young women for aging and ugly, previously married women in order to attain 'ett samliv och att aldrig vara ifrån varandra' (17) (because they desired to live together and never to be separated [19]). This sympathetic perception of divorce differs markedly from Axel's opinions about Maria in *A Madman's Defence*, where she is construed as a whore and a lesbian once she divorces her first husband and marries Axel. The social ramifications of divorce in *A Madman's Defence* threaten even the stability of material places, as if the domestic architecture of the time cannot contain the transgression against contemporary social norms implied by divorce in a national framework. In *The Cloister*'s Berlin, however, with its rapidly shifting locations, populated by transient and migrant artists and writers, divorce is naturalized, described as an expected result of a marriage. Transnational existence allows for different formulations of gender, including the renunciation of feminine beauty.

Yet, divorced men are stigmatized – their productivity diminished, their social function near exhaustion. They are presented as collectively spent, as unable to move beyond naturalistic verisimilitude and a rehashing of the so-called Woman's Question. The Scandinavian writers and artists (the protagonist included) are described by the narrator as having congregated in Berlin in search of something new and different, but seemingly finding only optical illusions, technological mediation, fleeting encounters, and idiosyncratic montages of conventional images in 'The Cloister.' The group is momentarily presented as a lifeless group of spineless opportunists who watch with detachment how:

infödingar ... lockats som malar till nordljuset, för att söka värme men funnit bara en isande köld ... Man var just i begrepp att rensa sig från den naturalistiska surdegen. Främlingarna funno sålunda endast faeces där de kommit att få näring. Alla sutto på lur att först finna den nya formeln för den stundande periodens konst- och litteraturverk. (17)

[the] natives ... attracted towards the northern light like moths in search of warmth, but all finding only icy cold ... its members were in the process of purging themselves of their naturalistic leaven. The strangers therefore only found faeces where they had come to obtain nourishment. Everyone was on the watch to see who could be the first to find a new formula for the artistic and literary works of the future. (19)

Alluding to the social realism and naturalism of the Modern Breakthrough Movement as old, as little better than excrement, the narrator here and elsewhere in *The Cloister* offers a markedly different view of the canonical legacy of the Scandinavian importance for the development of German modern literature and art, not least in the dramas of Hauptmann and Holz, and the extensive aesthetic criticism, published for example in *Freie Bühne* and *Zukunft*, that was a trademark of the Berlin avant-garde associated with the Scandinavian circles. Yet, in other instances, contemporary German, French, and British literature is not described as having anything to offer that has not already been initiated by Scandinavian writers (76, 106 [92, 131–2]). Although the narrator debunks idealism's combination of aestheticism and ethics, the next movement in literature and arts, the narrator implies, has little to do with intrinsic truth and beauty. Instead, the new literature will be all about pragmatism and formulaic constructions ('finna den nya formeln' / find a new formula). Literary modernism is implicitly construed as the possibility of 'the new.' In Strindberg's conception of Berlin, though, writers of different nationalities appear to be sitting around passively waiting for it.

The dissolution of domestic stability, the acceptance of divorces, and the inclusion of homosexual culture in *The Cloister's* first chapter emerge as constitutive of Strindberg's interest in new forms of literary representation at the end of the nineteenth century. Although critically disregarded and overlooked, the prose in *The Cloister*, followed eventually by *The Roofing Ceremony*, appears to search for new settings and formulas for describing dispassionately and self-reflexively cosmopolitan existence, insisting on the complexity of interpersonal relationships in a moment marked by transience and challenges to stable definitions of national belonging or national culture. Intensifying rhetoric in both Germany and Sweden at the end of the nineteenth century tended to link marriage not only with social stability, but also with the nationalistic project of securing offspring and the prospering of an ethnically homogenous indigenous population. This underlying ideology of nationalism cuts across the representation of interpersonal relationships in *The Cloister*. Stable and extended family relationships (as a nation-in-miniature) predicated on (heterosexual) marriage further a discourse that opposes homosexuality because homosexuality seemed to threaten through depopulation particularly Germany's military-based nationalistic desires (see Taeger).

Like settings, characters seem to be hastily construed in *The Cloister*. Although Axel quickly moves toward a normative courtship with Maria, in which he is first construed as an older mentor and father figure to her, these two characters actually form an unusual couple in Strindberg's writing. Maria is generally coded as active, productive, and competent, whereas he is passive, suffers from writer's block, and lives off her relatives – reflecting the 'spent' nature of the Scandinavians he criticizes in Berlin. Although from a wealthy Austrian family, Maria is a self-supporting newspaper correspondent who is clearly construed as a New Woman figure. Known in the press circles of Vienna and Berlin, Maria also has professional contacts in London and Paris. When Axel first meets her, she lives alone in a rented room, comfortably furnished with a 'rikt försett skrivbord' (28) (richly appointed writing desk [33]). She does not hesitate to see the protagonist in her home on her own, late at night, despite the serious breach of convention. She is also the first to kiss him, lowering the veil on her hat and kissing him through the fabric. *The Cloister's* interest in capturing aspects of modernity related to speed, travel, and social impermanence suggests new dimensions in Strindberg's writing and carries over to both setting and character construction. The narrative relates these aspects to a wide range of gendered practices. *The Cloister* introduces not only homosexuality, divorce, and New Woman figures as given aspects of the protagonist's everyday experiences in Berlin, but also formulates attraction and desire as predicated on significantly different premises, accelerated and formed by different spatial coordinates.

The Cloister formulates the attraction between Axel and Maria as technologically mediated. Attraction is not marked by physical eroticism but is construed both as disembodied and displaced into other mediums. Although fascinated by her, *The Cloister's* protagonist forgets what Maria looks like between the first and second time he meets her. He passes her on the street without recognizing her, locating her outside a pattern of visual spectatorship in the city that is also a sexualized relationship. As many commentators have noted, the prevalence of soliciting on Berlin's streets in the late nineteenth century was striking, in the northern working class as well as the western middle-class areas that Axel describes (see for example Richie 166–7). The difficulty Axel has recalling Maria's image is later resolved through the use of a technological metaphor about photography: He cannot 'framkalla "hennes" yttre' (recall what 'she' looked like) despite his practice 'att med ögat fotografera människor och scener' (27) ([of] photographing by eye people [and] scenes [32]). Instead, it was 'rösten han mindes, något djup, sorgsen, med små tonfall som drog en långt från storstad och väckte minnen från skogen och sjön' (27) (her voice he remembered, a rather deep and sorrowful voice, with little inflections that drew one far away from a great city, and awakened memories of forests and lakes [32]). Maria, idealized for a moment, is located outside the parameters of urban modernity and is implicitly reconnected with the location from which the protagonist hails – an unnamed natural haven.

Images of Maria as impermanent and displaced, particularly in *The Cloister*'s urban sections, correlate with other interpersonal relationships in Berlin, where alliances and friendships are made and broken quickly. Their accelerated courtship leads to marriage within a few months. This relationship is consistently marked as mediated, as formed by different experiences, backgrounds, and expectations. They acknowledge that they do not know and cannot know one another: 'de fingo aldrig reda på varann, så att de i riktigt allvarliga ögonblick kunde samtidigt utbrista: Vem är du? Vad är du för slag, egentligen? Och båda voro svarslösa' (44) (they never got to the bottom of each other and, at moments when they were quite serious, could burst out simultaneously with: 'Who are you? What kind of a creature are you really?' – questions which neither of them could answer [52–3]). The differences are never explored in detail in the narrative, but only fleetingly gestured to as inexplicable in terms of both traditional romantic and naturalist literary models. Instead, the spatio-temporal moment, marked by changing conceptualizations of gender roles and their different backgrounds come together also as an indication of life in Berlin in the early 1890s. As a married couple, Maria and Axel do not live for any extended period in Berlin or anywhere else but instead move from location to location, sometimes together but most often apart. The limited erotic or physical attraction between Axel and Maria is complemented by increasingly common references to the rapid communication pattern between the two, as if the speed of communication supplements physical attraction.

The technological mediation of attraction escalates between Maria and Axel. They communicate via rapidly exchanged telegrams, missives, and communiqués: 'depescher och ilbud haglade' (37) (a hail of telegrams and express letters [45]); 'breven haglade' (67) (the letters rained down like hail [81]); telegrams are sent off, letters are being written to maintain contact, and so on. *The Cloister* repeatedly emphasizes how disjointed spatio-temporal relationships speed up human interactions and dislodge those from the perceived necessity of being in the same place at the same time. The highly mediated practices of communication between Axel and Maria in Berlin (telegrams, missives, and so on) correlate implicitly with a desire for immediate psychological connections (telepathy) and concretely with the fact that the two characters are rarely in the same physical location. The relationship is equally rarely described figuratively as physically joined – just after their marriage they momentarily perceive of their union as having 'smält ihop som två bitar av samma metall. De hade förlorat sig och sin form, och de voro ett. Men minnet av ett självständigt väsen av en egen tillvarelseform fanns kvar' (51) (fused together like two pieces of the same metal. They had lost themselves and their individual shapes and they were one. But the memory of an independant being, of a personal existence still survived [62–3]). After only two weeks of married life and cohabitation in a cottage off the Baltic island of Helgoland, they start travelling around Europe, sometimes together, but most often apart.

The Cloister provides an important correlate to Georg Simmel's theories of the desensitization of contemporary urban life, which he formulated specifically with reference to Berlin as a *Großstadt*. In the well-known essay 'The Metropolis and Mental Life' (Die Großstädte und das Geistesleben) first published in 1903, Simmel emphasizes that it is the continual sensory input, and subsequent overload, which is the distinguishing factor of urban modernity. The result of this sensory input is alienation, exacerbated by practices of capitalist accumulation, which fundamentally estranges man from himself, other human beings, and his environment. *The Cloister's* Berlin descriptions illustrate different implications of Simmel's arguments. In Strindberg's fictional account of life in the modern metropolis, when character movement accelerates, descriptions of setting decrease in detail and frequency. It appears as if the sense of alienation and desensitization produced by the metropolis attaches not only to Maria and Axel, but also to construction of setting.

Concurrently, descriptions of exterior urban locations are brief, sparse, and laconic; the city looks as if marked by death in the first chapter, boulevards are empty and deserted and the two lovers walk little-populated streets in the western suburbs and dine in a side-street restaurant. Such descriptions of Berlin are motivated diegetically as appropriate for two lovers who seek anonymity to avoid being recognized by colleagues or countrymen, but are symbolically motivated as giving an alternate image of Berlin as out-of-joint, as far from the bustling, industrialized metropolis it had become by the early 1890s, and, more important, as separated from the problems of poverty, overcrowding, pollution, and crime of working class areas just north of Axel's boarding house and the restaurant 'The Cloister.' As part of its novelistic discourse, *The Cloister* shuns Berlin and seems to turn the *Großstadt* into an image befitting a northern small town – dreary, stifling, and with gossip flying fast.

On the other hand, the novel's initial descriptions of Axel's boarding rooms, the Wiener Ball, 'The Cloister' drinking establishment, and the displaced, mediated erotic attraction between Axel and Maria indicate formal attempts at marking disjointed spatio-temporal descriptions as modern, as befitting a narrative that searches for a new formula to describe an inconclusive contemporary moment in terms other than those allowed by realism and naturalism. Berlin thus represents more than its specific locality, the setting of *The Cloister*, but instead becomes a space in which the narrator is understood as experimenting with different perspectives. Here divorce is socially decoded, homosexuality is represented in a social context (rather than strictly from a religious or moral stance), and marriage is *not* existential.

In comparison to *A Madman's Defence*, published as *Die Beichte eines Thoren* in German in 1893, *The Cloister* offers a remarkably different and distinctly modern view of marriage as a pragmatic partnership, not least in its implicit connections with Simmel's theories of alienation. The heterosexual matrix in *The Cloister* appears formulated as already imbricated within the framework of capitalist alienation – desire is no longer existential in and of itself, but is always mediated and brought into existence via the transfer of money and technology. The work is explicit about the strain harsh economic circumstances put on romantic attraction and emotional fidelity: As Axel and Maria walk through London harbour on a hot day, weary from not having eaten and low on travel funds, Axel spitefully 'hoppades att hon skulle falla och stöta sig, bli knuffad av en hamnarbetare, önskade att en sjåare omfamnade henne och kysste, ja han trodde sig kunna med lugn åse hur en hamnbuse våldtog henne' (58) (hoped that she would fall and hurt herself, that harbourmen would bump into her. He wished that some docker would sieze her in his arms and kiss her, why, he even felt he could look on unmoved while a drunken loafer raped her [70]). The visualization of raw and sexual violence Axel imagines as an appropriate response to his own dejected situation is momentary; the striking effect is enhanced by the fact that the novel returns to its mode of detachment soon thereafter. Simmel's alienation travels along with the functions of capital.

The narrative strategies associated with Berlin carry forth to the travel narrative that follows. This suggests a model for Swedish city writing at the turn-of-the century formed by the convulsive resolution of previously conceived antithetical locations, such as oppositions between countryside and city, Sweden and Europe, provincialism and cosmopolitanism, travel and home, transience and permanence, naturalism and modernism, and so on. The novel bridges these oppositions in several important ways. Most clearly, the speed and fast mediation of diegetic events and their narration carry over from Berlin. Nothing slows down or gains in ideological permanence when the setting abandons the city – divorce, not stable marital coexistence, draws closer the longer the characters stay away from Berlin. Similarly, creativity and productivity diminish, sensations of homelessness increase, heterosexually normative gender roles decrease in stability, and so on. The desensitization Simmel describes as an aspect of modern urban living attaches itself to Maria and Axel and only increases in scope and magnitude when they leave the city. Their frustration with their own situations away from Berlin, travelling in Britain, Germany, and Austria, or living near her parents in rural Austria, is eventually directed as a desire for Paris. The novel thereby challenges ideologies of the European nation-state as it becomes consistently more emphasized at the end of the nineteenth century: cross-national travel is fast and easy, the languages of German and French are the vehicle for interaction among cosmopolitans, and although cultural boundaries may be difficult to transcend, such difficulties are not construed as existential, but as expected.

The Cloister exists as a fragment, and a final section of the last chapter has probably been lost. The narrative thus ends abruptly, but gestures toward two different but complementary spatial conceptualizations of the two main characters' respective futures. For Maria, the birth of their child has meant intellectual imprisonment and nearly professional suicide. She explains to Axel that 'detta liv dödar mig. Jag har icke läst en bok sen barnet kom och jag har icke skrivit något på ett år. Jag följer med dig till Paris' (110) (this life is killing me. I haven't read a book since the child arrived, and I haven't written anything for a year. I shall go to Paris with you [137]). For her, as for many other women in Europe and Scandinavia at the turn of the century, Paris stands as the desired, phantasmagorical location of personal and professional freedom, of a playing field somewhat more level in a brutal market economy of the printed word or artistic success (see Gynning on the Swedish context). The possibility that Paris stands as a feminized opposition to masculine Berlin is also offered as a reason for Maria's identification with Paris. Coming from Germany and Austria, and leaving for Paris connotes political revolt as well. Axel envisions Paris as an equally phantasmagorical location for 'grundandet av konfessionslösa kloster för [manliga] intellektuella, som i en tid, då industri och ekonomi trängt sig fram i första planet, ej kunde finna sig i den atmosfär av materialism som de själva låtit förleda sig predika' (106) (founding a non-confessional monastery for intellectuals who, at a time when industry and finance had pushed themselves so much to the fore, could not feel at home in the atmosphere of materialism which they themselves had been misled into preaching [131]). Berlin stands for the site of military might and commerce, while Paris is a median of culture. Yet both Axel and Maria have internalized the ideas of mobility, transience, and displacement that are implied in Simmel's theories of the desensitization of modern life in the big city. For a Swedish readership, Paris would still epitomize the centre of continental culture. It seems ironically fitting that Strindberg, who professed great fascination, as well as frustration, with Paris and French culture, did not actually become associated with any writing about Berlin for a Swedish readership at this time. *The Cloister* was published posthumously in 1966 and it is instead the metaconnection, Strindberg's being part of a Scandinavian group of writers in Berlin, that has become better known.

3 A New Literary Berlin of the Late Nineteenth Century: *The Cloister* as a Metaliterary Artefact

Usually overlooked by critics as a wasted period, Strindberg's period in Berlin came directly on the heels of a public divorce in Sweden from his first wife Siri von Essen. The subsequent flight from Stockholm into a second, extended period of vagabondage around Europe that started in Berlin also led to a brief marriage to the Austrian journalist Frida Uhl in 1893. The writer was more interested in experimenting in the natural sciences, photography, and painting in oil of primarily Swedish landscapes

while in Berlin, as Söderström shows (*Strindberg och bildkonsten* 191–3).
Strindberg's brief stay in Berlin has been mythologized as highly significant on other levels, however. In Berlin, Strindberg achieved the critical
success he had strongly desired in Paris. In 1895, Swedish critic Bengt
Lidforss writes in the Stockholm daily paper *Dagens Nyheter* that
Strindberg has become the Scandinavian most represented by Berlin
booksellers: his books are proudly displayed 'hvart man går' (cited in
Widell 40) (wherever you go [my trans.]). Emil Schering's German translations had a great impact from the 1890s onward and especially as collected in *Strindbergs Werke* (1908), while Karl Kraus introduced several
Strindberg texts in German translation to an Austrian readership in his
journal *Die Fackel* during the period 1903–12 (see Hansson). The reception of Strindberg's plays in Berlin – *The Father* at Freie Bühne in 1890;
Miss Julie in 1892; and *Creditors* at Rezidenztheater in 1893 – created a
name and legacy for Strindberg, which influenced the subsequent reception of dramatic productions by Otto Brahm and Max Reinhardt, including the expressionist plays during the 1920s. As a central figure in a bohemian coterie in Berlin in 1892–3, Strindberg's person has become
mythical as representative of an emergent Scandinavian modernism.

Berlin at the end of the nineteenth century was Europe's most industrialized, fastest-expanding capital, characterized by near-inconceiv-
able economic inequalities. Governed by Kaiser Wilhelm II's increasingly restrictive and nationalist acolytes, Berlin's cultural climate in the
1890s constituted a particularly intriguing aggregate of radicalism and
reaction, whose expressions, like the formal strategies of *The Cloister*,
oscillated between innovation and convention. The representation of
Berlin and its juxtaposition with continental Europe and Scandinavia in
The Cloister indicates Strindberg's fascination with the large urban aggregate in multiple ways. Berlin had already by this time become the
iconic engine of European industrial modernity. The enormous restitu-
tion fees France had to pay during the 1880s funnelled cash into enterprises and manufacturing. But the changing social fabric of Berlin in the
1880s, with its rapid industrialization, quick construction of enormous
and nearly identical apartment complexes in both working-class and
upper-class neighbourhoods, and large inequities between those newly
monied and those of the proletariat, found little expression in German
domestic cultural production.

Berlin in 1885 lacked any socially motivated literature or aesthetically sophisticated art forms according to Danish critic and author Georg
Brandes: 'simple and popular entertainment without artistic merit' was

the standard fare, he writes in his collection of essays *Berlin as the German capital* (*Berlin som tysk Rigshovedstad*) (1885, cited in Fuchs 340, my trans.). The period 1885–95 has been described by cultural historians of Scandinavian-German relations as 'a vacuum' (Fuchs 340) in which socially invested and aesthetically innovative Scandinavian writers could establish themselves, and continue to exert strong influences in literature, criticism, drama, art, and early film making until the start of the First World War (see for example, Englert; Fuchs; Schoolfield, 'Scandinavian-German Literary Relations'; Widell 16–40). Clearly Berlin had a lot to offer to migrant exile artists and writers who congregated there in the early 1890s, and perhaps one way to think of the city's cultural function includes the possibility of it figuring as a blank slate – in contrast to Paris or London, the city had few pretensions of being a cultural centre and had not yet been construed as a location of iconic metropolitan modernity. It was also a dynamic city in terms of its rapid immigration; many were newcomers in that city at the end of the nineteenth century, which allowed it the possibility of granting a different form of anonymity than that of Paris.

Germany, and particularly Berlin, also became the place where Scandinavian writers like Brandes, Ibsen, Strindberg, J.P. Jacobsen, Arne Garborg, Ola Hansson, Ellen Key, Selma Lagerlöf (and many others) gained international exposure, and, in some cases, where their national legacies were later established. Berlin filled a similar function for many artists and writers from Slavic regions, particularly for Polish and Czech writers, as Katherine David-Fox shows. Strindberg knew well, for example, Stanislaw Przybyszewski, 'the Polish *Wunderkind* of Berlin in the early 1890s' (McFarlane 106; see also Schoolfield, *A Baedeker of Decadence* 180–6). In 1889, Ibsen's *Ghosts* (*Gengangerne*) was the opening play at the inauguration of Brahm's radical theatre Freie Bühne in Berlin. Modelled on André Antoine's Théâtre Libre in Paris, Brahm's theatre, and his eponymous journal of criticism, prompted playwrights like Gerhart Hauptmann to begin exploring naturalist drama inspired at least partly by models provided by Scandinavian writers (Paul 194).[1]

Brandes had advocated for the emerging group of Scandinavian modernists in many German publications during the 1880s and his book of essays *Men of the Modern Breakthrough* (*Det moderne gjennembruds maend*)

---

1 See also the publication tables and bibliography in Paul's essay for more information about the significant exposure of Scandinavian writing in German, including translation, reception, and distribution practices.

(1883) gave an emergent group of young writers in Berlin motivation to take up the lance of the Modern. In a lecture to the Berlin literary circle Durch in 1886, Eugen Wolff launched the term *Die Moderne*, presumably as a direct response to Brandes and Scandinavian writers of the Modern Breakthrough, while articulating the self-reflexive, self-conscious, and transnational designs of the early Germanic movements of modernism (McFarlane 38–40). As the decade turned, the expressionistic style and a detachment from realism advocated by Strindberg, Hamsun, Hansson, and Garborg became major points of reference for writers and intellectuals in Berlin, as was Edvard Munch through his exhibition of expressionist painting in the fall of 1892. This transnational intellectual history is further illustrated by the fact that Friedrich Nietzsche first became known to German and European audiences in lectures and articles by the Danish Brandes and Swedish Hansson. McFarlane's chapter title in his coedited encyclopedic volume *Modernism* is illustrative: 'Berlin and the *Rise* of Modernism: 1886–1896' (105, emphasis added), indicating the foundational role Berlin played in the movements of European transnational modernism at the end of the nineteenth century.

The German literary market was thus ripe for exploration particularly by Scandinavian writers, who, often exiled on the continent, had difficulties getting recognized or even published in their home countries. The significance of the Scandinavian presence in Berlin, particularly during the period 1891–3, has been codified in Hermann Sudermann's expression 'Vom Norden kommt uns das Licht!' (The light comes from the North! [cited in Söderström, 'Zum' 353]). Yet outside the bohemian, socially informed, and avant-garde circles of Berlin, the legacy of Scandinavia in Germany at the end of the nineteenth century stood for a pervasive belief in a pan-Germanic shared history, which ideologically codified Scandinavia as Germany's primordial origin and where Nordic authenticity and roots – ethnically, racially, culturally, and geographically – became a preferred interpretive model. This was the image of Scandinavia that the kaiser and Berlin's upper crust wanted to promote, exemplified by an intense interest in Old Norse/Viking literature and culture. At this time, regular charter cruises took wealthy German tourists, including the kaiser for his yearly vacations starting in 1889, on the grand tour of Norway's fjords and magnificent, 'melancholic' nature (cited in Büchten 115).

Such idealized, undifferentiated constructs of Scandinavia contrasted sharply with the socially radical and aesthetically innovative 'light' that Scandinavian writers in exile were interested in reflecting. Indeed, the mythification of the Scandinavian presence in Berlin in the early 1890s has been quite formidable, aided at least partly by oft-cited expressions like Ola Hansson's admonition in a letter to Strindberg in 1889 that 'Germanien är stort och utan literatur. Der kunna vi ha både nöje och ära af att vara med' (cited in Widell 16) (Germany is large and without literature. There we should have both the pleasure and honour of participating [my trans.]). Hermann Bahr echoes this understanding of the presence of Scandinavian writers in Berlin. He writes in 1894 that 'Es gab keine deutsche Literatur mehr – das war die tägliche Klage der jungen Leute' (cited in Widell 17) (That there is no German literature anymore – that was the daily complaint by the young [my trans.]). The import to Berlin of Scandinavian literature in translation and of Scandinavian writers and artists, often themselves living various degrees of transnational, multilingual existences (Hansson, for example, returned only briefly to Sweden and wrote almost exclusively in German after 1890), necessarily complicates ideologies of national belonging. The relatively brief period of Scandinavian literary influence was also accelerated and intensified not least because it contrasted sharply with the formidable influence German literature, music, and philosophy had exerted in Denmark, Norway, and Sweden during the preceding decades of the nineteenth century – think Heine, Schiller, Goethe, Hegel, Marx, and Wagner, to name only a few. Strindberg's relationship with German culture is representative in this regard, since he, like most educated Swedes, had learned to associate more strongly with French culture as the representative of refined idealism and aestheticism, at least up until its defeat in the Franco-Prussian war of 1870. Then public opinion began to turn, and Germany became more closely associated with Sweden's desire to enter into paradigms of modernity when identified as beliefs in progress, technological and scientific innovations, and ideologies of economic development. In Prussia, the educated middle and upper classes joined in the 1880s with Kaiser Wilhelm II's deep hostility toward all matters French, directed in the literary sphere against the naturalism of Zola and emerging symbolist, or decadent, French literature and art.

This cultural context is important, since Berlin for Strindberg and his contemporaries was associated also with representations of modernity's underbelly – poverty, pollution, industrialization, capitalism, and overpopulation. The literary market economy of Germany, however, was to serve Strindberg very well. This inverted centre-margin paradigm, where the marginal but modern arts of Scandinavia revitalized

German culture in its new capital, Berlin, has been quite strongly canonized. This image was promoted also at the time, and *The Cloister* both embraces and rejects this legacy. Keeping this socio-cultural background in mind, *The Cloister*'s straightforward references to the reception of Scandinavian writers in Berlin takes on added meaning. The text refers explicitly to establishment resistance – when Axel is invited to dinner by a professor who is also an associate of the kaiser's, he senses the conservative rebuttal: 'Skandinaverna voro nämligen illa anskrivna på högre ort' (33) (The fact was that Scandinavians in particular were out of favour in high circles [40]). Axel nevertheless discredits his own achievements, labelling them as old-fashioned, as only modern within the thoroughly reactionary cultural sphere of Berlin: 'Men den litteratur som hon [Maria] kallade modern, var just vorden omodern i Norden, och det blev honom som åhörare olidligt höra de nyss avlagda idéerna hälsas som fruktbringande' (13) (But the literature that she [Maria] called modern was now outmoded in the North, and he found it excrutiating to hear her greeting as new, and capable of bearing fruit, ideas that had so recently been abandoned [14]). Literature written in and about Berlin in the early 1890s, McFarlane shows, became unusually focused on the programmatic – on ideology, philosophy, and aesthetics, as discussed in literary clubs and in *Programschriften*, rather than on the creation of formally innovative novels or drama (113, 112). This contrasts starkly with *The Cloister*, which is one of the least programmatic and most detached in tone of all Strindberg's prose works. It is as if he, in hindsight, writing in Sweden after a prolonged stay in Paris in the mid-1890s, seeks to write an alternate narrative of modern Berlin literature, avoiding the panoramic or tendentious in favour of the fleeting, the subjective, and the transient.

Berlin novels of the 1880s generally portray the city panoramically, from the point of view of all walks of life, to comment on the larger economic and social movements of the time. As Schutte and Sprengel argue, long descriptive street scenes and a Darwinian 'survival of the fittest' economic model are some of the characteristics seen in Max Kretzer's *Die Verkommenen* (1883) and in Alberti's *Wer ist der Stärkere* (1888), part of the cycle *Der Kampf ums Dasein* (310–11). In this naturalistic scheme, the individual can only find sanctuary outside of the city limits, if at all. Alberti's writings of the mid-1890s, as exemplified by the novel *The Machines* (*Maschinen*) (1895), continue this stance, as machines threaten the existence of the human within the city. Sprengel argues that 'Alberti's representation mythifies the machines by making them, in a sense, personally responsible for social problems, which result from their employment in a specific economical environment' (Sprengel 28, my trans.). Technology is used in *The Cloister* as well, but to portray the speed of modern society as a narrative technique rather than as a social explanation for inequalities. Arno Holz's extensive plans in 1893 for a ten-part series of plays called *Berlin in Drama*, modelled expressly on Zola's Rougon-Macquart series illustrates the epigonous stance – the one and only play conceived was eventually called *Berlin, the End of an Age in Dramas* (1896). Cosmopolitan and transnational heterogeneity seemingly presented the Berliner Moderne movements with problems, as German culture oscillated between embracing an emergent *national* culture of unification post 1871, which was simultaneously construed as both *inter*-national (not least in its connections to Scandinavia and ensuing efforts of pan-Germanification) and as counter-bourgeois. A resolution to the tension between the poles of 'consistent naturalism' in Arno Holz's terminolgy, that is, between the 'slice of life' and 'the author's temperament,' seemed by 1891 not only impossible, but irrelevant; and, the contradictions between the 'passionate and the dispassionate' in art seemed equally out of date in the early 1890s (McFarlane, 113, 112). *The Cloister* arguably bypasses this debate in its detachment.

The literary group 'Friedrichschagener Kreis,' led in part by the philosophical ideas of Bruno Wille and Wilhelm Bölsche, rose partly in reaction to negative views of the *Großtadt*. Both Strindberg and Ola Hansson were peripherally associated with the group and Strindberg stayed for six weeks in the suburb Friedrichshagen when he first arrived in Berlin in 1892. As far as depictions of the city were concerned, the call from Wille (as later exemplified in his *Einsiedelkunst aus der Kiefernheide*, 1897) was to poeticize the *Großstadt* from the subjective viewpoint of a lonely wanderer, who longs for the happiness of nature's harmony (Sprengel 24). Similarly, in Julius Hart's 1898 poem 'Triumph des Lebens,' the city is beautiful and full of atmosphere only from a distance. The cultural affirmation of country life was, it has been argued, intended to help Germany reclaim its past and set German literature apart from French influence (Barnes 236–41; see also Bergmann). *The Cloister* largely disregards the tensions of a burgeoning *Heimat*-movement in German literature to focus instead on thematization and formal strategies associated with transience, speed, technological mediation, and displacement. Berlin in *The Cloister* thus appears to differ from earlier Berlin depictions and to prefigure expressionistic accounts of the early twentieth century. Aspects of transnational European mobility join in *The Cloister* with recurring thematic emphasis on speed, transience, and technological mediation, and narratologically achieves this effect by moving quickly from one scene to another, and from one location to the next. The novel shuns psychological complexity and dialogue. Yet, even with these suggestions of alternate models of everyday existence, *The Cloister*'s main character adheres to a known pattern for the social organization of life. His previous marriage is only briefly mentioned; the second marriage is one of detachment, impermanence, mediation, and expected divorce. *The Cloister*'s narrative mediation of life in Berlin, the protagonist's travels through the European continent, and his anticipated departure for Paris, however, suggest that strategies for the composition of transience have also changed. In fact, it may be that it was the modernist representational strategies, rather than the presumed autobiographical content, that made Strindberg withhold the narrative from publication. A similar story, but with most geographical markers and identifying characteristics removed, was in fact published as a story-within-a-story in *Fair Haven and Foul Strand* (*Fagervik och Skamsund*) (1902). In this version, called 'The Quarantine Master's Second Story' (Karantänmästarens andra berättelse) Berlin has become Copenhagen, Austria rural Denmark, Helgoland an unnamed island in the British Channel, and Axel is now 'The Norwegian' and Maria Danish rather than Austrian, and so forth. The first extended Berlin chapter of *The Cloister* has been completely removed. As Walter Berendsohn has shown, Strindberg's rapid editing of the manuscript left geographical inconsistencies that are remarkably striking ('Studier i manuskriptet'). This narrative loses much of what I see as its modernist qualities by being inserted into a frame of oral storytelling in which it is just one of many stories told, rather than relating a specific experience of urban modernity (see also Stounbjerg 39–42).

To conclude, then, *The Cloister* is a literary work marked by displacements. Life in the big city is understood by the characters and narrator not only as formative, but also as transformative, as allowing for the tantalizing possibility of the beyond, and thereby also of conquering the disjointed spatio-temporal existence that is modernity. The novel describes Berlin as an utterly modern location: as curiously empty, as being of a blank nature. Chosen by Scandinavian artists and writers as giving opportunities for an avant-garde existence, and for allowing them to make an impact and provide recognition outside their home countries, it is a given in *The Cloister*'s Berlin that women work, unmarried couples cohabit, divorce is an established social practice, that homosexuals are allowed to interact but under controlled circumstances, and prostitution is solicited openly. But Berlin is also repressive. Nothing gets written or produced; Axel and his compatriots rest on old laurels. The social landscape in *The Cloister* changes quickly. People move, resettle, reconvene, and the urban setting allows an alternate model of interaction, where sexual relationships are quickly struck up and then die off. In *The Cloister*, the setting of Berlin is displaced and detached from realistic spatial markers, which allows it in addition to become construed as explicitly metaliterary, as part of Scandinavian cultural context in Berlin. Strindberg's last long prose narrative, *The Roofing Ceremony*, builds on *The Cloister's* figurations of displacement and transience. I turn to this tale of travel, colonialism, and interiority conceits next.

5 Recording, Habitation, and Colonial Imaginations in *The Roofing Ceremony*

As a transnational writer and émigré with personal experience of the centre-periphery paradigm that unevenly shaped European discourses about literary innovation in the late nineteenth century, Strindberg returns again and again in his writing to reinscribe complex relationships with Stockholm, Paris, and Berlin. It seems that the full extent of Strindberg's authorial identity as transnational, as fluid and dynamic, was quickly suppressed in Swedish culture at the time and has been in Strindberg scholarship since then. Complex and multilayered factors of geography, location, culture, aesthetics, and literary innovation coalesce in new ways in Strindberg's writing upon his permanent return to Stockholm in 1898, after years of vagabondage around Europe.

The specific setting of a modern apartment building carries high symbolical and structural value in Strindberg's late writing. In one of his last fictional prose pieces, *The Roofing Ceremony* (*Taklagsöl*) (1906), a modern, standardized, middle-class Stockholm apartment provides the exclusive setting. The novel operates on the premise that it is the private, stationary, and (relatively) permanent location of a domestic apartment that allows for narrative experimentation – extended monologues, jumbled chronology, flashbacks, and emulation of morphine-induced, semiconscious, first-person speech. These strategies are meant to be understood as experimental, as seeking to investigate how drugs and dying affect consciousness and the retelling of events and experiences. The apartment setting is not an empty container waiting to be filled with narrative meaning in *The Roofing Ceremony*, however. Figurations of transnational settings include in *The Roofing Ceremony* references to Swedish colonial imaginations of Congo, including ethnographic collecting, which correlates Strindberg's novella thematically with Joseph Conrad's *Heart of Darkness* (1902). In addition, the narrative's attempts to relay psychological interiority complement our understanding of Strindberg's contemporary experimentation with setting in the sequence of chamber plays (1907–9) and monodramas. As a composite, spatial representation in *The Roofing Ceremony* indicates literary modernism's interest in disassembling boundaries between interiority and exteriority, and suggests how these must be conceived as part of a transnational literary paradigm, even if the experiencing consciousness hardly leaves his bed, as is the case in *The Roofing Ceremony*.

The plot of *The Roofing Ceremony* is simple. The main character, called the curator, is propped up in his bed and dazed by morphine to dim the pain incurred from an accident. During four days, he sleeps, talks, and hallucinates. The curator's story is conveyed through monologues, dialogue, and in a third-person narrative frame, where we learn that he has lived an expansive life as an explorer, scientist, author, and world traveller. He cherishes his personal Baedeker copy and reminisces repeatedly about his experiences in Africa. In the monologues, the curator tells in flashback form three primary stories. These centre on problematic domestic spaces: his failed marriage and difficult relationship with his son; a parallel marriage of his downstairs architect neighbour; and the curator's relationship to 'the Green Eye,' an enemy from his time as an explorer in Congo who now resides in an apartment within view of his own. A parallel plot line involves the rapid construction of a new apartment building coming up opposite the curator's. In the moment of his death, the last pole of the new building is put into place and celebrated with a workmen's feast (hence the novel's title). At that time, the view to the Green Eye is obstructed.

This chapter explores how the interiority conceit of modernist narration evoked in the novella depends not only on the apartment setting, but even more so on a sophisticated understanding of setting's mediation through period architectural discourse, audio and recording technology, colonial travel, and metatextual genre construction. This chapter illustrates features of transnational prose modernism by addressing four areas: first, the form and function of architecture and corporeality; second, recording devices like the grafophone and phonograph conceived as containers and playback devices of human voice; third, colonial rhetoric and ethnographic objects that mediate the apparently stable boundaries of the apartment (particularly in relation to Joseph Conrad's *Heart of Darkness*, 1902); and fourth, literary genres that emphasize spatialized figurations, such as chamber plays and monodramas. Seen through these perspectives, setting can be understood as instrumental for the development of experimental narrative techniques, and it can also help elucidate the complexity of transnational modernist prose forms as they evolve in Strindberg's late writing.

1 The Interior

As in Franz Kafka's later *Metamorphosis* (1915) or Marcel Proust's *Swann's Way* (begun in 1909, first published 1913), a bedroom is introduced as the point of origin for novelistic narration in *The Roofing Ceremony*. The curator lies immobile in 'sin sängkammare' (his own bedroom) and later awakens for a moment to search 'efter ett visst mönster på tapeten' (9, 14) (after a certain pattern in the wallpaper [*The Roofing Ceremony*, trans. Paul and Paul 3, 9]). Resembling the head of his friend the museum director, the wallpaper shape becomes an imagined interlocutor, a backdrop to the extended flashback monologues. This construction remains stable in the numerous recollections that follow. In these recollections, the curator extensively describes three apartments – his own, his wife's, and that of his architect neighbour, located directly below his own. These apartment descriptions link the moment of narration with the interiority conceit of the flashbacks. In the first person voice, the curator realistically describes furniture and decorations, light falling through the windows, the garden outside, the view toward his 'enemy' in the building opposite, as well as the charting and measurements taken in preparation for the new apartment building. These descriptions cover several pages and contrast with the notion of supposedly disordered, unmediated thought representation (17–19 [13–16]). The mediation inherent in domestic architecture and interior design emerges through this contrast – it appears impossible, even for a drugged, feverish, and partly hallucinating protagonist, not to describe domestic architecture in ways that are recognizably realist. The power of spatial determination is, however, countered by linguistic markers that juxtapose the present with the past tense to locate two temporal realms in one space, the apartment: 'Nu gick jag ensam i våningen' (16, emphasis added) (*Now* I *was* alone in that apartment [13, emphasis added]). Linguistic markers that indicate hallucinatory confusion are also spatial: The speaker interjects 'Var var jag?' (19) (*Where* was I? [16]) to indicate that he has lost his narrative thread. In its first section, devoted to descriptions of apartments in seemingly unmediated first-person form, *The Roofing Ceremony* confirms architecture's ordering function. Spaces must be described in order for narrative function to emerge, it appears. But the narrative also departs from this model by imagining a parallel universe, in which events repeat themselves and the modern apartment building creates stories as a given aspect of its location.

The Roofing Ceremony's many descriptions of apartments, of the architecture of private life, indicate fascination with the most common urban form of dwelling – the modern, standardized, reproducible apartment. Indeed, the text begins close to home, in the very familiarity of a bedroom. Self-reflexively, the text ties literary representation to architecture's legibility, by which the two forms of representation become explicitly related. Events in the curator's apartment and those in the identically laid-out apartment below resemble one another, so that the unravelling of the speaker's and his downstairs neighbours' marriages propel the narration. Sounds transfer between the apartments and tell stories of their inhabitants that none could visually know – like a grafophone recording could be imagined to do. One day, the curator recalls in a monologue, he had ample time to observe for the first time the downstairs apartment, waiting there alone for hours to place an outgoing telephone call. The apartment belongs to an architect. The curator's experiences there shape his understanding of both literary and architectural registers of meaning:

> Det är hans rum, men det är en pendang till mitt; hans rum äger något naket, abstrakt, såsom arkitekten ju rör sig med geometriska storheter, linjer, ytor. Jag ser endast byggnadsritningar, men inga hus; inga levande föremål, inga växter, ingen färg. Gardiner för fönstren saknas, ty han söker ljus för sitt arbete; därigenom tycker jag mig sitta ute, oskyddad för den råa väderleken, och detta gör rummet banalt, avskräckande, utom det att ledsnaden vilar över det hela. Jag ser mitt varma rum, med färgat ljusdunkel, fyllt av levande växter och uppstoppade djur … [D]et är mitt rum, övergivet, plundrat, ostädat. (23)

> It is his room, but it is a counterpart of mine; his room has something naked, abstract about it, as an architect works with geometrical quantities, lines, and planes. I see only house drawings, but no houses; no living objects, no growing things, no color. Curtains at the windows are lacking, because he needs the light for his work; because of this, I feel as though I am sitting outdoors, unsheltered from the raw force of the weather, and this makes the room banal, repellent, beyond the fact that boredom weighs

upon the whole place. I see my warm room, with its colored light and shadow, filled with living plants and stuffed animals ... [T]his is my room, abandoned, plundered, in disarray. (22)

The curator's and the architect's rooms are identical but could not be coded more differently – both the space and the practices of the architect are coded negatively in double registers of meaning. His room is naked, cold, and empty, just as 'byggnadsritningar' (house drawings [sic]; architectural/technical drawings) are empty representations, not real 'houses.' Filled with light, the room is simultaneously unsheltered and lacking in original creativity ('boredom'); it is 'plundered' and 'in disarray.' The architect's room is like a distorted mirror image of the speaker's own study. This image ties in with several other references to visual distortion – the curator can see the growing apartment building only through a mirror on the wall of his bedroom, while the nurse's sign of a red cross on a white background confuses him and makes him think of the Swiss flag (white cross on a red background). The cold rationality implied in the architect's space and practice contrasts with the curator's study, filled with oxymoronic 'levande föremål' (living objects). For the curator, representations of architecture appear so abstract that they are empty of meaning, while he himself constantly refers to the production of emotions and experiences generated by built environments, and particularly by residential buildings.

The experience with the architect's apartment is in *The Roofing Ceremony* tied to literary representation that turns the tables on a reflection theory in which experiences with certain forms of locations have an impact on the person who has experienced them. Though the architect's portait is 'vardagligt' (23) ([characterized by] ordinariness [22]) and that of his wife is anonymous, 'en grisaille-varelse' (a study in grey [22]), the curator asks whether his experience of their apartment has changed not himself, but *them*: 'Motsvarade dessa människor mina föreställningar, eller hade jag diktat om dem till oigenkännlighet? Man gör ju homunkler av de människor man icke känner, och de man känner bli spöken' (26) (Did these people match my images of them, or had my imagination [had I literarily recreated them] made them unrecognizable? One makes homunculi of the people one doesn't know, and those one knows become ghosts [26]). The confrontation with the process and site where buildings are first conceived, which comprises the work of an architect, transforms the curator's image of his own site of literary creativity; the experience turns characters from anonymous grey visages to ones with personal stories. Compared with what he perceives to be the architect's lonely and dreaded place, his own apartment – inhabited only by himself and decorated with inanimate objects – turns around paradoxically to become a place of organic growth – 'fyllt av levande växter' (filled with living plants). Yet his study also serves as the site of reversal of this organic process by which exteriority becomes incorporated into interiority, exemplified by the cherished 'uppstoppade djur' (stuffed animals).

The location of narration – the curator's bedroom – and the domestic setting of the number of flashback stories he tells in extended first-person monologues are intrinsically connected in *The Roofing Ceremony*. These connections also tie the architecture of domestic life to novelistic forms of narration. In a related argument about genre expectations and Henry James's novelistic techniques, Elizabeth Boyle Machlan argues that James creates 'a literary phenomenology that reveals the centrality of architectural metaphors to human understanding, and the ways in which genre not merely categorizes, but helps interpret, experiences' (395). *The Roofing Ceremony* similarly posits that the conceit of first-person unmediated thought narration depends on architecture and functions as an attempt, extrapolating on Machlan's argument, also to take seriously 'genre's taxonomic purposes as inseparable from, instead of at odds with, its hermeneutic functions' (395). *The Roofing Ceremony* seeks to relay the function of particular locations – in this case standardized, seemingly identical, apartment dwellings – as a way to produce an unmediated interior monologue that is inseparable from its setting.

The curator's recollection of his architect neighbour's apartment is also coded in other ways, which indicate how architecture mediates between literary representation and its own cultural function. The natural light and naked, geometrical, and abstract features of the neighbour's apartment seem to indicate that the curator's neighbour is an architect of the modern continental European school, whose new directions – anti-ornamental, functional, ordered, pragmatic – had been clearly delineated by Otto Wagner in his treatise *Modern Architecture* (1896), published shortly after his inaugural lecture as a professor in Vienna. For Wagner and his followers around Europe, new architecture was meant to 'represent our modernity, our capabilities, and our actions through forms created by ourselves,' particularly in metropolitan aggregates (cited in Frisby 3). The curator's apartment, on the other hand, reflects mid-nineteenth-century bourgeois decorative ideals of domestic design, in which nature is domesticated and interiorized in the form of potted plants and stuffed wild animals, and a harsh reality is blocked by heavy dark curtains. The speaker interprets both the architect neighbour and his drawings as generic and old-fashioned, however: 'Ser på hans tidningar, vars andas barn han är, att han lever omkring 1840, icke haft kraft att växa; ser på hans ritningar att han stannat vid 1860' (23) (I see now by his magazines with whose spirit he is kindred, that he is living around 1840, not having had the strength to grow; see by his drawings that he has stopped at 1860 [22]). The curator ascribes plenty of importance to dwelling spaces, and *The Roofing Ceremony* depends on the apartment for its narrative configuration, but the ideals of modernist architecture are neither recognized nor appreciated.

For Wagner, new architecture was not to be nostalgically historicist, but had a social role to fill that was pragmatic and which could let the practical function of the metropolis be visible to its inhabitants, for whom architecture was to be 'intelligble, and by implication legible' (Frisby 18). His Viennese apartment buildings shun stucco decorations for flat facades; his *Postsparkasse* building uses required aluminium bolting as ornaments. Structure and form conjoin in Wagner's buildings, as narrative structure and setting conjoin in *The Roofing Ceremony*. Assumptions that underscored metaphorical connections between architecture and legibility, and between architecture and narrative, were part of the conception of residential architecture for modernist architects at the time. *The Roofing Ceremony* appears to address directly the fact that domesticity, and by implication domestic space, has been shunned in a tradition of aesthetic modernism that emphasizes speed and movement (Thacker; Kern) or the *avant-garde* (a military term), in which 'being undomestic came to serve as a guarantee of being art' (Reed 7). In *Modernism and the Architecture of Private Life*, Victoria Rosner argues instead that in English high modernism, 'spaces of private life are a generative site for literary modernism,' since, in fact, the 'modernist novel draws a conceptual vocabulary from the lexicons of domestic architecture and interior design, elaborating a notion of psychic interiority, to take one example, that rests on specific ideas about architectural interiors' (2). In *The Roofing Ceremony*, the apartment is such a generative site, since the narrative shifts the framework away from a presumed marginality of certain settings, such as a standardized middle-class apartment in turn-of-the-century Stockholm, into a specific condition for experiments with interiority conceits – the pretence of direct and unmediated thought transfer in novelistic form.

Wagner's designs for Vienna contrast with the contemporary Arts and Crafts-related, neo-Romantic (*nationalromantisk*) building design in

Stockholm. Gradually continental architectural ideals began to take hold in Sweden, especially as Stockholm faced a residential construction boom during the rapid expansion of the Östermalm borough – where Strindberg lived and wrote *The Roofing Ceremony* – during the first decade of the twentieth century (cf. Eva Eriksson 172, 308, 426–30). During the period from 1890 to 1915, Stockholm's population grew by 60 per cent, from 245,000 to 392,400, and housing shortages were severe (Eva Eriksson 426; Ingemar Johansson 310–15; see also Pred, *Recognizing European Modernities* 55–95). This puts into relief the class-marked, if not elitist, aspects of the curator's extended descriptions of the pleasure of dwelling in a new, spacious, light-filled, and clean apartment. His reclusive solitude, as he lies dying alone without visits from friends, his son, or former wife, stands in contrast to the crowded and dismal living arrangements of the urban poor, but forms a necessary backdrop to the text's interiority conceit. The conceit of unmediated thought transfer in an extended monologue, directed to a figure on the wall paper, is also part of the ideology of modernist narration – that supreme, exclusive, even elitist subjectivity is conveyed through narration.

That critics have continued to overlook the intriguing aspect of *The Roofing Ceremony*'s interest in domestic architecture seems aligned with a predominant drive in scholarship about Strindberg's prose that emphasizes identity formation and constructions of selfhood and subjectivity, along the lines of biographically influenced scholarship. The novel, however, demonstrates conceptions about the function of architecture that ties it to later European literary modernism. The most obvious way in which it does so is by refusing any other diegetic setting than the modern apartment itself. The minute section in which the plot leaves the apartment deserves closer scrutiny in this respect: 'Den sjuke fördes till lasarettet i en vagn, öppnades och undersöktes, syddes igen och fördes tillbaka' (44) (The patient was brought to the hospital in a wagon, was opened and examined, sewn up again, and brought home [55]). The passage indicates that once outside the apartment, there is no access to the curator's thoughts. As a literary construction, he does not exist outside his setting. After the operation, the speed of retelling and the disparate content of the curator's recollections increase, moving from coherent reminiscing about a summertime stay at a house in the archipelago, to dissociated fragmented speech covering topics from disease, bacteria, chemical compounds, literature, personal relationships, and musical composition. The curator's operation and impending death triggers an exteriorization process that not only marginalizes spatial description, but also bars pretence at psychological coherence. While the curator is screaming in pain, propped up in bed not to drown from the fluid collected in his chest, the body's materiality takes over to the extent that 'hans eget jag upplöstes' (61) (his own personality was dissolved [72]) (cf. Olsson, *Jag blir galen* 277). At the moment of death, the building opposite the curator's is completed, while the curator's imagination, unfettered by a body in pain, leaves the constraints of the apartment for dreams of pristine green meadows, sunshine, and blue water. At the moment of death, setting has come full circle – from enclosure in the bedroom in the narrative's first sentence to a fantasy of freedom outside the modern urban environment in the last; from realistic spatial descriptions that contain a fear of losing control, to hallucinations of the pastoral dissociated from the modern apartment.

Scholars have recognized that *The Roofing Ceremony* offers a break from the more conventional approaches of Strindberg's narrative techniques, but generally overlook the static setting as critical to this construction. Some argue that the novel 'can be counted among the precursors to newer novelistic techniques' (Brandell cited in Ståhle Sjönell, 'Kommentarer' 168, my trans.), that it foreshadows the method 'Joyce used in the triumphant ending of *Ulysses*' (Lagercrantz 330), and that because of the prominent first-person 'I' form, the novella can be considered as an originator of the stream of consciousness technique (Perelli 143). *The Roofing Ceremony* is not an interior monologue, however. Although the vast majority of text is construed in the protagonist's first-person speech as monologues, these are inserted within a frame. This frame also contains dialogue and third-person narrative commentary.[1]

It is instead the interplay between an attempt at first-person unmediated narration, modernism's interiority conceit, and the setting that allows for *The Roofing Ceremony*'s self-reflexive and experimental status. The apartment is not an empty container waiting to be filled with narrative meaning in *The Roofing Ceremony*. Rather, the setting signals

---

1 Another group of critics argues that *The Roofing Ceremony* is not quite experimental enough to qualify as an illusion of a 'flow of consciousness' (Johannesson, *The Novels* 246) and that the epic components of the novella prevent such readings, since the third-person frame and extended monologue operate in a dialectic relationship that structures both form and content (Tjäder, 'Det växande huset' 31–2). Most critics agree, though, that *The Roofing Ceremony* is a modernist work, primarily because of the unusual narrative complexity that leaves questions unanswered and riddles unsolved (cf. Boëthius, 'Gröna ögat' 49; Jacobs).

the text's spatial complexity in ways that challenge boundaries of architecture, narrative form, and geography in transnational modernism by showing exactly how constructions of setting in and of themselves are mediated. Moreover, we cannot understand *The Roofing Ceremony*'s interest in conceiving a strategy, and formulating a range of tropes (like those of audio recording and playback technology) to relay the disordered and irrational thoughts of a dying and drugged person, without realizing that the premise for this attempt is conventional, prosaic, domestic space: a middle-class Stockholm apartment.

2 The Grafophone

Dying necessitates storytelling in *The Roofing Ceremony*. While memories spill out in the monologue sections, the third-person frame draws on the trope of audio-recording technology to contain the stories. Although domestic architecture may appear to house the mind as represented by the novel's first-person narration, the grafophone, a popular turn-of-the-century mechanical recording and playback device, is explicitly evoked as a construction used to instrumentalize the text's interiority conceit. Featuring a cylinder container, the grafophone is both a playback 'talking machine' and a device whose inscription stylus 'writes the voice' of the recorded. As the dying curator seeks to speak his mind in an attempted re(p)lay of unmediated interiority, he becomes coded (by the third-person frame) as such a mechanical playback device. He is presented in the first paragraph as 'talande ut varje uppkommen föreställning' (9) (speaking aloud every image that arose [3]), while metaphors of recording, repetition, and transmission of memories attach to the curator's speech, as if he were a grafophone incapable of stopping the cylinder from rolling and words from emerging. Later 'började den sjuke att spela opp igen likt grafofonen utan spärrhake' (18) (the patient began again to play, like a grafophone that lacked a stop [15]). Toward the end, the curator is completely mechanized: 'När han vaknade började åter rullen i hjärnfonografen att gå; gav ifrån sig alla sista minnen och intryck, men i sträng ordning alldeles så som de blivit "inspelade"' (48) (When he awoke, the cylinder in his brain-phonograph began again to turn; it gave out all the latest memories and impressions, but in exact order, just as they had been 'recorded' [55]), while the monologues seem to be produced by the technological device itself: 'Nu släppte hakarne ... så att monologen återtog sin fart' (59) (Now the hooks loosened ... so that the monologue picked up speed again [70]). The curator's stories are produced by the grafophone, while contained in an apartment.

The actual recording technology repeatedly invoked in *The Roofing Ceremony* is most likely a cylinder-shaped device. This kind of recording and replaying device, increasingly called a grafophone, was the most popular in Europe until around 1908. Several different versions were invented and manufactured in Europe and the United States and the name, brand, and technology distinctions are almost impossible to trace completely (see Read and Welch, Gelett, and Kjellgren).[2] *The Roofing Ceremony's* terminology reflects this confusion – most often called 'grafophone,' it is nevertheless referred to once as a 'phonograph' (48 [55]). Numerous examples of early reports on the grafophone assign agency to the device, rather than to the human voice it recorded. An 1878 article in *Harper's Bazaar* posits that the 'phonograph never speaks until it has first been spoken to ... It has no original ideas to advance ... The phonograph only consents to astonish the world at the instance of some dominant and controlling mind' (Read and Welch 22; Jewell 8–9). At the end of *The Roofing Ceremony*, the curator remains in his bed, and having gone without food or drink for forty-eight hours, approaches the stage of an automaton with words streaming out of him.

In the novel, seemingly unrelated metaphors increasingly take on the shape of a cylinder or a disc-shaped recording device, so that the trope of the grafophone influences the figurative language in multiple registers. 'Hjärnan gick som tomma kvarnstenar, kastade gnistor som ville den ta eld' (54) (his brain spun around like empty millstones, throwing off sparks as though it was going to catch fire [63]); this trope remains at the end, when the curator is described as suffering from an uncontrollable need to play back his memories: 'han yrar ju; det är som att ta ur en propp ur sodaflaskan' (53) ([he] is babbling; it's like taking the cork out of a soda bottle [61]). In one of the last descriptions, just before dying, the third-person narrator frames the curator as interiorized, just

---

2 Other sources mention various technical differences between these three terms. For Jewell, the difference between the phonograph and the grafophone is in the composition of the cylinder (13); for Read and Welch, the early grafophones were mechanically operated by the turn of a hand crank or foot pedal, while the Edison phonographs were run by electric motors (46) but after 1895 the two machines used interchangeable records (56). A gramophone was always a disc-based machine but a phonograph or grafophone was based on the cylinder until 1910–16.

like the cylinder-shaped phonograph with its recording tracks inside, and its outside blankly reflecting metal: 'Han uttalade ... millioner, millioner ord, hela hans liv flöt ut i ord ... minnet svek aldrig. De inre sinnena skärptes otroligt, allteftersom de yttre släcktes' (60) (He uttered ... millions upon millions of words, his whole life streamed out in words ... his memory never failed him. His inner senses were unbelievably sharpened as his outer senses were extinguished [71]). The speaker becomes like a cylinder containing prerecorded words. The first-person monologue, increasingly disorganized, corresponds as well to an increasing mechanization of the speaker as he approaches death. *The Roofing Ceremony*'s third-person narrative frame establishes tight connections between the grafophone as a playback device and the curator's first-person monologues. It is as if this popular recording device makes the attempt at unmediated narration of interiority understandable, as if it makes it possible formally to capture this interior narration.

Technological mediation of narration, and implicitly of human speech, is a well-known figuration of high-modernist literature; Samuel Beckett's *Krapp's Last Tape* (1958) provides a suggestive point of comparison with *The Roofing Ceremony*. Sara Danius argues in *The Senses of Modernism* that this mediation includes the ways in which 'the image of technology attaches itself to the image of death' (87). The curator's speech accelerates death in *The Roofing Ceremony*: this narrative offers no talking-cure. Mechanization drains life out of the character, whose last words come to illustrate Thomas Edison's conjecture that recording 'the last words of dying persons' would be a priority application for his invention (cited in Kittler 12). *The Roofing Ceremony*'s first-person interiority conceit is construed along these lines as well, as the incessant talking hastens the curator's death. As a structural device, the grafophone's figuration combines utterance and narrative, recording and playback, with a setting that it also domesticates: the modern, standardized, and easily reproducible apartment building.

At the time, the grafophone was quickly anthropomorphized also as a means to reproduce memories and thereby construe consciousness as a dynamic process, rather than as a passive container. Strindberg wrote at the time that 'Minnet reproducerar genom en Grafofon' (cited in Ståhle Sjönell, Diss. 'Strindbergs Taklagsöl' 48) (Memory reproduces through a grafophone [my trans.]). This formulation echoes French philosopher Jean Marie Guyau's proposition in an essay from 1880 'to define the brain as an infinitely perfected phonograph – a conscious phonograph' ('Memory and Phonograph,' quoted in Kittler 30–3; see also Hockenjos, 'Das Grauen im Speicher'; and Ståhle Sjönell, ibid. 52). Grafophones in *The Roofing Ceremony* seem to produce certain experiences of space, and of creating memories seemingly of their own accord. Simple inexpensive portable grafophones were common when Strindberg wrote *The Roofing Ceremony* and the very reproducibility of the device is important, as it functions both as topic and formal figuration for the curator's first extended monologue: 'Jo, jag hade köpt en liten grafofon för tio kronor åt min gosse till hans födelsedag' (9) (Yes, I had bought a little grafophone for ten crowns, for my boy's fourth birthday [3]). The explicit reference to spoken language, 'Jo' (Yes), marks a linguistic connection between a spoken word and its subsequent recording. The device is first introduced as a triviality in the text, as a toy for a young child, but when the curator listens to it, the recording appears distorted. The intrusion of a loud recorded voice into his 'ensamma våning' (lonely apartment) creates a 'fasans intryck ... infernaliskt' (9, 10) (a dreadful [ghastly] impression ... devilish [10]). The voice in *The Roofing Ceremony*'s first grafophone scene is coded as haunted, as a decorporealized aural spectre that both prefigures and eventually produces the curator as a babbling, dying, mechanized shell of a human being.

Connections between the phonograph and childhood (as indicative of a temporal regression or of retraction to a naive or authentic state) are an important part of its history and indicate the sense of spatio-temporal annihilation associated with the device. The first thing ever recorded and reproduced on Edison's phonograph was the nursery rhyme 'Mary Had a Little Lamb' (Schwartzman 10). Strindberg also associated Edison's invention with children – he described it in a prose fragment as a toy: 'Edison ej gjort guld, endast en dålig leksak: fonografen' (cited in Hockenjos, 'Das Grauen' 127) (Edison has not made gold, only a bad toy: the phonograph [my trans.]). Strindberg's objection to the fonograph/grafophone as a 'bad toy' indicates its function in *The Roofing Ceremony*; it is a device that threatens to deconstruct boundaries not only between humans and machines, but also between literary innovation and convention, and between a world an individual imagines as private and one that threatens to impose itself on it it (for a related argument about the function of telephones in Strindberg's late writing, see Ulf Olsson, *Invändningar* 65–6).

In *The Roofing Ceremony*, the grafophone and the apartment setting are figured as permeable containers that make the problems of modernism's interiority conceit tangible. *The Roofing Ceremony* uses the grafophone as both a metaphor and a device intrinsic to its apartment setting, which helps contextualize modernism's interest in recording technology. In a Swedish brochure from 1901, published by a distributor of Edison's phonographs and Columbia's grafophones, the device is described as having four primary uses. These correlate thematically and structurally with the device's function and role in *The Roofing Ceremony*. The brochure describes the phonograph first as an entertainment device for home or domestic use, as a way to listen both to prerecorded songs and to record the beloved voices of family and close friends for eternal preservation. The second description presents it as a concert device for a public performance, the third as an office stenographer that copies accurately and tirelessly, and the fourth as an early form of jukebox for use in a public setting, promising an excellent 'return on investment' (Numa Petersons Handels & and Fabriks-Aktiebolag).

In a pragmatic sense, grafophones helped mediate domestic space by bringing into a supposed private sphere the recorded voices of others, so that a public form of entertainment became interiorized within the architecture of private life. Recorded songs and novelty acts popular in Sweden at the time were often imported and recorded in other languages, particularly English and German, and so this particular form of entertainment related to popular culture trends outside the boundaries both of a domestic space and of Sweden. Simultaneously, the grafophone is a spectacularly delocalized invention. Competing near-identical versions were developed simultaneously in the United States and in Europe, with recordings not sold according to national origin or national language. Discourse about the device is remarkably similar whether conceived in America, France, Germany, or Sweden. These facets are thematically incorporated in the *The Roofing Ceremony*. The first flashback monologue explicitly connects apartment living with figurations of disembodiment and displacement, including references to the curator's impending death and figurations of danger and ghostly presences that haunt his wife's apartment.

The Roofing Ceremony introduces this mechanical device as a mediator of the traumas of domestic space – such as divorce or the discontinuation of parental-child relationships. These traumas spill over to the text's metaphorical registers. Not only does the curator's wife's apartment seem inhabited by the spectre of divorce, but the descriptions of their interactions echo the form and function of a grafophone repetitiously playing the same tune. A scene of marital discord seems to have 'upprepats sextio gånger' (10) ([been] (repeated sixty times [5]). Similarly, 'måste tystnaden brytas, och frun i huset tog upp sina klago-visor, på välkända melodier och med text som icke var ny' (11) (the silence had to be broken and the lady of the house took up her lament, to familiar tunes and with lyrics not new [6]). Later, the protagonist describes how he rents a small summerhouse for his family in the archipelago, but it is a 'spökhus' (31) (a haunted house [33]). The curator describes how the ghost appears to have an uncanny relationship to a brother he has not maintained any contact with, but upon whose yacht a 'kolossal grafofon spelade upp' (35) (colossal grafophone started playing [38]). An image of a grafophone on the deck of a small sailing vessel is featured in the Numa Peterson catalogue of grafophones, which signals the device's portability also between different registers of textual production – from an advertising catalogue to this novel's attempts to bridge the haunting of the past with a technological device.

Through the figuration of the grafophone, sound waves appear to transcend boundaries between different dwelling spaces – the apartment and the summerhouse – in a way that signals its close connection to functions of setting. Ghosts (a black lady and her companion) appear at the summerhouse, while scenes, marriages, and relationships (including finding anew a long-lost brother) repeat as if they were prerecorded according to a script. Similarly, the curator hears 'grafofonens repertoar' (20) (the grafophone's repertoire [18]) in the apartment below, as if it were replaying a recording of his own failed marriage. The architect's wife is like a grafophone with only a limited number of tunes; her playing has stagnated into a set number of prerecorded performances: she 'sitter då ensam och spelar sin begränsade repertoar' (22) (is sitting alone and playing her limited repertoire [21]). Critics have remarked on The Roofing Ceremony's interest in the grafophone, but tend to relate it to the psychology of the main character (Johannesson, The Novels 250–1; Olsson, Jag blir galen 274–7). Its connections to the architecture of private life, or the ways its specific transnational qualities bridge the customary divide between public and private, have been overlooked.

The grafophone and the architecture of private life are thus intimately connected in The Roofing Ceremony, since both are figured as premises for experiments in narration. Both include aspects of repetition as well – the curator's recollections and reminiscing repeat, as he returns again and again to retell stories only with slight variations, just as his apartment building is replicated by the construction of another one.

The apartment and the grafophone figure both as inanimate containers and mediated settings, which allow for the narrative experimentation in *The Roofing Ceremony*.

3 The Colonial Apartment and Transnational Literary Modernism

The Roofing Ceremony's third-person frame allows for an eerie 'playback' of the dying curator's first-person monologues. While introspective in its emphasis on dwelling spaces and recording devices (as containers and mediators of consciousness), *The Roofing Ceremony* also gestures outward from its own conceits, particularly toward a late nineteenth-century culture of colonial exploration. These aspects relate to modernist literary representation of world travel, and specifically to contemporary constructions of a white European man's Congo. In this section, I discuss how *The Roofing Ceremony* reflects the prominent Swedish presence in the Belgian Congo Free State around 1900, as this aligns the narrative closely with contemporary Scandinavian colonial and ethnographic discourse, as well as with Joseph Conrad's short novel *Heart of Darkness* (1899, first published in book form in 1902).

Transnational travel, Africa, and Congo are immediately juxtaposed with the stationary apartment setting of *The Roofing Ceremony*. The curator's first monologue includes references to his 'Kongovistelse' (12) (stay in Congo [7]), which is reffirmed in the third-person frame. When the nurse studies his face, for example, she sees 'spår av Afrika' (13) (trace[s] of Africa [9]) and perceives his strong jaws to illustrate, in typical colonial rhetoric, 'den starke mannens okänslighet för egna och således också för andras lidanden' (13) (the strong man's indifference to his own, and thus to others', suffering [9]). Further described as a hunter, fisherman, sportsman, Africa-traveller, and seaman (13 [9]), the third-person narrator affirms that the curator's reputation as a trophy hunter of humans in Africa, where he used to 'samla hjärnor' (28) (collect their brains [28]), has followed him back to Stockholm. The source of his enmity with the man in the apartment building opposite his own, called 'gröna ögat' (28) (Green-Eye [28]), is a business venture gone sour during their stay in 'Kongostaten' (28) (the Congo State [28]). Perhaps, the curator speculates, the Green Eye, whose Congo flag he sees from his bedroom, orchestrated the accident that caused a horse to kick him unconscious (28 [30]). Congo is present in the apartment, as the curator's speech brings up the location and the third-person frame affirms its importance.

The connections between the curator and Congo are manifest as connected explicitly with apartment dwelling in Stockholm; this is where the curator and his fellow Congo traveller are ending their days. The curator in *The Roofing Ceremony* has decorated his apartment with ethnographic objects, collected from his world travels. One striking passage intertwines his apartment and Africa explicitly. A lion's skin is placed as a centerpiece of the protagonist's parlour, right in the centre of the apartment's big room. 'På salsgolvet låg min lejonhud, jag hade själv skjutit djuret; denna begagnade vi förr som gräsmatta' (17) (On the floor of the room lay my lion pelt, an animal I had shot myself; this, we had formerly used as our lawn [14]). Described as a 'trofé' (17) (trophy) (14), the lion's skin complements the curator's prized stuffed animals. The remnants of a wild feline are domesticated and incorporated into the bourgeois apartment's interior, just as Africa becomes a manicured front lawn outside a generic Stockholm apartment in a reversal of colonialism's geography.

Drifting into drugged semi-consciousness, the curator's monologues address more and more directly the transgressions involved in his presence there. Having at first accepted as complimentary Stockholm rumours about his being a human trophy hunter as 'snobbigt, urstyvt' (53) (chic and very clever [62]), his remarks indicate that colonial exploration and exploitation in turn-of-the-century Swedish scientific and academic culture still held quite a bit of cachet – the curator is, after all, imagining himself as speaking to a museum director. After a new shot of morphine, however, traumatic memories emerge from 'det där med Kongo! Jag har aldrig jagat mänskor, fastän jag samlat hjärnor' (53) (that Congo business. I have never hunted men, though I have collected brains [62]). But the curator is dying alone, likened to an automaton-mannequin, and functioning like a recording device that repeats the discourse of colonial rhetoric but lacks any agency, as he remains immobile in his bedroom.

The multiple references to Africa relate *The Roofing Ceremony* to Sweden's long-standing involvement in Congo from the early 1880s onward, including representations in Swedish publications and ethnographic exhibitions. It also indicates, however, what appears to be the first-person speaker's unease with images of Africa current in Sweden. 'Congo' was a term widely used in Sweden at the time, but as a geographical delimitation it referred primarily to parts of what became in 1885 L'État Indépendant du Congo, the personal property of King Leopold II of Belgium. Roughly translated as the Congo Free

State, the region remained under King Leopold's supreme and tyrannical rule until 1908. The establishment of this state in Bismarck's international conference in 1884 was not a national colonial project, but was framed officially in Sweden and elsewhere in Europe as an international civilization project, through which it was 'alla civiliserade staters plikt och möjlighet att motarbeta arabernas slavhandel, sprida kristendom och höja utvecklingsnivån' (cited in Reinius Gustafsson 11; cf. Hochshild) (the duty and possibility of all civilized nations to fight the Arab slave trade, evangelize, and increase progress [my trans.]). The atrocities committed in the Congo Free State have been well documented. Swedes and Scandinavians began playing significant roles in Congo in the early 1880s, when Sweden, still governing Norway in a union until 1905, had no other colonies, nor any official colonial involvement in Congo. Nevertheless, at the end of the nineteenth century, Scandinavians were the third largest group present in Congo after Belgians and Italians (Reinius Gustafsson 11).[3]

Swedes in Congo generally belonged to one of four groups. The first comprised seamen, skippers, or administrators on the Congo River or in settlements; the second evangelical or Baptist missionaries; the third officers in King Leopold of Belgium's army; and the fourth, explorers in service of the 'scientific' expeditions that charted the last blank spots on the map of Africa. The two first groups were the largest. Skippers and seamen from the Scandinavian countries were so prominent on the river, sought after for dependability and expertise, that they were described in 1905 as the group of people that had made the Belgian conquest of Congo possible (Jenssen-Tusch 184). The captain on board the first ship that takes Marlow up the Congo River in *Heart of Darkness* is indeed only called 'the Swede' (14), which represents his anonymity – as one of many working the river, a witness of and complicit in the colonial exploitation. This Swede is one of the first to voice a critical opinion in Conrad's novel. With 'considerable bitterness,' the Swede complains about the '[f]ine lot, these government chaps' (14). That

---

3 For a general introduction to the Belgian involvement in Congo and the Congo Free State, see Hochschild *King Leopold's Ghosts*. For information in English about the Swedish and Scandinavian involvement in central Africa around 1900, see Kajsa Ekholm Friedman, *Catastrophe and Creation*, and for a more personal account, Sven Lindvist, *'Exterminate All the Brutes'* 11–30. Recent relevant secondary sources in Swedish include Axelsson, Reinius Gustafson, Tygesen and Waehle, and Tell.

Conrad describes this Swedish skipper as critical of the Belgian rule probably has less to do with any particular Swedish individual in the river business on the Congo, and more to do with the Swedish evangelical missionary E.V. Sjöblom, who in 1896–7 had written in English several highly critical eye-witness reports about the atrocities committed in Congo in the name of 'civilization.' In the essay 'Startling News from the Dark Congo,' published in the United States and in Britain, as well as in letters, reports, and memoirs, Sjöblom referred extensively to the inhuman conditions of the rubber extraction industry and the violations committed by Belgian forces in the Congolese-Arab war in 1891–4. Sjöblom spoke at the Aborigines' Protection Society in London in May of 1897, an event covered in the British press and followed by an editorial in The Times (Axelsson 224–7; cf. Lindqvist 18, 27). Although Conrad had personal experience of Congo from his tour in 1890, his descriptions of violence, butchering, and cannibalism were most likely influenced by subsequent reports, like those of Sjöblom, which claimed in the British press that the atrocities were less indicative of native Congolese practices than those of their oppressors who meant to intimidate them (Brantlinger 280–1). That Kurtz-figures – renegade European warlords – were a prominent figuration of the Western presence in Congo is supported by The Roofing Ceremony's casual description of the curator as a grim-faced hunter of brains. It is unlikely that Strindberg, by the time he wrote The Roofing Ceremony in early 1906, had read Conrad's Heart of Darkness, published in book form in 1902 and only translated into Swedish in 1949. Instead, the novella's explicit figuration of a Swedish presence in Congo most likely had other roots.

Swedish seamen and missionaries were not the only prominent foreign group in the Congo state. Swedish officers participated either directly or indirectly in King Leopold's project, often invited to do so by the Belgian consul von Schwerin in Stockholm, a member of the Swedish nobility. In 1883–6, four officers travelled through Congo in close association with the Belgian army, as described in the two-volume extensive collection of notes called Three Years in Congo (Tre år i Kongo) (Möller et al), published in 1887. At the height of the Congolese-Arab war, during which many of the accusations of cannibalism, violence, butchering, and inhuman conditions began to spread more widely in Europe, the Swedish officer Axel Svinhufvud signed up to serve a three-year terme in King Leopold's official army, 'La Force Publique.' In his memoirs, Svinhufvud describes how he led battles against villagers in Congo's southeastern jungles, but denies any allegations that the

Belgian army behaved in any way cruelly toward the Congolese population. Yet one evening several of his own troops bring him a sack 'ur vilket rullade inte mindre än sju avhuggna huvuden. Även många andra sådana exempel skulle jag kunna berätta, men jag avstår härifrån' (174) (out of which rolled no less than seven decapitated heads. I could tell stories about many other related examples, but I refrain from doing so here [my trans.]). Not objecting to practices like these, Svinhufvud receives in 1897 L'ordre Royal du Lion, the Congo State's highest medal, as well as official recognition by the Swedish king (Svinhufvud 254).

Sweden's and Scandinavia's connections to Congo ran along multiple social, cultural, and geographical lines – from the royal family and nobility, to military officers, maritime working classes, and the mostly rural missionaries who had been sent from provincial congregations to Congo. As in Conrad's *Heart of Darkness*, fantasies of domination, as well as actual mercenary exploitation and violent subjugation, become near synonymous with Congo exploration in *The Roofing Ceremony*. The transnational literary modernism that is part of *The Roofing Ceremony*'s conceptions of literary setting, its tension between domestic architecture and Congo, for example, also relates to the specific literary forms we have come to associate with the modernist representation of the colonial experience in *Heart of Darkness*. The two narratives share structural similarities that relate explicitly to the first-person conceit of unmediated interiority. The basic set-up shares some similarities, with extended monologues contained in a narrative frame. In *Heart of Darkness*, the frame is a first-person account rather than *The Roofing Ceremony*'s third-person narrator. Marlow is presented as cogently addressing a group of four listeners, whereas the curator in *The Roofing Ceremony* ostensibly tells his story under the influence of morphine to an imaginary interlocutor. Performative metaphors are embedded in the respective texts, in the sense that the curator describes how he reacts to accusations that he had been a cannibal in Congo and that this became a part he felt obligated to play, a role he had to perform, just as Kurtz appears to be performing, with some self-reflection, the part of a white explorer gone mad, in which his final words 'the horror,' are uttered as much to himself as to Marlow. Similarly, the curator, like Kurtz, is a writer – he describes how he might have 'diktat om' (26) (literarily reconstructed [my literal trans.]) his downstairs's neighbours; Kurtz has written an account of his experiences that seems to have transformed the image of himself into a mouth-piece for a ruthless colonial project that legitimizes exploitation. The main character of *The Roofing Ceremony* is ambiguous also in terms of identification, which is exactly how *Heart of Darkness* has been perceived (ref Brantlinger). As a figure, the curator is both Kurtz (collector of brains) and Marlow (a witness who retells his innocence), while his self-image is ultimately deconstructed at the end of the novella.

The Roofing Ceremony's deliberate juxtaposition of the apartment in Stockholm and the curator's Congo experiences illustrates transnational European phenomena that also associate Congo with a highly specific form of exoticization. That form involves the ethnographic collections brought back to Scandinavia from Congo. The officer Svinhufvud describes in his memoirs with pride how his 'stora vackra samling etnografiska föremål' (250) (large beautiful collection of ethnographic objects [my trans.]) has survived intact the five-month ocean passage; the curator of *The Roofing Ceremony* cherishes his lion skin and his reputation as a trophy hunter. Bringing back ethnographic collections from Congo to Scandinavia was a well-established and legitimate practice at the time. Since 1880, 400 individual collections and nearly 40,000 objects have been received or accepted by Scandinavian ethnographic museums; in total probably around 50,000–60,000 objects have come from Congo to the North (Tygesen and Waehle 8). *The Roofing Ceremony* is in fact closely aligned with this practice. The main character's title is curator, and he speaks at length to his friend the museum director, whom he imagines present in the room. These terms relate to a specific scientific culture in Stockholm at the end of the nineteenth century, during a period when geographical exploration and the ethnographic preservation of objects collected around the world gained increasing public presence (cf. Ljungström).

The long-standing Scandinavian engagement in Congo came into widespread public awareness for the first time in the summer of 1907, during a four-month exhibit called 'Etnografiska missionsutställningen' (The Ethnographic Missionary Exhibit) held at the Royal Academy of Science in Stockholm and sponsored by the National Museum of Natural History. The exhibit included more than 10,000 objects from around the world, but the primary emphasis was on objects collected by Swedish missionaries in Congo (Reinius Gustafsson 10). The young explorer and scientist Erland Nordenskiöld, head of the ethnographic division of the Natural History Museum, had begun encouraging the two largest Swedish missionary groups in 1905 to think actively about ethnographic representation of foreign cultures in Sweden and to bring back objects that could form the basis of an independent ethnographic museum in Sweden (Reinius Gustafsson 7). The exhibit coincided with the first publication in Swedish of Sjöblom's memoirs from his experiences during the Congolese-Arab war, the missionary K.A. Laman's extensive description of the Congolese language and life, and a collection of descriptions of Congolese stories, tales, and linguistic features edited by Nordenskiöld. Nordenskiöld explains in the preface to this collection that missionaries, in fact, were uniquely qualified to understand and describe foreign cultures, since they in most cases had a better understanding than the visiting scientific explorer.

With these projects, Nordenskiöld attempted to bridge the wide gap in Swedish culture regarding Congo, in which official Sweden (including the king as the primary sponsor of the Royal Academy of Science), academics, explorers, and military officers were often critical of missionary activities and regarded the popular culture of the missions with a great deal of suspicion (Axelsson 215). In the Swedish establishment, there were strong proponents of the white colonial masculinity project of mercenary exploitation, whether in the form of scientific exploration or military careers. Encouraging active participation of missionary culture in a national exhibit was thus controversial, not least because official Sweden for so long had neglected to acknowledge the transgressions of the Belgian regime. The curator of *The Roofing Ceremony* must be understood as part of, or at least desiring to be part of, this official conservative movement. He self-identifies with the legacy of the 'courageous' explorer who takes pride in accusations of being a trophy hunter of human brains, and for whom a stay in Congo was to be understood as a means to both monetary compensation and an academic career. This career does not materialize for the curator in *The Roofing Ceremony*; he explains this failure as caused by his violation of decorum in the academic hierarchy, rather than as a result of questionable practices in Congo.

Strindberg wrote *The Roofing Ceremony* during the period January to March 1906 and the novella was first published in instalments in the popular weekly magazine *Hvar 8:e dag* during the summer of 1906; in book form, the work was published at the end of 1907. Any direct influence from the ethnographic exhibit in 1907 is thus ahistorical. As contemporary events, the exhibit and the novella – aimed in its instalment version for a broad and popular audience – align to show the conflicted status of colonial representation in Sweden, however. Reports about the Belgian violations were prominent in the European press by then, and international public opinion against King Leopold's venture had become so strong in 1908 that he was forced to relinquish his personal control of Congo to the Belgian government. As the publication of *Heart of Darkness* in book form in 1902 shows, Congo had a strong transnational presence as the source of both fantasies and fears of white colonial rule in Africa. In 1902, Harald Jenssen-Tusch, the brother of a Danish military officer killed in Congo, began publishing his periodical *Scandinavians in Congo* (*Skandinaver i Kongo*) at the prestigious Gyldendals press in Copenhagen. Thirty-three issues were published in Sweden, Norway, and Denmark until 1904, when they were collected in two large volumes and published in book form in January 1905. The publication, Jenssen-Tusch writes, is dedicated to the 922 Danish, Norwegian, and Swedish men and women who since 1880 had served in Congo, and is intended to commemorate their contributions to the civilization process of Congo, as well as provide an overview of the history, practices, languages, and customs of Congo. Jensen had not himself visited Congo but draws on a number of primary sources that include interviews with former visitors, such as Svinhufvud and Ebonne Sjöblom, the missionary's wife, and the standard international sources on Congo, such as Stanley's *In Darkest Africa* (1890) and the official publications of the Belgian government in Brussels. In the addendum to the collected volume, Jenssen-Tusch affirms that any allegations that the Belgians have mistreated any Africans 'mangle fodfaeste' (are without source).

In December of 1904, *Scandinavians in Congo* was reviewed in *Ymer*, the official journal of The Swedish Association of Anthropology and Geography. Both Nordenskiöld and von Schwerin, the Belgian consul in Stockholm, were members of the board of this association; this is also exactly the kind of Stockholm-based academic association that a figure like the curator of *The Roofing Ceremony* would have desired to be a member of. The review of *Scandinavians in Congo* in *Ymer* is overwhelmingly positive. Described as objective and impartial, the reviewer lauds the work for three main reasons. First, the work fills an important public information gap, since, with the exception of small notices in the papers about individuals who have signed up to serve a *terme*, died of fever, or had been devoured by a crocodile or 'en segerdrucken kannibal' (Stenfelt 412) (a victorious cannibal [my trans.]), little information about recent developments in the Congo state had previously been available. Second, the work introduces for the first time the number of people who have served in Congo without any previous official recognition, who, unlike well-known Scandinavian explorers like Sven Hedin, Fridtjof Nansen, Axel Nordenskiöld, or S.A. Andrée have only been known 'i en trängre krets av vänner' (412) (among a smaller group of friends). Third, the work allows the reader to immerse himself in the Congo experience, as if he himself were making the journey from Belgium to Central Africa: 'så spirituellt och naturtroget skildrad, att man omöjligt kan föreställa sig, att den berättas i andra hand' (413) (so imaginatively and realistically told, that one can hardly imagine that it is told in second hand; my trans.). A story of this kind is what Marlowe tells his audience in *Heart of Darkness*; the connections to a culture of exploration and of scientific missions around the world tie the review to Strindberg's geographical location at the time of writing *The Roofing Ceremony*. Nordenskiöld's interest in the ethnographic exhibition of 1907 signals an increasing awareness of the transnational as political, offering academic circles different perspectives than the exoticized colonial fantasy of Congo that also permeates the representation of the curator's experiences in *The Roofing Ceremony*.

The apartment setting in *The Roofing Ceremony* is part of an aggregate of transnational locations that tie the novella's modernist experiments in narrative technique to emergent ethnographic recording practices. In the first issue of Jenssen-Tusch's *Scandinavians in Congo*, two particular explorers are mentioned – Dr Falkenstein and Dr Nachtigal (5, 7, 8). Both were German explorers in Congo in the late 1870s, around the time of Stanley's expeditions there. 'Falkenstein' and 'Nachtigal' are in fact the titles of the grafophone recordings the curator plays, although no such actual titles of recordings have been found (Ståhle Sjönell, 'Kommentarer' 185). Like the stuffed animals and the lion's skin, these two names function as memory triggers that connect the curator's immobility in his apartment with Congo. The names also serve as historical references that transcend the fictional universe of the novella – Strindberg had likely come across them in the first issue of *Scandinavians in Congo*. Reinscribed in Strindberg's narrative as titles of grafophone recordings, the names correlate ethnographic preservation and recording techniques with modernist literary strategies. In *The Roofing Ceremony* the grafophone, as discussed above, serves as a figurative container of consciousness, memory, and a first-person narrative interiority conceit. As a technological device, the grafophone mediates the literary form with other forms of ethnographic representations that are both modernist and transnational. Around this time, the grafophone began to be used extensively for ethnographic music recordings all over the world, as Brady shows in *The Spiral Way*. Reliable and dependable, the mechanical grafophone became a standard feature also in

Swedish ethnographic expeditions in the first decades of the twentieth century (see Kjellgren 3; Boström). Although it is not entirely clear whether audio recordings were part of the exhibit in 1907, the desire to expand the ethnographic representation of foreign cultures beyond written reports or two-dimensional visuality (drawings and photographs) was clearly manifest in the exhibit's use of objects and a large model of a Congolese village for example. That desire is also an important aspect of *The Roofing Ceremony*.

The transnational gestures of *Roofing Ceremony* thus extend far beyond Strindberg's legacy as a 'Swedish' writer, or the setting as a generic apartment in 'Stockholm,' to include a wider narrative paradigm that ties Strindberg's prose composition to European prose modernism and colonialism. Incorporating to some extent the author's experiences as a transnational writer who has returned to settle permanently in the capital of his native country, *The Roofing Ceremony* becomes an important contemporary counterpart to Conrad's *Heart of Darkness*. Conrad's native language was Polish, his second language French, and through his world travels and a literary career in English, Conrad self-identified as a transnational writer. Strindberg's experimental prose is important not only in a Swedish context, but also for situating his proto-modernist prose experiment in a European context that also included the narratives, sometimes lauded to a near-mythological level, of the Scandinavian explorers who were also Strindberg's contemporaries. The main character of *The Roofing Ceremony* was once a (failed) explorer and is now a museum curator, and thereby engaged in the collecting, preserving, and classifying of artefacts, rather than in the active exploration of new locations. As such, the character conjures up the strong ethnographic and anthropological interest of late nineteenth-century Scandinavia, a movement in which Strindberg participated very extensively during the 1880s (see chapter 2 of this book, for example). The tension in *The Roofing Ceremony* between stasis and movement, between containers and actions, between recording devices and memories thus also resonates on the level of near-suppressed references to world travels, explorations, and transnational movement in the narrative. While Scandinavian explorers like Hedin and Nansen became world famous during their lifetime, and Hedin, in particular, very rich, Strindberg did not. The main character of *The Roofing Ceremony* lies immobile in his apartment, 'imprisoned,' it would seem, and soon to be buried. On the one hand, the narrative appears haunted by its colonial references, as if these are half-way buried but threatening to rise to the surface. At the same time,

The Roofing Ceremony's narrative constructions gesture toward an expansive, transnational, intertextual, and metacritical complexity. They thereby give us a different perspective on European colonialism's relation to literary modernism. They also give an alternate perspective to Strindberg's experience of a static life in Stockholm upon his return there from many years of vagabondage around Europe, but they also involve *The Roofing Ceremony*'s mediation between experimental narrative prose techniques and modern drama, which I shall examine next.

4 Genre Transitions

Strindberg's return to Stockholm in 1898 after a long period of self-imposed exile in Europe also meant a return to writing fiction. During the following decade, Strindberg had an extremely productive period and wrote many of his best-known experimental plays, such as the *Damascus* trilogy (1898–1901), *Dance of Death* I–II (1898), *A Dream Play* (1902), and the sequence of chamber plays, of which *Ghost Sonata* (1908) is the best known, as well as a series of historical plays. In the sequence of five chamber plays, four are set in modern and generic apartment buildings, and one in an older single-family house. Never geographically specified as Stockholm, that location is assumed, while the dramas also implicitly address the fact that apartment living was a general feature of European urban life by this time. In a drama fragment from 1902, Strindberg portrays a residential apartment building as a metaphor for the anonymity of human life generally, while implying that this particular setting is uniquely suited to represent modern human life: 'Så många mänskoöden samlade i detta hus, trafvade på hvarandra, der den ena familjen trampar ofvanom de andras hufvuden ... endast skilda af ett lag bjelkar och lite sågspån' (cited in Ståhle Sjönell, 'Strindbergs Taklagsöl' 185) (So many human destinies collected in this building, stacked one above the other, where one family walks on the heads of another ... separated only by beams and some wood shingles [my trans.]). The specific setting of a modern apartment building thus carries high symbolical and structural value in Strindberg's late drama.

Between *A Dream Play* and *Ghost Sonata*, Strindberg had founded in 1907 with August Falck his own theatre company in the basement of a recently constructed apartment building in central Stockholm. Its name, The Intimate Theatre, draws on Max Reinhardt's two scenes in Berlin, Kleines Theater and the Kammerspiele annex to Deutsches Theater. Both theatres clearly inspired Falck and Strindberg (Stam 265). The transnational connections that are always part of Strindberg's productions and legacy are illustrative here. Reinhardt had been greatly inspired by Strindberg's earlier plays and had staged *The Stronger* (1889) and *Crimes and Crimes* (1899) at Kleines Theater in 1902; some years later, Strindberg appears to have derived part of his inspiration for his own theatre from him. The term 'chamber play,' *Kammerspiel* in German and *kammarspel* in Swedish, has largely been understood with reference to chamber music. The title term '*Sonata*'and the supplementary titles Opus I–IV are a case in point. Strindberg also conceived of the plays as a sonata form: intimate, filled with meaning, and carefully executed (Stam 265). Yet, the word *kammar* (chamber, *Kammer*) has a spatial component, referring generally to a small room and specifically to a private bedroom. This spatial connection is implied in the name of the Intimate Theatre as well. It reflects Strindberg's interest in dramas of high psychological intensity that centre on the hidden secrets of the modern bourgeois family, to be performed by an ensemble cast whose close collaboration also reflects the intimacy of domestic family space.

The apartment setting of a play like *Ghost Sonata* and other chamber plays allows the complexity of modernist theatre practices to emerge. Performed at the Intimate Theatre, the plays' settings reflect the apartments located on the floors above, as well as those in which its audience dwells. The small scale of theatre, the psychological themes of the plays that often centre on familial conflicts, and the limited production circumstances create further intimacy. The Intimate Theatre becomes an example of how modernist theatre, as it develops on the northern margins of Europe, echoes the domestic architecture of urban middle-class life. Such an understanding of modernist art goes counter to the reception of European avant-garde aesthetics, which has taken the suppression of the domestic as a primary motivator. Dramatic and performative expression, as Moi argues in *Henrik Ibsen and the Birth of Modernism* while drawing on Puchner's seminal work, was also suppressed in the formulation of modernist aesthetic theory, in which literary modernism became understood as 'anti-theatrical,' as against theatre as both form and institution (28–30).

Through the Intimate Theatre, Strindberg could visualize and concretize the function of architecture in modernist representation, which aligns his dramatic experimentation at the time with the setting of *The Roofing Ceremony*. Strindberg expressed in a letter to his German translator Emil Schering that '*The Roofing Ceremony* is a Chamber Play, but I do not have the strength to redo it. I have the plan, but I don't have the energy to do it' (my translation cited from Ståhle Sjönell, 'Kommentarer,' *Taklagsöl* 167; see also Johannesson, *The Novels* 247–8; Lamm 465–6; and Ståhle Sjönell, 'Strindbergs Taklagsöl' 162–70). *The Roofing Ceremony*, as a highly complex narrative work in multiple layers, appears antithetical to a dramatic work in some ways, but the apartment setting makes the connections between narrative and dramatic form relevant. Strindberg does not comment explicitly on the formal aspects of tension between first-person narration and the dramatic form, but through the idea of publicizing the private, the curator's seemingly unmediated thoughts in first-person narration bridge dramatic expression with the literary representation of psychological interiority. Strindberg's later dramas focus on mediating between public and private, for which the apartment setting is a location particularly ripe with meaning. In prose form, his work at this time seeks also to publicize the private – particularly an individual's consciousness – but they do so in forms that must be construed as intimate and unmediated rather than public. This conceit, of intimacy and interiority, underlies modernism's prose construction. Seeing the base for this conceit in the theatrical first-person monologue, *The Roofing Ceremony* turns the tables on the performative interiority conceit of literary prose modernism.

In *The Roofing Ceremony*, the curator's apartment and his experiences of the architect's study help frame the first-person monologue as a mediation between a desire to formulate narration and the expression of interiority. The genre's dramatic monologue or monodrama could also be possible precursors to *The Roofing Ceremony's* experiments in narrative technique. Dramatic monologue was until the late nineteenth century most closely associated with poetry, while monodrama had been an established European dramatic form, particularly as a one-person operatic performance, since the late eighteenth century (Dwight, especially 368 and 370–82). In neither case was implied setting or formalized scenography judged to be of particular importance to the literary form of expression. As monodrama begins to evolve as a more experimental form around 1900, the representation of psychological interiority becomes a fundamental aspect (Taroff 146–52, expanding on Evreinov's well-known 1909 'An Introduction to Monodrama'). For Evreinov, plot and dramatis personae should be relayed through the subjectivity of a single character. The development of monodrama is cotemporaneous with experiments in narrative interior monologue techniques. Taroff suggests that also Conrad's *Heart of Darkness* 'might well be read as a monodrama' (152). Strindberg's play *The Stronger*

(1889), with two characters set in a continental café, has been presented as exemplary of modern monodrama and as correlating to the novelistic *monologue intérieur* (Törnqvist 145, 156). Strindberg was working on several monodramas around the time of the composition of *The Roofing Ceremony* – indeed, as Ståhle Sjönell shows, one from 1905 is called 'Huset' ('The Residential Building,' 'Strindbergs Taklagsöl' 52, 10) and shares thematic and plot aspects with the description of the downstairs neighbours' marriage in *The Roofing Ceremony*. It thus seems that Strindberg's interest in novelistic prose experimentation correlates strongly with developments around 1900 in monodrama as the retelling of one mind's experience or thoughts.

The setting of the domestic in European modernism – its architecture, objects, practices, and functions – is as mediated by modernity as any other location. Like the apartment setting that is so important for *The Roofing Ceremony*, the many references to a recording device have important precursors in Strindberg's experimental drama. The chamber plays, as I discussed above, depend to some extent both formally and thematically on tropes of musical composition, while *A Dream Play* incorporates music and song as distinctive features. In the middle section of that play, set in Fingal's Cave, performative aspects of music are also coded as stored and recorded. In the cave, shaped like an enormous shell-shaped ear, Indra's daughter channels the music and translates lyrics conveyed through this particular space. Thinking about this location as a large cylindrical storage device for sound, like a grafophone, or alternately as the conveyor of sound through the shell-like form of the grafophone's speaker may be a stretch, yet such a tentative correlation would parallel the interiority conceit of *The Roofing Ceremony*'s experimental narrative techniques as well as the anthropomorphization that the popular phonograph/grafophone technology it was originally associated with.

When figured as material sets, the importance of setting in literary representation becomes clear. It is arguably in his innovative scenography, particularly in *A Dream Play* and the chamber plays, that Strindberg helps establish the spatial forms that contain modernist drama. I would argue that this emphasis on scenography led to further experimentation with spatial formations in novelistic prose, particularly in *The Roofing Ceremony*. The scenography of Strindberg's later plays differs significantly from his earlier plays. Much more extensively described, props and architectural features that are symbolically important also figure prominently as concrete aspects of the scenography, as Ann Charlotte Hanes Harvey outlines (61–2, 74–5). The realistic scenography in the experimental plays conveys a milieu that readers and audience would have been personally familiar with, as demonstrated by the prevalence of such upper-middle class props as the 'chiffonjé, schäslong, kakelugn, skvallerspegel' (75) (secretaire, chaiselongue, tiled stove, window mirror [my trans.]). Here we can add the prevalence of thick curtains, pots of plants, decorative trinkets, and so forth, which also figure prominently in *The Roofing Ceremony*. Harvey shows how Strindberg's scenography relies on symmetry in plane and perspective, as well as on the spatial separation of genders into a male and female sphere on stage (62–5). These features connect explicitly with ideals of home decoration and apartment building architecture at the turn of the century in Stockholm (see Gejvall on the structure and outline of the Stockholm bourgeois apartment). The domestic interior of the modern apartment building is not a blank space for the conception of Strindberg's most sophisticated plays but speaks explicitly to building and design practices at the time. As such, they also have aesthetic implications for developments in the transnational literary representations of European modernism.

A *Dream Play* is often described as modernist with respect to Strindberg's subjective and fluid character construction, as well as to the notion in the oft-quoted short prefatory remark that in this play, 'tid och rum existera icke … and … Personerna klyvas, fördubblas, dubbleras, dunsta av, förtätas, flyta ut, samlas' (7) (time and space do not exist … and … characters split, double, multiply, evaporate, condense, disperse, and converge [176]). *A Dream Play*'s conceit, the annihilation of time and space in a dream, is thereby also effected through the multitude of concrete sets and a very specific scenography. The particular spatiality of this play, moreover, mediates explicitly between the domestic and the public. Scenes transition from a prison, to a kitchen, to a street scene, to a lawyer's office, to a kitchen, and so on, while the public performance of a sleeper's dream also ties the construction to domestic space – that most dreaming occurs while asleep in a bed in one's bedroom is hardly surprising, and a reworking of the image of a consciousness contained in an immobile body structures the interiority conceit of *The Roofing Ceremony*'s. The use of setting, implied as well as concrete, in both the play and the novella thus share intriguing connections.

Ghost Sonata's realistic scenography moves the set from the exterior of an apartment building to a drawing room in the interior of that building, providing a countermovement to *The Roofing Ceremony*'s exteriorization process, which begins in a bedroom and at the moment of death transcends the apartment building. *Ghost Sonata's* Hummel character, moreover, is not a cannibal or trophy hunter. The characterization of Hummel as a combination of vampire and building speculator, whose faulty apartment building designs have killed scores of people, bridges the expressionistic with the realistic (faulty building practices were a serious problem in Stockholm at the time). *Ghost Sonata's* scenography is described in great detail, particularly in the design of the domestic space. In both *A Dream Play* and the chamber plays, the architecture of intimate life helps produce concretely the modernist idiom Strindberg explores during the first decade of the twentieth century. This modernist idiom, coded as unique and innovative, in fact depends on an intriguing paradox, namely, that it relies to a large extent on sets that draw on the most generic and typical of architectural development in late nineteenth-century Europe: the modern apartment.

The Roofing Ceremony, as I have shown in this chapter, offers a model for understanding anew the importance of the domestic as a critical location for European modernism. We would be mistaken in thinking that the apartment setting of *The Roofing Ceremony* is a stable, passive container waiting to be filled with formal experimentation, however. Reifying the notion that it is architecture that contains the attempted first-person representation of a dying consciousness would cement the opposition between public and private that Strindberg and European prose modernism seek to deconstruct. Indeed, the novella offers multiple ways of understanding how the construction of setting is also mediated. Architectural discourses, technologies of audio recording and playback, colonialism and ethnographic presentation, and developments in modern drama transcend, in *The Roofing Ceremony*, constructions of architectural stability in the 'suppressed' domestic setting and of national demarcation, construing modernism's narrative interiority conceit as always located within and constructing the setting which it seeks to transcend. Without an understanding of setting, we cannot understand European modernism. Neither can we begin to grasp the contributions of Strindberg as a transnational writer.

Works Cited

Abolgassemi, Maxime. 'August Strindberg et André Breton à la lumière du hasard objectif.' *Mélusine*. Vol 27. *Le Surréalisme et la science*. Paris: Éditions l'Âge d'Homme, 2007. 245–55.

Adamson, Walter L. *Embattled Avant-Gardes: Modernism's Resistance to Commodity Culture in Europe*. Berkeley: U of California Press, 2007.

Anderson, Benedict. *Imagined Communities*. London and New York: Verso, 1983.

Ahlström, Gunnar. *Det moderna genombrottet i Nordens litteratur*. Stockholm: Kooperativa Förbundet, 1947.

Ahlström, Stellan. 'Strindbergs erövring av Paris: Strindberg och Frankrike 1884–1895.' Diss. U of Stockholm, 1956. Stockholm: Almqvist and Wiksell, 1956.

Allen, Julie Kalani Smith. 'Parole Dänemark: Symbolic Re-presentations of Denmark in Fin-De-Siecle German and Austrian Literature.' Diss., Harvard U, 2005, Dissertations & Theses: Full Text. ProQuest. University of Illinois Libraries, Urbana, IL. 30 Nov. 2008. http://www.proquest.com.

Armstrong, Tim. *Modernism: A Cultural History*. Cambridge: Polity P, 2005.

Axelsson, Lasse Berg. *När Sverige upptäckte Afrika*. Stockholm: Rabén Prisma, 1997.

Bachelard, Gaston. *The Poetics of Space*. Trans. Maria Jolas. Boston: Beacon, 1994.

Bahun-Radunović, Sanja Pourgouris, and Marinos Pourgouris, eds. *The Avant-Garde and the Margin: New Territories of Modernism*. Newcastle, UK: Cambridge Scholars Press, 2006.

Bakhtin, Mikhail. *The Dialogic Imagination: Four Essays*. Ed. Michael Holquist. Trans. Caryl Emerson and Michael Holquist. Austin: U of Texas P, 1981.

Bal, Mieke. *Narratology: Introduction to the Theory of Narrative*. 2nd ed. Toronto: U of Toronto P, 1997.

Balakian, Anna Elizabeth. *Surrealism: The Road to the Absolute*. 3rd ed. Chicago: U of Chicago P, 1986.

Balzamo, Elena. 'Le substrat français dans *Utopies dans la réalité.' Strindberg och det franska språket. Strindberg et la langue française. Föredrag från ett symposium vid Växjö universitet 22–23 maj 2003*. Ed. Olof Eriksson. Växjö: Växjö UP, 2004. 35–47.

Barnes, Meghan Woodbury. 'Fashion and Nationalism in Berlin Novels, 1870–1895.' Diss. Washington U, 2003. Dissertations & Theses: Full Text. ProQuest. University of Illinois Libraries, Urbana, IL. 23 May 2008. http://www.proquest.com.

Battail, Jean-François. 'Avènement de la machine et nostalgies pastorales: Strindberg témoin critique de son temps.' *Germanica* 4 (1988): 53–64.

Begam, Richard, and Michael Valdez Moses. Introduction to *Modernism and Colonialism: British and Irish Literature, 1899–1939*. Ed. Richard Begam and Michael Valdez Moses. Durham: Duke UP, 2007. 1–16.

Behschnitt, Wolfgang. *Die Autorfigur: Autobiographischer Aspekt und Konstruktion des Autors im Werk August Strindbergs*. Basel: Schwabe, 1999.

Berendsohn, Walter A. 'Studier i manuskriptet till Strindbergs *Karanänmästarens andra berättelse.' Samlaren* 32 (1951): 16–28.

Bergmann, Klaus. *Agrarromantik und Grossstadtfeindschaft*. Meisenheim am Glan: A. Hain, 1970.

Bettrell, Richard R. 'The Fields of France.' *A Day in the Country: Impressionism and the French Landscape*. Ed. Richard R. Bettrell. Los Angeles: Los Angeles County Museum of Art, 1983. 241–72.

– 'The Impressionist Landscape and the Image of France.' *A Day in the Country: Impressionism and the French Landscape*. Ed. Richard R. Bettrell. Los Angeles: Los Angeles County Museum of Art, 1983. 27–52.

Bezucha, R.J. 'The Urban Image of the Countryside in Late Nineteenth-Century French Painting: An Essay on Art and Political Culture.' *The Rural Vision: France and America in the Late Nineteenth Century*. Ed. Hollister Sturges. Omaha: Joslyn Art Museum: U of Nebraska P, 1987. 13–31.

Björklin, Mats. 'Remarks on Writing and Technologies of Sound in Early Cinema.' *The Sounds of Early Cinema*. Ed. Richard Abel and Rick Altman. Bloomington: Indiana UP, 2001. 32–8.

Bleibtreu-Ehrenberg, Gisela. *Homosexualität – Die Geschichte eines Vorurteils*. Frankfurt: Fisher, 1981. Cited in http://www.heinz-sandmann.de/frame3/schwul2/homhista.html#VI. 20 Sept. 2007.

Boëthius, Ulf. '"Gröna ögat": Det paranoida mönstret i Strindbergs *Taklagsöl.' Tidskrift för litteraturvetenskap* 2–3 (1986): 48–62.

– 'Strindberg och kvinnofrågan tom Giftas I.' Diss. U of Stockholm, 1969. Stockholm: Prisma, 1969.

Borgström, Eva. *Kärlekshistoria: Begär mellan kvinnor i 1800-talets litteratur.* Göteborg: Kabusa, 2008.

Boström, Mattias. 'The Phonogram Archive of the Stockholm Ethnographic Museum (1909–1930): Another Chapter in the History of Ethnographic Cylinder Recordings.' *Fontes artis musicae* 50.1 (2003): 22–35.

Bourguignon, Anne. 'Entre Balzac et Kafka: *Inferno* d'August Strindberg.' *Le Prisme du Nord: Pays du Nord, France, Allemagne (1750–1920).* Ed. Michel Espagne. Tusson: Du Lerot, 2006. 259–77.

Boyer, Régis. 'En lisant *Bland franska bönder*: En français dans le texte.' *Strindberg et la France.* Ed. Gunnel Engwall. Stockholm: Almquist & Wiksell, 1994. 15–28.

Bradbury, Malcolm, and James McFarlane. 'The Name and Nature of Modernism.' *Modernism: A Guide to European Literature 1890–1930.* Ed. Malcolm Bradbury and James McFarlane. Harmondsworth, UK: Penguin, 1976. 19–55.

Brady, Erika. *A Spiral Way: How the Phonograph Changed Ethnography.* Jackson: UP of Mississippi, 1999.

Brandell, Gunnar. *På Strindbergs vägar genom Frankrike.* Stockholm: Wahlström & Widstrand, 1949.

– *Strindberg – ett författarliv.* 4 vols. Stockholm: Bonnier, 1983–9.

– *Strindberg in Inferno.* Trans. Barry Jacobs. Cambridge, MA: Harvard UP, 1974.

Brandes, Georg. 'Inaugural Lecture, 1871.' Trans. Evert Sprinchorn. *The Theory of the Modern Stage.* Ed. Eric Bentley. New York: Applause, 1997. 381–402.

Brantlinger, Patrick. 'Heart of Darkness: Anti-Imperialism, Racism, or Impressionism.' *Heart of Darkness: Joseph Conrad.* Ed. Ross C. Murfin. Boston: St Martin's P, 1996. 277–98.

Brantly, Susan. 'Into the Twentieth Century: 1890–1950.' *A History of Swedish Literature.* Ed. Lars G. Warme. Lincoln: Nebraska UP, 1996. 273–379.

Bravo, Michael, and Sverker Sörlin, eds. *Narrating the Arctic: A Cultural History of Nordic Scientific Practices.* Canton, MA: Science History Publications, 2002.

Breton, André. 'Manifesto of Surrealism.' *Manifestoes of Surrealism.* Trans. Richard Seaver and Helen R. Lane. Ann Arbor: U of Michigan P, 1972. 3–47.

– *Oeuvres complètes.* Ed. Marguerite Bonnet. Bibliothèque de la Pléiade. Vol. 1. Paris: Gallimard, 1988.

Briens, Sylvain. *Paris Laboratoire de la littérature Scandinave moderne 1880–1905.* Paris: L'Harmattan, 2010.

Brooker, Peter, and Andrew Thacker. 'Introduction: Locating the Modern.' *Geographies of Modernism: Literatures, Cultures, Spaces.* Ed. Peter Brooker and Andrew Thacker. London: Routledge, 2005. 1–5.

Büchten, Daniela. 'Opp mot Nord! Tyske turister i Skandinavia.' *Skandinavien och Tyskland 1800–1914: Möten och Vänskapsband.* Trans. Arve H. Thorsen. Ed. Bernd Henningsen. Stockholm: Nationalmuseum, 1997. 113–14.

Bulson, Eric. *Novels, Maps, Modernity: The Spatial Imagination, 1850–2000*. New York: Routledge, 2007.

Burgin, Victor. 'Chance Encounters: *Flâneur* and *Détraquée* in Breton's *Nadja*.' *Qui Parle: Literature, Philosophy, Visual Arts, History* 4.1 (1990): 47–61.

Carlson, Harry G. *Out of Inferno: Strindberg's Reawakening as an Artist*. Seattle: U of Washington P, 1996.

Carroll, Noël. 'On the Narrative Connection.' *New Perspectives on Narrative Perspective*. Ed. Willie van Peer and Seymour Chatman. Albany: State U of New York P, 2001. 21–42.

Casanova, Pascale. *The World Republic of Letters*. Trans. M.B. DeBevoise. Cambridge, MA: Harvard UP, 2004.

Caws, Mary Ann, ed. *City Images: Perspectives from Literature, Philosophy, and Film*. New York: Gordon and Breach, 1991.

– *A Metapoetics of the Passage: Architextures in Surrealism and After*. Hanover: UP of New England, 1981.

Chénieux-Gendron, Jacqueline. *Surrealism*. Trans. Vivian Folkenflik. New York: Columbia UP, 1990.

Clark, Timothy J. *The Painting of Modern Life: Paris in the Art of Manet and His Followers*. Princeton: Princeton UP, 1984.

Cohen, Margaret. 'Panoramic Literature and the Invention of Everyday Genres.' *Cinema and the Invention of Modern Life*. Ed. Leo Charney and Vanessa R. Schwartz. Berkeley: U of California P, 1995. 227–52.

– *Profane Illumination: Walter Benjamin and the Paris of Surrealist Revolution*. Berkeley: U of California P, 1993.

Collier, Peter. 'Surrealist City Narrative: Breton and Aragon.' *Unreal City: Urban Experience in Modern European Literature and Art*. Ed. Edward Timms and David Kelley. New York: St Martin's P, 1985. 214–29.

Conrad, Joseph. *Heart of Darkness*. *The Complete Short Fiction of Joseph Conrad: The Tales*. Vol. 3. Ed. Samuel Hynes. New York: Ecco P, 1992.

Crang, Mike, and Nigel Thrift. 'Introduction.' *Thinking Space*. Ed. Mike Crang and Nigel Thrift. London and New York: Routledge, 2000. 1–30.

Danius, Sara. *The Senses of Modernism: Technology, Perception, and Aesthetics*. Ithaca: Cornell UP, 2002.

David-Fox, Katherine. 'Prague-Vienna, Prague-Berlin: The Hidden Geography of Czech Modernism.' *Slavic Review* 59.4 (2000): 735–60.

De Certeau, Michael. *The Practice of Everyday Life*. Trans. Steven F. Rendall. Berkeley: U of California P, 1984.

Deleuze, Gilles, and Felix Guattari. *A Thousand Plateaus: Capitalism and Schizophrenia*. Trans. Brian Massumi. Minneapolis: U of Minnesota P, 1987.

Dijkstra, Bram. *Idols of Perversity: Fantasies of Feminine Evil in Fin-de-Siècle Culture*. New York: Oxford UP, 1986.

Edwards, Elizabeth. *Raw Histories: Photographs, Anthropology, and Museums.* Oxford: Berg, 2001.

Ekholm, Per Erik. 'Kommentarer.' *Bland franska bönder: Subjektiva reseskildringar.* August Strindberg, *Samlade verk.* Vol. 23. Stockholm: Almqvist & Wiksell, 1985. 187–260.

Eklund, Torsten. 'Kommentarer.' *Vivisektioner* [French-Swedish edition]. Ed. Torsten Eklund. Stockholm: Bonnier, 1958. 194–210.

Ekner, Reidar. 'Rilke, Obstfelder och "Malte Laurids Brigge."' *Obstfelder: Fjorten essays.* Ed. Asbjørn Aarnes. Oslo: Aschehoug, 1997. 213–33.

Englert, Uwe. 'Det moderna genombrottet.' *Skandinavien och Tyskland 1800–1914: Möten och Vänskapsband.* Ed. Bernd Henningsen. Berlin: Jovis, 1997. 209–12.

Engwall, Gunnel. '"Det knastrar i hjärnan": Strindberg som sin egen franske översättare.' *August Strindberg och hans översättare.* Ed. Björn Meidal and N.Å. Nilsson. Stockholm: Kungliga Vitterhets Historie och Antikvitetsakademien, 1995. 35–51.

– '"Le Plaidoyer d'un fou!" Un Plaidoyer de Strindberg ou de Loiseau?' *Studier i modern språkvetenskap* 6 (1980): 29–54.

– ed. *Strindberg et la France.* Stockholm: Almqvist & Wiksell International, 1994.

Eriksson, Eva. *Den moderna stadens födelse: Svensk arkitektur 1890–1920.* Stockholm: Ordfront, 1990.

Eriksson, Olof, ed. *Strindberg och det franska språket. Strindberg et la langue française. Föredrag från ett symposium vid Växjö universitet 22–23 maj 2003.* Växjö: Växjö UP, 2004.

– 'Strindbergs franska: en språklig paradox.' *Strindberg och det franska språket. Strindberget la langue française. Föredrag från ett symposium vid Växjö universitet 22–23 maj 2003.* Ed. Olof Eriksson. Växjö: Växjö UP, 2003. 112–25.

Eysteinsson, Astradur. 'Borders of Modernism in the Nordic World: Introduction.' *Modernism.* Vol. 2. Ed. Astradur Eysteinsson and Vivian Liska. Amsterdam: Benjamins, 2007. 833–5.

Facos, Michelle. *Nationalism and the Nordic Imagination: Swedish Art of the 1890s.* Berkeley: U of California P, 1998.

Farland, Maria. 'Modernist Versions of Pastoral: Poetic Inspiration, Scientific Expertise, and the "Degenerate" Farmer.' *American Literary History* 19.4 (2007): 905–36.

Fahlgren, Margaretha. *Kvinnans ekvation. Kön, makt och rationalitet i Strindbergs författarskap.* Stockholm: Carlsson, 1994.

Fjelkestam, Kristina. 'Ungkarlsflickor, kamrathustrur och manhaftiga lesbianer: Modernitetens litterära gestalter i mellankrigstidens Sverige.' Diss. U of Stockholm. Eslöv: B. Östlings bokförl. Symposion, 2002.

Forsell, Håkan. *Property, Tenancy, and Urban Growth in Stockholm and Berlin, 1860–1920.* Aldershot, UK: Ashgate, 2006.

Frank, Joseph. 'Spatial Form in Literature.' *The Theory of the Novel: A Historical Approach.* Ed. Michael McKeon. Baltimore: Johns Hopkins UP, 2000. 784–802.

Friedman, Kajsa Ekholm. *Catastrophe and Creation: The Transformation of an African Culture.* Philadelphia: Harwood, 1991.

Friedman, Susan Stanford. 'Cultural Parataxis and Transnational Landscapes of Reading: Toward a Locational Modernist Studies.' *Modernism.* Vol. 1. Ed. Astradur Eysteinsson and Vivian Liska. Amsterdam: Benjamins, 2007. 35–52.

Frisby, David. 'Analyzing Modernity: Some Issues.' *Tracing Modernity: Manifestations of the Modern in Architecture and the City.* Ed. Mari Hvattum and Christian Hermanson. London: Routledge, 2004. 3–22.

Fritzsche, Peter. *Reading Berlin 1900.* Cambridge, MA: Harvard UP, 1996.

Frykman, Jonas, and Orvar Löfgren. *Culture Builders: A Historical Anthropology of Middle-Class Life.* Trans. Alan Crozier. New Brunswick, NJ: Rutgers UP, 1987.

Fuchs, Robert. 'Skandinaviska författare i Berlins kulturliv vid sekelskiftet.' Trans. Lars W. Freij. *Skandinavien och Tyskland 1800–1914: Möten och Vänskapsband.* Ed. Bernd Henningsen. Berlin: Jovis, 1997. 340–6.

Gaonkar, Dilip Parameshwar. 'On Alternative Modernities.' *Alternative Modernities.* Ed. Dilip Parameshwar Gaonkar. 2nd ed. Durham: Duke UP, 2001. 1–23.

Gavel Adams, Ann-Charlotte. 'The Generic Ambiguity of August Strindberg's Inferno: Occult Novel and Autobiography.' Diss. U of Washington, 1990.

– 'Kommentarer.' *Inferno.* August Strindberg, *Samlade verk.* Vol. 37. Stockholm: Norstedt, 1994. 321–457.

– 'Strindberg and Paris 1894–1898: Barbarian, Initiate, Self.' *August Strindberg and the Other: New Critical Approaches.* Ed. Paul Houe, Sven Hakon Rossel, and Göran Stockenström. Amsterdam: Rodopi, 2002. 91–100.

– 'Strindberg and Rimbaldian Poetics: *Inferno* as a French *poème en prose.*' *The Moscow Papers.* Ed. Michael Robinson. Stockholm: Strindbergssällskapet, 1998. 77–83.

Gejvall, Birgit. '1800-talets stockholmsbostad: En studie över den borgerliga bostadens planlösning i hyreshusen.' Diss. U of Stockholm, 1954. Stockholm: Stockholms kommunalförvaltning, 1954.

Gelatt, Roland. *The Fabulous Phonograph 1877–1977.* New York: Macmillan, 1977.

Gerson, Stéphane. *The Pride of Place: Local Memories and Political Culture in Nineteenth-Century France.* Ithaca: Cornell UP, 2003.

Gikandi, Simon. 'Preface: Modernism in the World.' *Modernism/Modernity* 13:3 (2006): 419–24.

Glienke, Bernhard, and Annika Krummacher. *Metropolis und Nordische Moderne: Grossstadtthematik als Herausforderung literarischer Innovationen in Skandinavien seit 1830*. Frankfurt am Main: Lang, 1999.

Götselius, Thomas. 'Helvetet lössläppt: Strindberg skriver!' *Strindbergs förvandlingar*. Ed. Ulf Olsson. Stockholm/Stehag: Brutus Östlings bokförlag Symposion, 1999. 95–136.

Granath, Olle, ed. *August Strindberg: Painter, Photographer, Writer*. London: Tate Pub., 2005.

Gravier, Maurice. 'Strindberg et Kafka.' *Etudes Germaniques* 8 (1953): 118–40.

Grimal, Sophie Isabelle. 'The Alchemy of Writing: A Stylistic Analysis of August Strindberg's 'Inferno': I, II and III.' Diss. U of California, Los Angeles, 1995. Dissertations & Theses: Full Text. ProQuest. University of Illinois Libraries, Urbana, IL. 13 Dec. 2008. http://www.proquest.com.

Gustafson, Lars. 'Strindberg as a Forerunner of Scandinavian Modernism.' *The Hero in Scandinavian Literature*. Ed. John M. Weinstock and Robert T. Rovinsky. Austin: U of Texas P, 1975. 125–41.

Gynning, Margareta. 'Paris – självförverkligandets stad.' *De drogo till Paris: Nordiska konstnärinnor på 1880-talet*. Ed. Louise Robbert and Lollo Fogelström. Stockholm: Liljevalchs Konsthall, 1988. 29–34.

Hackett, Robin. *Sapphic Primitivism: Productions of Race, Class, and Sexuality in Key Works of Modern Fiction*. New Brunswick, NJ: Rutgers UP, 2004.

Håkansson, T. 'Strindberg and the Arts.' *Studio International* 181.930 (1971): 62–7.

Halberstam, Judith. *In a Queer Time and Place: Transgender Bodies, Subcultural Lives*. New York: New York UP, 2005.

Hamon, Philippe. *Expositions: Literature and Architecture in Nineteenth-Century France*. Trans. Katia Sainson-Frank and Lisa Maguire. Berkeley: U of California P, 1992.

Hamsun, Knut. *The Cultural Life of Modern America*. Trans. Barbara Morgridge. Cambridge, MA: Harvard UP, 1969.

– *Hunger*. Trans. Sverre Lyngstad. Edinburgh: Cannongate, 2001.

Hansson, Thelma. *Karl Kraus och Strindberg*. Göteborg: Kungl. Vetenskaps-och Vitterhets-Samhället, 1996.

Harvey, Anne-Charlotte Hanes. 'Strindbergs scenografi.' *Strindbergiana* 5 (1990): 56–86.

Harvey, David. 'Cosmopolitanism and the Banality of Geographical Evils.' *Millenial Capitalism and the Culture of Neoliberalism*. Ed. Jean Comaroff and John L. Comaroff. Durham: Duke UP, 2001. 271–309.

– *Paris, Capital of Modernity*. New York: Routledge, 2003.

Hemmingson, Per. *Strindberg som fotograf*. Åhus: Kalejdoskop, 1989.

Higonnet, Patrice. *Paris: Capital of the World*. Trans. Arthur Goldhammer. Cambridge, MA: Belknap P of Harvard UP, 2002.

Hochschild, Adam. *King Leopold's Ghost: A Story of Greed, Terror, and Heroism in Colonial Africa*. New York: Mariner, 1999.

Hockenjos, Vreni. 'Das Grauen im Speicher: August Strindbergs Funktionalisierung des Phonographen.' *Historisierung und Funktionalisierung: Intermedialität in den skandiavischen Literaturen um 1900. Berliner Beiträge zur Skandinavistik*. Vol. 8. Ed. Stephan Michael Schröder and Vreni Hockenjos. Berlin: Nordeuropa-Institut der Humboldt-Universität, 2005. 125–58.

– 'Money, Monney, Monet: Om rörelse, teknologi och perception i Strindbergs "Från Café de l'Ermitage till Marly de Roi och så vidare."' *Tidskrift för litteraturvetenskap* 1 (2004): 4–24.

– 'Picturing Dissolving Views: August Strindberg and the Visual Media of His Age.' Diss. Stockholm U: Acta Universitatis Stockholmiensis, 2007.

Hogan, Steve, and Lee Hudson. *Completely Queer: The Gay and Lesbian Encyclopedia*. New York: Henry Holt, 1998.

Huyssen, Andreas. 'Geographies of Modernism in a Globalizing World.' *Geographies of Modernism*. Ed. Peter Brooker and Andrew Thacker. New York: Routledge, 2005. 6–18.

– 'Paris/Childhood: The Fragmented Body in Rilke's *Notebooks of Malte Laurids Brigge*.' *Modernity and the Text: Revisions of German Modernism*. Ed. Andreas Huyssen and David Bathrick. New York: Columbia UP, 1989. 113–41.

Ishikawa, Kiyoko. *Paris dans quatre textes narratifs du surrealism: Aragon, Breton, Desnos, Soupalt*. Paris: L'Harmattan, 1999.

Jacobs, Barry. 'Strindberg's Binoculars: Narrative Perspectives in *The Roofing Ceremony*.' *Narrative Ironies*. Ed. Adolph Prier and Gerald Ernest Paul Gillespie. Amsterdam: Rodopi, 1997. 123–38.

James, Henry. [1884]. *A Little Tour in France*. http://www.gutenberg.org/etext/2159. Accessed 20 January 2009.

Jansson, Mats, Jacob Lothe, and Hannu Riikonen, eds. *European and Nordic Modernisms*. Norwich: Norvik Press, 2004.

Jenssen-Tusch, Harald. *Skandinaver i Congo: svenske, norske og danske Mænds og kvinders virksomhed i den uafhængige Congostat*. Copenhagen: Gyldendals, 1902–5.

Jewell, Brian. *Veteran Talking Machines: History and Collectors' Guide*. Kent, UK: Midas, 1977.

Johannesson, Eric O. *The Novels of August Strindberg: A Study in Theme and Structure*. Berkeley: U of California P, 1968.

Johansson, Ingemar. *Stor-Stockholms bebyggelsehistoria: Markpolitik, planering och byggande under sju sekel.* Stockholm: Gidlund, 1991.

Jones, James W. *'We of the Third Sex': Literary Representations of Homosexuality in Wilhelmine Germany.* New York: Peter Lang, 1990.

Jonsson, Ulf. 'Det franska jordbrukets efterblivenhet: En seglivad myt.' *Historisk tidskrift* 2 (1997): 224–50.

Kern, Stephen. *The Culture of Time and Space 1880–1918.* Cambridge, MA: Harvard UP, 1983.

Kerr, Alfred. *Mein Berlin: Schauplätze einer Metropole.* Berlin: Aufbau Verlag, 1999.

Kittler, Friedrich A. *Gramophone, Film, Typewriter.* Trans. Geoffrey Winthrop-Young and Michael Wutz. Stanford, CA: Stanford UP, 1999.

Kjellén, Alf. *Flanören och hans storstadsvärld: Synpunkter på ett litterärt motiv.* Stockholm: Almqvist & Wiksell International, 1985.

Kjellgren, Hans. *Grammofonen och dess föregångare fonografen.* Stockholm: Samlarförbundet Nordstjärnan, 1980.

Kylhammar, Martin. 'Maskin och idyll: Teknik och pastorala ideal hos Strindberg och Heidenstam.' Diss. Linköping U, 1985. Malmö: Liber, 1985.

– *Den tidlöse modernisten: en essäbok.* Stockholm: Carlsson, 2004.

Lagercrantz, Olof. *August Strindberg.* Trans. Anselm Hollo. London and Boston: Faber and Faber, 1984.

Laman, Karl Edvard. *Några drag ur Kongofolkets lif från Svenska Missionsförbundets arbetsfält i Kongo.* Stockholm: Utg., 1907.

Lamm, Martin. *August Strindberg.* Trans. and ed. Harry G. Carlson. New York: B. Blom, 1971.

Lefebvre, Henri. *The Production of Space.* Trans. Donald Nicholson-Smith. Oxford: Blackwell, 1991.

Lehning, James R. *Peasant and French: Cultural Contact in Rural France during the Nineteenth Century.* Cambridge: Cambridge UP, 1995.

Lewis, Pericles. *The Cambridge Introduction to Modernism.* Cambridge: Cambridge UP, 2007.

Lindqvist, Sven. *'Exterminate All the Brutes': One Man's Odyssey into the Heart of Darkness and the Origins of European Genocide.* Trans. Joan Tate. New York: New Press, 1997.

Lindvåg, Alf. 'August Strindbergs *Inferno* i den nordiska kritiken.' *Samlaren* (1986): 59–81.

– 'Strindbergs *Inferno* i den nordiska kritiken.' *Samlaren* (1986): 58–81.

Ljungmark, Lars. *Swedish Exodus.* Trans. Kermit B. Westerberg. Carbondale: Southern Illinois UP, 1996.

Ljungström, Olof. *Oscariansk antropologi: Exotism, förhistoria och rasforskning under sent 1800-tal.* Hedemora: Gidlund, 2004.

Lönngren, Ann-Sofie. 'Att röra en värld: en queerteoretisk analys av erotiska trianglar i sex verk av August Strindberg.' Diss. Uppsala U, 2008. Lund: Ellerström, 2007.

Lucey, Michael. *Never Say I: Sexuality and the First Person in Colette, Gide, and Proust*. Durham: Duke UP, 2006.

Luthersson, Peter. *Svensk litterär modernism: en stridsstudie*. Stockholm: Atlantis, 2002.

MacDougall, David. *The Corporeal Image: Film, Ethnography, and the Senses*. Princeton: Princeton UP, 2006.

Machlan, Elizabeth Boyle. '"There Are Plenty of Houses": Architecture and Genre in *The Portrait of a Lady*.' *Studies in the Novel* 37.4 (2005): 394–410.

Marcus, Sharon. *Apartment Stories: City and Home in Nineteenth-Century Paris and London*. Berkeley: U of California P, 1999.

Marmus, Roger. 'Från kupéfönstret under full fart: Landsskapskildring i rörelse i *Bland franska bönder*.' *Strindberg and His Media: Proceedings of the 15th International Strindberg Conference*. Ed. Kirsten Wechsel. Leipzig: Edition Kirchhof & Franke, 2003. 279–89.

Matthews, J.H. 'Du surnaturalisme au surréalisme.' *French Forum* 5.1 (1980): 48–55.

McFarlane, James. 'Berlin and the Rise of Modernism 1886–96.' *Modernism*. Ed. Malcolm Bradbury and James McFarlane. Harmondsworth: Penguin, 1978. 105–19.

McPhee, Peter. *A Social History of France, 1789–1914*. 2nd ed. New York: Palgrave Macmillan, 2004.

Meidal, Björn. 'Odalmannen och vikingen: bonden i svensk litteratur.' *Bonden i dikt och verklighet*. Ed. Bo Larsson. Stockholm: Nordiska museet, 1993. 5–21.

Melberg, Arne. 'Barbaren i Paris.' *Strindbergs förvandlingar*. Ed. Ulf Olsson. Eslöv: B. Östlings bokförl. Symposion, 1999. 73–94.

– 'Strindberg stiger ner: Inferno.' *Ästhetik der skandinavischen Moderne: Bernard Glienke zum Gedenken*. Ed. Annegret Heitmann and Karin Hoff. Frankfurt am Main: Lang, 1998. 231–41.

Mesch, Rachel. *The Hysteric's Revenge: French Women Writers at the Fin de Siècle*. Nashville: Vanderbilt UP, 2006.

Miller, Neil. *Out of the Past: Gay and Lesbian History from 1869 to the Present*. 2nd ed. New York: Alyson Books, 2006.

Mitchell, P.M. 'The Concept of Modernism in Scandinavia.' *Facets of European Modernism: Essays in Honor of James McFarlane*. Ed. Janet Garton. Norwich: U of East Anglia P, 1985. 243–56.

Moi, Toril. *Henrik Ibsen and the Birth of Modernism: Art, Theater, Philosophy*. Oxford: Oxford UP, 2006.

Möller, P., G. Pagels, and E. Gleerup. *Tre år i Kongo*. 2 vols. Stockholm: P.A. Norstedt, 1887–8.

Moretti, Franco. *Atlas of the European Novel 1800–1900*. London: Verso, 1999.

Nerval, de Gérard. *Aurélia, où le rêve et la vie*. 1855. Ed. Jean Richer. *Aurélia où le rêve et la vie; lettres d'amour*. Paris: Minard, 1965. 2–127.

– *Aurélia*. Trans. Geoffrey Wagner. *Aurélia and Other Writings*. Boston: Exact Change, 1996. 1–70.

Nordenskiöld, Erland, ed. *Etnografiska bidrag af svenska missionärer i Afrika*. Stockholm: Palmquist, 1907.

– 'Företal.' *Några drag ur Kongofolkets lif från Svenska Missionsförbundets arbetsfält i Kongo*. Stockholm: Utg., 1907. 3–5.

Numa Petersons Handels and Fabriks-Aktiebolag. *Columbia Grafofoner med tillbehör*. Stockholm: n.p., 1901.

Olsson, Ulf. 'En nordlig Strindberg?' *Strindbergiana*. Vol 24. Ed. Per Stam. Stockholm: Atlantis, 2009. 59–68.

–*Jag blir galen: Strindberg, vansinnet och vetenskapen*. Eslöv: B. Östlings bokförl. Symposion, 2002.

– *Levande död: Studier i Strindbergs prosa*. Eslöv: B. Östlings bokförl. Symposion, 1996.

Parmée, Douglas. 'Introduction.' *The Earth*. Harmondsworth: Penguin, 1980. 5–19.

Paul, Fritz. 'Tyskland: Skandinaviens port till världslitteraturen.' Trans. Ingrid Windisch. *Skandinavien och Tyskland 1800–1914: Möten och Vänskapsband*. Ed. Bernd Henningsen. Berlin: Jovis, 1997. 193–202.

Pedersen, Jean Elisabeth. *Legislating the French Family: Feminism, Theater, and Republican Politics, 1870–1920*. New Brunswick, NJ: Rutgers UP, 2003.

Perelli, Franco. 'Taklagsöl: Strindberg's Last Tape.' Trans. Rosangela Baronne. *Strindbergiana*. Vol. 2. Stockholm: Strindbergssällskapet, 1985. 130–45.

Poulenard, Elie. 'Among French Peasants.' *Essays on Strindberg*. Ed. Carl-Reinhold Smedmark. Stockholm: Strindberg Society, 1966. 161–75.

Pred, Allan Richard. *Recognizing European Modernities: A Montage of the Present*. London: Routledge, 1995.

Prendergast, Christopher. *Paris and the Nineteenth Century*. Oxford: Blackwell, 1992.

Puchner, Martin. *Stage Fright: Modernism, Anti-Theatricality, and Drama*. Baltimore: Johns Hopkins UP, 2002.

Read, Oliver, and Walter L. Welch. *From Tin Foil to Stereo: Evolution of the Phonograph*. Indianapolis: H.W. Sams, 1976.

Reed, Christopher. Introduction to *Not at Home. The Suppression of Domesticity in Modern Art and Architecture*. Ed. Christopher Reed. London: Thames and Hudsen, 1996. 7–17.

Reinius Gustafsson, Lotten. *Förfärliga och begärliga föremål: Om tingens roller på Stockholmsutställningen 1897 och Etnografiska missionsutställningen 1907. Kulturperspektiv 15.* Stockholm: Etnografiska museet, 2005.

Réja, Marcel. 'Avant-Propos.' *Inferno* by Auguste Strindberg. Paris: Société de Mercure de France, 1898. 5–11.

Renan, Ernest. 'What is a Nation?' [Qu'est ce-que une nation? 1882]. Trans. unknown. 18 September 2008. http://www.cooper.edu/humanities/core/hss3/e_renan.html.

Richie, Alexandra. *Faust's Metropolis: A History of Berlin.* London: HarperCollins, 1999.

Ricoeur, Paul. *Time and Narrative.* Trans. Kathleen McLaughlin and David Pellauer. 3 vols. Chicago: U of Chicago P, 1984–8.

Rilke, Rainer Maria. *Die Aufzeichnungen des Malte Laurids Brigge.* http://www.gutenberg.org/etext/2188. Accessed 12 Aug. 2008.

– *The Notebooks of Malte Laurids Brigge.* Trans. Stephen Mitchell. New York: Random House, 1983.

Robb, Graham. *Strangers: Homosexual Love in the 19th Century.* New York: Norton, 2004.

Robinson, Michael. 'Among French Peasants.' *Essays in Memory of Michael Parkinson and Janine Dakyns.* Ed. Christopher Smith. Norwich Papers 4. Norwich: U of East Anglia P, 1992. 169–174.

– *Strindberg and Autobiography: Writing and Reading a Life.* Norwich: Norvik P, 1986.

Rosner, Victoria. *Modernism and the Architecture of Private Life.* New York: Columbia UP, 2005.

Rossholm, Göran. 'Axel och Axel: Strindbergs användning av perspektiv i *En dåres försvarstal.*' *Tijdschrift voor skandinavistiek* 21.2 (2000): 195–220.

– 'Kommentarer.' *En Dåres Försvarstal.* August Strindberg, *Samlade verk.* Vol. 25. Stockholm: Norstedt, 1999. 521–641.

Roy, Matthew. 'August Strindberg's Perversions: On the Science, Sin and Scandal of Homosexuality in August Strindberg's Works.' Diss. U of Washington, 2001.

Rugg, Linda. 'August Strindberg: The Art and Science of Self-Dramatization.' *The Cambridge Companion to August Strindberg.* Ed. Michael Robinson. Cambridge: Cambridge UP, 2009. 3–19.

– *Picturing Ourselves: Photography and Autobiography.* Chicago: U of Chicago P, 1997.

– 'A Self at Large in the Hall of Mirrors: Rilke's *Malte Laurids Brigge* as Autobiographical Act.' *Seminar* 29:1 (1993): 43–54.

Russell, Stephen J. *Agriculture, Prosperity, and Modernization of French Rural Communities, 1870–1914: Views from the Village*. Lewiston, NY: Edwin Mellen, 2004.

Sandberg, Mark B. *Living Pictures, Missing Persons: Mannequins, Museums, and Modernity*. Princeton: Princeton UP, 2003.

Saussy, Haun. *Comparative Literature in an Age of Globalization*. Baltimore: Johns Hopkins UP, 2006.

Schnurbein, Stefanie von. *Krisen der Männlichkeit: Schreiben und Geschlechterdiskurs in skandinavischen Romanen seit 1890*. Göttingen: Wallstein, 2001.

– 'Maskulinitetens kris och *En Dåres Försvarstal.*' *Det gäckande könet: Strindberg och genusteori*. Ed. Anna Cavallin and Anna Westerståhl Stenport. Stockholm/Stehag: Symposion, 2006. 39–68.

Schoolfield, George C. *A Baedeker of Decadence: Charting a Literary Fashion 1884–1927*. New Haven: Yale UP, 2003.

– 'Rilke and the Fall of the House of Schulin.' *The Enlightenment and Its Legacy: Studies in German Literature in Honor of Helga Slessarev*. Ed. Sara Friedrichsmeyer and Barbara Becker-Cantarino. Bonn: Bouvier, 1991. 139–53.

– 'Scandinavian-German Literary Relations.' *Yearbook of Comparative and General Literature* 15 (1966): 19–35.

Shattuck, Roger. 'Introduction: Love and Laughter: Surrealism Reappraised.' Maurice Nadeau, *The History of Surrealism*. Trans. Richard Howard. New York: Macmillan, 1966. 11–34.

Schutte, Jürgen, and Peter Sprengel. *Die Berliner Moderne 1885–1914*. Stuttgart: Reclam, 1987.

Schwartzman, Arnold. *Phono-graphics: The Visual Paraphernalia of the Talking Machine*. San Francisco: Chronicle, 1993.

Simmel, Georg. 'The Metropolis and Mental Life.' *Classic Essays on the Culture of Cities*. Ed. Richard Sennett. New York: Appleton-Century-Crofts, 1969. 48–60.

Sjöblom, Edvard Wilhelm. *I palmernas skugga: självbiografi, dagboksanteckningar m. fl. efterlämnade manuskript*. Stockholm: Hellström, 1907.

Smedmark, Carl Reinhold. 'Kommentarer.' *Röda Rummet*. August Strindberg, *Samlade verk*. Vol. 6. Stockholm: Norstedt, 1981. 293–321.

Smith, Neil, and Cindi Katz. 'Grounding Metaphor: Towards a Spatialized Politics.' *Place and Politics of Identity*. Ed. Michael Keith and Steven Pile. London and New York: Routledge, 1993. 66–81.

Söderström, Göran. *Strindberg och bildkonsten*. Stockholm: Forum, 1972.

– 'Zum schwarzen Ferkel.' *Skandinavien och Tyskland 1800–1914: Möten och Vänskapsband*. Ed. Bernd Henningsen. Berlin: Jovis, 1997. 353–6.

Soja, Edvard. *Thirdspace: Journeys to Los Angeles and Other Real-and-Imagined Places.* Oxford: Blackwell, 1996.

Sörlin, Sverker. 'Bonden som ideal.' *Bonden i dikt och verklighet.* Ed. Bo Larsson. Stockholm: Nordiska museets förlag, 1993. 22–36.

– 'Prophets and Deniers: The Idea of Modernity in Swedish Tradition.' *Utopia and Reality: Modernity in Sweden 1900–1960.* Ed. Cecilia Widenheim. New Haven: Yale UP, 2002. 16–25.

Spivak, Gayatri Chakravorty. *The Death of a Discipline.* New York: Columbia UP, 2003.

Sprengel, Peter. *Geschichte der deutschsprachigen Literatur 1870–1900: Von der Reichsgründung zur Jahrhundertwende.* München: Beck, 1998.

Sprinchorn, Evert. 'Introduction.' *A Madman's Defence,* ed. Evert Sprinchorn. Gloucester, MA: Peter Smith, 1981. vii–xxvi.

– 'Introduction: Strindberg 1892 to 1897.' *Inferno, Alone, and Other Writings.* Ed. Evert Sprinchorn. Garden City: Anchor Books, 1968. 1–96.

Stam, Per. 'Kommentarer.' *Teater och Intima Teatern.* Ed. Per Stam. August Strindberg, *Samlade verk.* Vol. 64. Stockholm: Norstedt, 1999. 245–65.

Ståhle Sjönell, Barbro. 'Kommentarer.' *Klostret: Fagervik och Skamsund.* August Strindberg, *Samlade verk.* Vol. 50. Stockholm: Norstedt, 1994. 285–370.

– 'Kommentarer.' *Taklagsöl.* August Strindberg, *Samlade verk.* Vol. 55. Stockholm: Norstedt, 1994. 159–201.

– 'Strindbergs Taklagsöl: ett prosaexperiment.' Diss. U of Stockholm. *Stockholm:* Almqvist & Wiksell International, 1986.

Stanford Friedman, Susan. 'Cultural Parataxis and Transnational Landscapes of Reading: Toward a Locational Modernist Studies.' *Modernism.* Vol 1. Ed. Astradur Esteinsson and Vivian Liska. Amsterdam: John Benjamins, 2007. 35–52.

Stenfelt, Gustaf. Review of 33 published issues of *Skandinaver i Congo. Ymer* 4 (1904): 412–13.

Stenport, Anna Westerståhl. 'Inledning: Strindberg som genuskonstruktion.' *Det gäckande könet: Strindberg och genusteori.* Ed. Anna Cavallin and Anna Westerståhl Stenport. Stockholm/Stehag: Östlings Bokförlag Symposion, 2006. 7–15.

– 'Making Space: Stockholm and Paris in the Urban Prose of Strindberg and His Contemporaries.' Diss. U of California at Berkeley, 2004. http://www.cafepress.com/stenport.

Stierle, Karlheinz. *Der Mythos von Paris: Zeichen und Bewusstsein der Stadt.* Munich: Hanser, 1993.

Stounbjerg, Per. 'Between Realism and Modernism: The Modernity of Strindberg's Auto-biographical Writings.' *The Cambridge Companion to*

August Strindberg. Ed. Michael Robinson. Cambridge: Cambridge UP, 2009. 47–57.

– 'A Modernist Hell: On Strindberg's *Inferno.*' *Scandinavica* 38.1 (1999): 35–59.

– 'Ett subjekt intrasslat i världen. Om Strindbergs självbiografiska prosa.' *Strindbergiana.* Vol 23. Ed. Per Stam. Stockholm: Atlantis, 2008. 23–45.

– 'Uro og Urenhed: Studier i Strindbergs selvbiografiske prosa.' Diss. U of Aarhus. Århus: Aarhus universitetsforlag, 2005.

Strindberg, August. 'Des Arts Nouveaux!' 1894. *Vivisektioner.* Ed. Torsten Eklund. Stockholm: Bonnier, 1958. 56–73.

– 'Är detta icke nog?' Ed. John Landquist. *Samlade skrifter.* Vol. 22. Stockholm: Bonnier, 1914.

– *Bland franska bönder: Subjektiva reseskildringar.* Ed. and commentary Per Erik Ekholm. *Samlade verk.* Vol. 23. Stockholm: Almqvist & Wiksell, 1985.

– *Brev.* Ed. Torsten Eklund. Vols 1–15. Stockholm: Bonnier, 1948–76.

– *The Cloister.* Ed. C.G. Bjurström. Trans. Mary Sandbach. New York: Hill and Wang, 1969.

– *Creditors. Selected Plays I.* Trans. and ed. Evert Sprinchorn. Minneapolis: U of Minnesota P, 1986.

– 'Deranged Sensations.' *Selected Essays by August Strindberg.* Ed. and trans. Michael Robinson. Cambridge: Cambridge UP, 1996. 122–34.

– *A Dream Play. Selected Plays II.* Trans. and ed. Evert Sprinchorn. Minneapolis: U of Minnesota P, 1986.

– *Ett drömspel.* Ed. and commentary Gunnar Ollén. *Samlade verk.* Vol. 46. Stockholm: Norstedt, 1988.

– *Fadren; Fröken Julie; Fordringsägare.* Ed and commentary Gunnar Ollén. *Samlade verk.* Vol. 27. Stockholm: Almkvist & Wiksell, 1984.

– *Fair Haven and Foul Strand.* Trans. unknown. London: T. Werner Laurie, 1914.

– *The Father. Selected Plays I.* Trans. and ed. Evert Sprinchorn. Minneapolis: U of Minnesota P, 1986.

– *Gamla Stockholm: Anteckningar ur tryckta och otryckta källor.* Ed. and commentary Hans Söderström. *Samlade verk.* Vol 8. Stockholm: Norstedt, 2007.

– *Ghost Sonata. Selected Plays II.* Trans. and ed. Evert Sprinchorn. Minneapolis: U of Minnesota P, 1986.

– *Giftas: äktenskapshistorier.* Vol. 1. Ed. and commentary Ulf Boëthius. *Samlade verk.* Vol. 16. Stockholm: Almkvist & Wiksell, 1982.

– *Inferno.* Ed. and commentary Ann-Charlotte Gavel Adams. *Samlade verk.* Vol. 37. Stockholm: Norstedt, 1994.

– *Inferno.* Trans. Derek Coltman and Evert Sprinchorn. *Inferno, Alone, and Other Writings.* Ed. Evert Sprinchorn. Garden City: Anchor Books, 1968. 177–284.

– *Klostret: Fagervik och Skamsund.* Ed. and commentary by Barbro Ståhle Sjönell. *Samlade verk.* Vol. 50. Stockholm: Norstedt, 1994.

– *A Madman's Manifesto.* Trans. Anthony Swerling. University: U of Alabama P, 1971.

– 'The New Arts!' Trans. Albert Bermel. *Inferno, Alone, and Other Writings.* Ed. Evert Sprinchorn. Garden City: Anchor Books, 1968. 99–103.

– *Parmi les paysans français.* Trans. Eva Ahlstedt and Pierre Morizet. Arles: Actes sud, 1988.

– 'Les Perverts.' *Vivisektioner II.* Trans. Tage Aurell. Ed. and commentary Torsten Eklund. Stockholm: Bonnier, 1958. 152–69.

– *Le plaidoyer d'un fou.* Ed. Göran Rossholm and Gunnel Engwall. *Samlade verk.* Vol. 25. Stockholm: Norstedt, 1999.

– *The Red Room: Scenes of Artistic and Literary Life.* Trans. Elizabeth Sprigge. London: Dent, 1967.

– *The Roofing Ceremony.* Trans. David Mel Paul and Margareta Paul. *The Roofing Ceremony and The Silver Lake.* Lincoln: U of Nebraska P, 1987. 1–74.

– *Röda Rummet: Skildringar ur artist- och författarlivet.* Ed. and commentary Carl Reinhold Smedmark. *Samlade verk.* Vol. 6. Stockholm: Norstedt, 1981.

– *Samlade verk* [nationalupplagan]. Main editors, Lars Dahlbäck and Per Stam. Stockholm: Almquist & Wiksell, 1981–5; Stockholm: Norstedt, 1986–.

– 'Sensations détraquées: 1894–1895.' *Le Figaro Littéraire.* 17 November 1894, 26 January 1895, and 9 February 1895. No pagination.

– *Spöksonaten. Kammarspel.* Ed. and commentary Gunnar Ollén. *Samlade verk.* Vol. 58. Stockholm: Norstedt, 1991.

– *Strindberg's Letters.* Ed. and trans. Michael Robinson. Vol. 1. Chicago: U of Chicago P, 1992.

– *Strindbergs Werke.* Trans. Emil Schering. Munich: Müller, 1908.

– *Svenska folket i helg och i söcken, i krig och i fred, hemma och ute eller Ett tusen år av svenska bildningens och sedernas historia.* Ed. and commentary Camilla Kretz and Per Stam. *Samlade verk.* Vol. 10. Stockholm: Norstedt, 2002.

– *Taklagsöl. Strindbergs förarbeten till Taklagsöl: Förslag till avsnitt som skall ingå i avhandlingen Strindbergs Taklagsöl.* Ed. Barbro Ståhle Sjönell. *Samlade verk.* Vol. 55. Stockholm: Norstedt, 1984.

Svinhufvud, Axel. *I Kongostatens tjänst.* Stockholm: Lindfors, 1942.

Swahn, Sigbrit. 'Pigbrevet i *Röda rummet.* Balzacs griset i Strindbergs roman.' *Svensk Litteraturtidskrift* 46.2 (1983): 3–6.

Swerling, Anthony. *In Quest of Strindberg: Letters to a Seeker.* Cambridge: Trinity Lane P, 1971.

– *Strindberg's Impact in France, 1920–1960.* Cambridge: Trinity Lane P, 1971.

Taeger, Angela. 'Homosexual Love between "Degeneration of Human Material" and "Love of Mankind": Demographical Perspectives on

Homosexuality in Nineteenth-Century Germany.' *Queering the Canon: Defying Sights in German Literature and Culture*. Ed. Christoph Lorey and John L. Pews. Columbia, SC: Camden House, 1998. 20–35.

Taroff, Kurt 'The Mind's Stage: Monodrama as Historical Trend and Interpretive Strategy.' Diss. City University of New York, 2005. ProQuest Digital Dissertations. ProQuest. University of Illinois at Urbana-Champaign Library. Urbana, IL. 8 Feb. 2008 http://www.proquest.com.

Tate Modern. Website. 18 Apr. 2008. http://www.tate.org.uk/about/tatereport/2006.

Taylor, Charles. 'Two Theories of Modernity.' *Alternative Modernities*. Ed. Dilip Parameshwar Gaonkar. Durham: Duke UP, 2001. 172–96.

Teilmann, Katja. 'Hekseproces og ægteskabsroman: Om *"Le Plaidoyer d'un fou."'* *Tidskrift för litteraturvetenskap* 30.4 (2001): 78–97.

– 'Når genrer mødes: generiske interferenser – særligt hos Strindberg.' *Edda* 1 (2002): 63–72.

Tell, Per Erik. *Detta fredliga uppdrag: Om 522 svenskar i terrorns Kongo*. Umeå: hström, 2005.

Thacker, Andrew. *Moving through Modernity: Space and Geography in Modernism*. New York: Palgrave, 2003.

Theis, Wolfgang, and Andreas Sternweiler. 'Alltag im Kaiserreich und in der Weimarer Republik.' *Eldorado: Homosexuelle Frauen und Männer in Berlin 1850–1950. Geschichte, Alltag, Kultur*. Ed. Michael Bollé. Berlin: Frölich & Kauffmann, 1984. 48–73.

Tidström, Karin. 'Cette fameuse *Sonate des spectres* ... *Une* pièce de chambre d'August Strindberg en France: traduction et réception.' Diss. U of Stockholm, 1989.

Tjäder, Per Arne. 'Det växande huset. Kommentar till strukturen i Strindbergs *Taklagsöl.' Tidskrift för litteraturvetenskap* 1 (1978): 30–43.

Tygesen, Peter, and Espen Waehle. *Kongospår: Norden i Kongo – Kongo i Norden*. Stockholm: Etnografiska museet, 2005.

Törnqvist, P.E. (Egil). 'Monodrama: Term and Reality.' *Essays in Drama and Theater: Liber Amicorum Benjamin Hunningher*. Ed. Paul Binnerts. Amsterdam: Moussault, 1973. 145–59.

Unglaub, Erich. 'Rilke und das Dänemark seiner Zeit.' *Blätter der Rilke-Gesellschaft* 16/17 (1989/90): 93–118.

Vidler, Anthony. *The Architectural Uncanny: Essays in the Modern Unhomely*. Cambridge, MA: MIT P, 1992.

– *Warped Space: Art, Architecture, and Anxiety in Modern Culture*. Cambridge, MA: MIT P, 2001.

Waelti-Walters, Jennifer. *Damned Women: Lesbians in French Novels 1796–1996*. Montreal: McGill-Queen's UP, 2000.

Walkowitz, Rebecca L. *Cosmopolitan Style: Modernism beyond the Nation.* New York: Columbia UP, 2006.

Weber, Eugen. *Peasants into Frenchmen: The Modernization of Rural France, 1870–1914.* Stanford: Stanford UP, 1976.

Webster's New Universal Unabridged Dictionary. New York: Random House, 1996.

Weinstein, Arnold. *Northern Arts: The Breakthrough of Scandinavian Literature and Art from Ibsen to Bergman.* Princeton: Princeton UP, 2008.

Wescher, Paul. 'Strindberg and the Chance-Images of Surrealism.' *The Art Quarterly* 16:2 (1953): 93–105.

Widell, Ove. 'Ola Hansson i Tyskland: En studie i hans liv och diktning åren 1890–1893.' Diss. Uppsala U, 1979.

Williams, Elisabeth A. 'Anthropological Institutions in Nineteenth-Century France.' *Isis* 76 (1985): 331–48.

Wollaeger, Mark, ed. *The Oxford Handbook of Global Modernisms.* Oxford: Oxford UP, forthcoming.

Zola, Émile. *The Earth* [*La Terre*, 1887]. Trans. Douglas Parmée. London: Penguin, 1980.

Index

Adams, Lotta Gavel, 100–1, 101n3
Adorno, Theodor, 102
Africa, 156–7, 171–9
Ahlström, Stellan, 5, 102n4
Albert, Henri, 50
Alberti, Conrad, 128, 152–3
Among French Peasants (1889):
  overview, 55–6; agrarian setting
  of, 16; approach to peasantry in,
  74–86; ethnographic travel in, 56,
  62–73, 79, 81, 87; literary modernism and, 72–4; naturalism and,
  74–6; publication of, 56–7;
  Strindberg exile status and, 84–5;
  translations of, 57, 57n2
Anderson, Benedict, 80
Andrée, S.A., 178–9
anthropometrics, 76–7
Antoine, André, 149
apartments: apartment building
  design, 33–4; apartment building
  failures in *Ghost Sonata*, 186;
  apartment interiors as private
  space, 17, 20, 30–6, 156–65, 179,
  183; as theatrical settings, 181–3.
  See also domestic space
Aragon, Louis, 104, 107, 111

architecture: absence of architectural
  description in *Madman* travel
  narrative, 45; architect's room in
  Roofing Ceremony, 159–60;
  architectural corporeality in
  Roofing Ceremony, 157; architectural shifters, 31–2, 41–2; gendered urban architectural
  markers, 28–9; modern architecture movement, 161–3; Parisian
  architectural tourism, 63; psycho-
  architectural mapping in *Madman*,
  19–20, 25–6; representation of
  bourgeois detachment, 32; social
  transgressions in *Madman* and, 20.
  See also domestic space
Arrabal, F., 112
art. *See* painting and drawing;
  photography
Artaud, Antonin, 109, 112
Auguier, Emile, 40
Austria, 117–18, 121–2, 148
authenticity: authenticity/perform-
  ance boundary, 38, 44; outsider
  credentials in *Peasants*, 59–60;
  rupture of domestic authenticity,
  41–2